The Pre-Raphaelite Trail In Kent

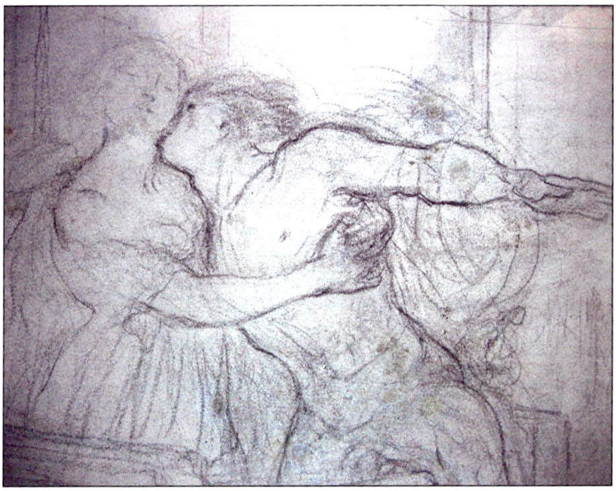

Peter Wise

S. B. Publications

DEDICATION

This book is dedicated to my partner Sally, my daughters Isobel and Verity and to my mother Jessie.

First published in 2009 by S. B. Publications
Tel: 01323 893498
Email: sbpublications@tiscali.co.uk
www.sbpublications.co.uk

ISBN 978-185770-3412

Designed and Typeset by EH Graphics, East Sussex (01273) 515527

FRONT COVER: *RED HOUSE FROM THE GARDEN - PHOTO BY KIND PERMISSION OF THE NATIONAL TRUST.*

DETAIL OF THE MARY MAGDALENE WINDOW DESIGNED BY WILLIAM MORRIS AT LANGTON GREEN CHURCH - PHOTO BY AUTHOR.

OPUS SECTILE COMMEMORATIVE PLAQUE PRODUCED BY POWELL IN FOUR ELMS CHURCH.

KNOLE - PHOTO BY KIND PERMISSION OF THE NATIONAL TRUST.

TITLE PAGE: *PRELIMINARY DRAWING FOR 'ROMEO AND JULIET' BY FORD MADOX BROWN - PHOTO BY AUTHOR.*

BACK COVER: *DETAIL OF LUDDESDOWN MURALS - PHOTO BY AUTHOR.*

Contents

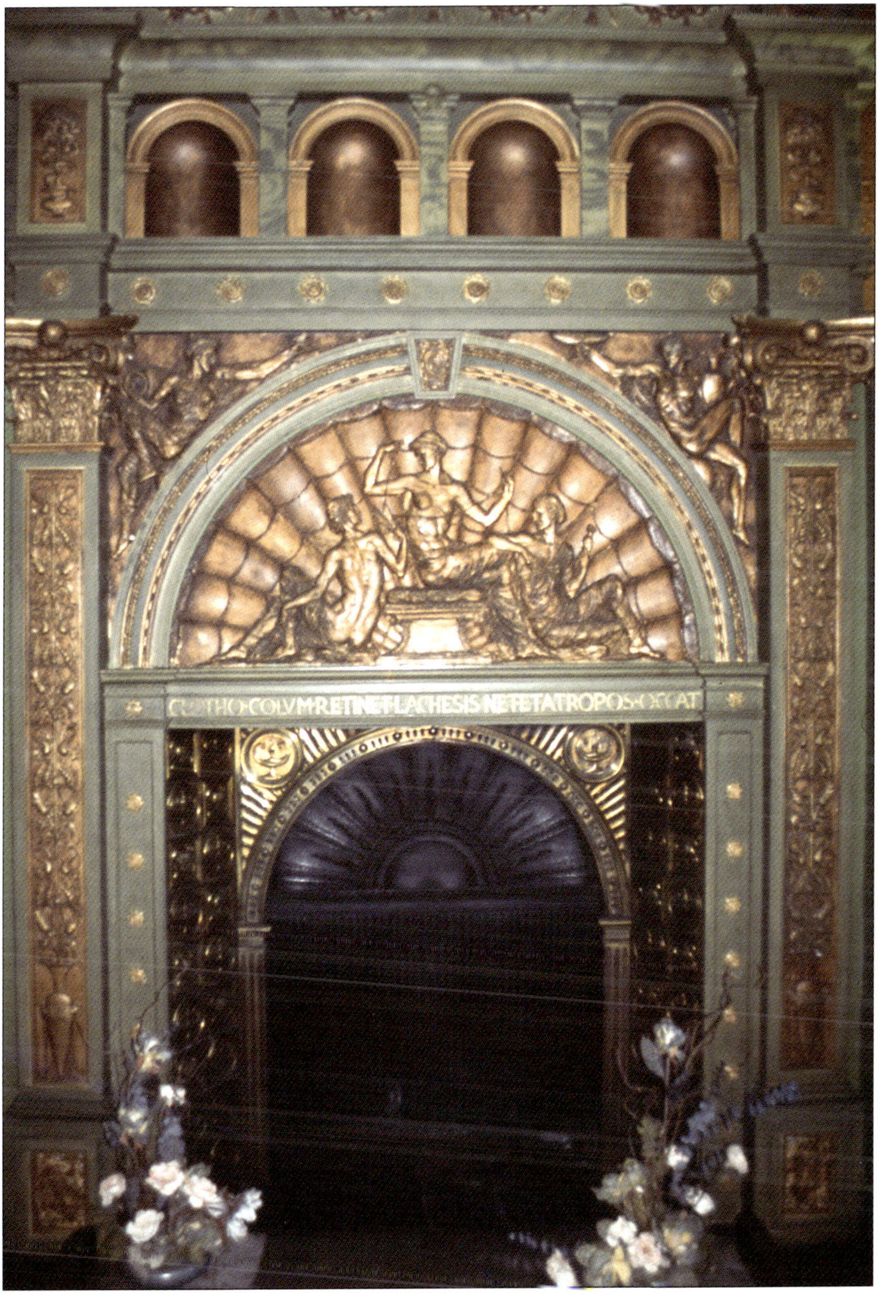

FIRE PLACE AT COMBE BANK DESIGNED BY WALTER CRANE - PHOTO BY AUTHOR

The Author

Peter Wise is an art historian with a particular interest in Victorian art. He is a member of the William Morris Society, The Pre-Raphaelite Society and the Kempe Society. Peter has lived in Sussex virtually all his life and being so close has frequently visited its adjacent county of Kent and appreciated its variety and charm. Although he continues to visit often he now lives with his family in Invergowrie, NSW, Australia.

The author is most grateful to the rectors and vicars of all the churches concerned as well as to the many professionals, academics and other individuals who provided invaluable help and assistance with this book. The author would like to thank in particular Robert Eberhard for sharing his knowledge of stained glass.

The author encourages comments about this book from readers, in particular any new information about the subjects discussed. E-mail address: peterrwise@yahoo.com

Introduction

This book is a companion volume to The Pre-Raphaelite Trail in Sussex (2003, revised 2008) but can also be used as a completely independent guide. It explores how painters associated with Pre-Raphaelite art had links with the people and places of the county of Kent.

Artists found herein include Dante Gabriel Rossetti whose paintings of sensual voluptuous women seem to many to epitomise everything Pre-Raphaelite. However, the term is a far reaching one encapsulating pictures with subjects such as Arthurian legend, with early Pre-Raphaelite pictures having a serious and moral message. The term also describes an innovative way of painting outdoors developed years before the Impressionists. Another artist who spent some significant time in the county was Ford Madox Brown, sometimes referred to as a father figure to the original Pre-Raphaelite Brotherhood. A slightly older man, his paintings provided the three most important members of that brotherly association (William Holman Hunt, John Everett Millais and Rossetti) with early inspiration. Two of his daughters, Lucy and Cathy, became artists themselves after learning their craft from their father in his studio and workshop.

Another well-known figure associated with the movement is of course William Morris whose important home Red House is found within the more expansive boundaries of Kent. This house was designed by Morris' friend, Philip Webb, and was essentially his first commission but which has subsequently become a modern architectural icon.

This book examines aspects of the lives of the men connected with Pre-Raphaelitism but does not forget the women whose lives were intertwined with them. These include figures such as Phoebe Traquair and Rosa Brett whose contact with the movement may have been transitory or of greater longevity, as well as the wives and partners of the principal artists such as Janey Morris and Georgiana Burne-Jones.

As with its neighbouring county Sussex, attention should be given to the churches in Kent for it is these buildings which so often highlight the legacy of the Pre-Raphaelites and William Morris or the Arts & Crafts Movement that followed. The gift they give to us may take the form of stained glass or mural work or may be seen through the close attention to detail in the whole design of a building. Time and time again it is through a visit to a church that the beauty of the work of this group of artists and designers is much appreciated.

All the churches in this book (except those in the appendices) are rated for their importance, the nature of their contents and overall atmosphere on a one to five star rating. Simply, the more the stars the better.

The book includes details of glass by companies and designers who were contemporaries of Morris so that the reader can see differences in style and make comparisons between them. It is not however a comprehensive list of all the work by firms and their craftsmen other than by Morris & Co. as there would be too many churches in Kent which have perhaps one window by a Victorian company and this is not the main focus of the book. The interested researcher will no doubt find a number of other churches which have glasswork by lesser known artists and designers or ones whose style is far removed from the subject of this volume.

HOW TO USE THIS BOOK

The second part of this book has details of ten trails that the reader may like to explore. On all of these there are a number of churches listed as these buildings now provide one of the best opportunities to see at first hand examples of the artists' work. The trails sometimes include visits to houses open to the public such as Ightham Mote and Knole and also local art galleries. The areas around Sevenoaks and Tunbridge Wells are particularly rich in associations and artefacts and those short of time are therefore directed to these earlier trails in the book. However to do a whole trail in these densely packed areas will take time so the reader may wish to select those locations of special interest to them beforehand.

Maps that are useful include the Ordnance Survey Landranger 177/8/9 and 188/9 and the Explorer 136/7/8, 147/8/9 and 150. The Philip's Street Atlas for Kent provides good detail in one handy volume.

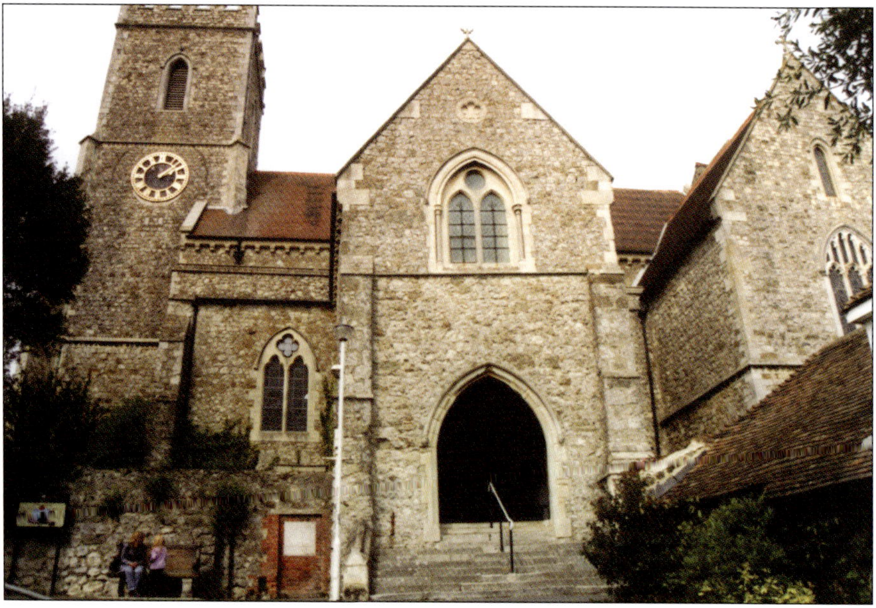

HYTHE CHURCH - PHOTO BY AUTHOR

The Early Days of the Pre-Raphaelites

The year 1848 saw a number of revolutions in Europe. A Second Republic was established in France, there were revolts against the Austrian Empire and there were rebellions in a number of Italian cities. The nearest that England came to such an event was the Chartist demonstrations that called for greater political representation for the disadvantaged and poor. They largely failed through lack of support so perhaps the most significant revolution was in the world of art led by a group of seven individuals to be known as the Pre-Raphaelite Brotherhood.

In this group there were three main protagonists who were all students at the Royal Academy. They were John Everett Millais, aged nineteen and a precociously talented painter, William Holman Hunt, a conscientious and moral young man, and Dante Gabriel Rossetti who was more charismatic and Bohemian but of similar age. Invited to join them was James Collinson, another painter, and the sculptor Thomas Woolner. Also asked to join was Frederick Stephens, a more occasional painter, and Gabriel's brother Michael who would act as secretary.

These young men felt that the Academy (which was then by far the most influential institution in the British art world) was outdated in its teaching practices and thus producing artists who were formulaic in the execution of their work. They felt that the practice of copying from the Old Masters was producing generations of uninspired students and they singled out the Renaissance painter Raphael as the prominent artist around when the rot set in. He was at the time considered to represent the peak of perfection in European art. However, the Brotherhood preferred to admire artists of the so called 'primitive' school for their honesty and truth (such as Van Eyck and Memling)who were active prior to Raphael. Hence they were dubbed 'Pre-Raphaelite' by their fellow students.

The Brotherhood's stated aims included the principle of 'truth to nature' whereby they wished to reproduce the world around them with great fidelity and without resorting to the established artistic methods that were in vogue at the time. This led them to work directly from nature outdoors and also to use innovative techniques that enabled their works to be highly coloured with great detail. The subjects that they chose for their early paintings and drawings had serious sources. They included Biblical scenes and subjects drawn from Shakespeare, Keats and contemporary novelists.

Their work caused considerable hostility, for example in their use of the abbreviation PRB in order to sign their pictures. In addition, the way that they chose to depict incidents from the Bible caused pronounced criticism. The most obvious example of this was Charles Dickens' comments on Millais' *Christ in the House of his Parents* (Tate Britain) exhibited at the Royal Academy in 1850. This painting shows the Holy Family in a non-idealised way which has been described as 'with warts and all'. An example is how Millais chose to portray the figure of Joseph with the correct musculature for a carpenter (and copied from a man of this employment) with other features such as callouses on the workman's hands. Dickens wrote about the picture in his journal

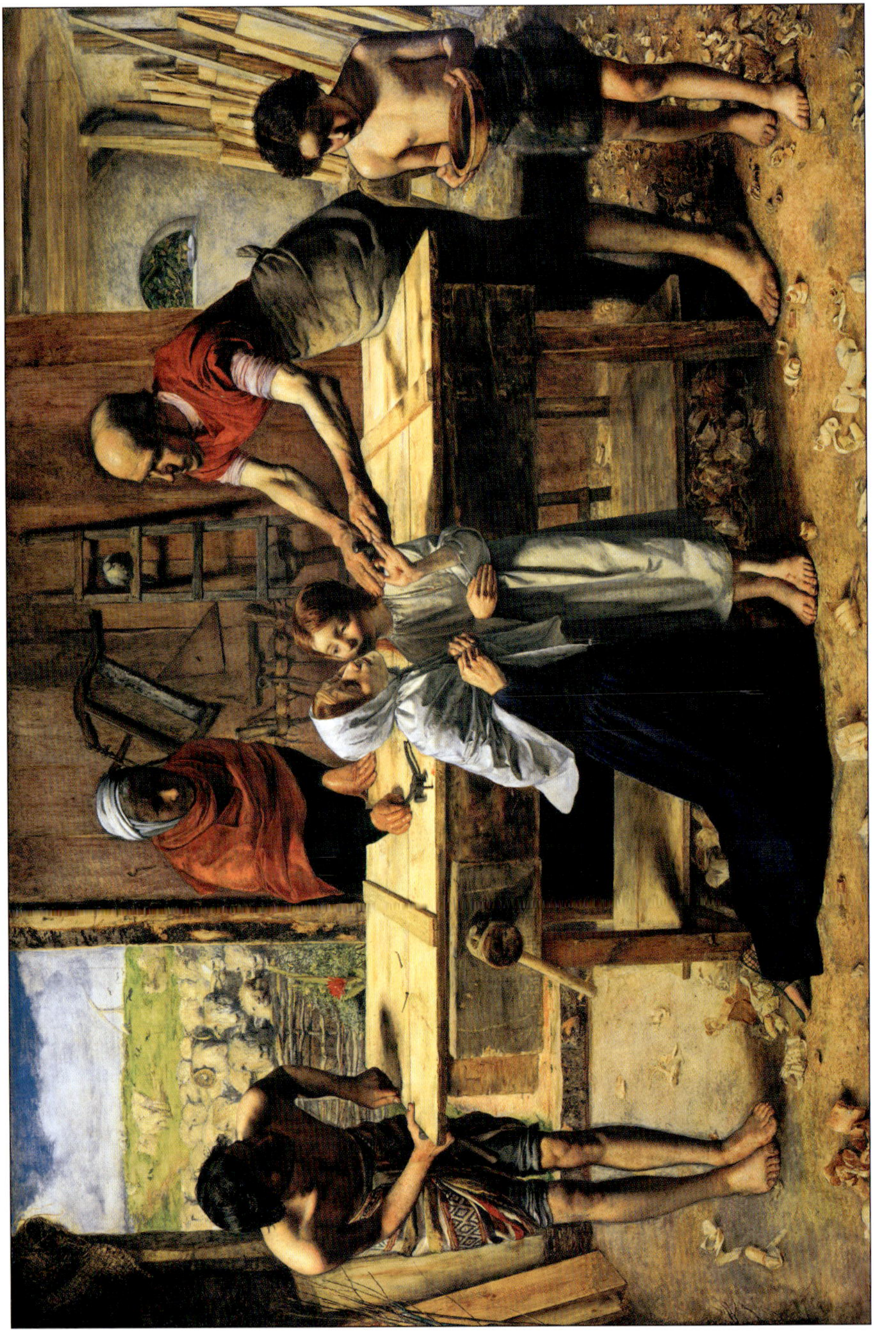

Household Words-

'wherever it was possible to express ugliness of feature, limb or attitude you have it expressed. Such men as the carpenters might be undressed in any hospital where dirty drunkards in a high state of varicose veins are received'.

The controversy continued into the next year but then the influential art critic John Ruskin intervened on behalf of the Brotherhood. He wrote to The Times in defence of the techniques used by the Pre-Raphaelites and this led other critics to reconsider their work.

'CHRIST IN THE HOUSE OF HIS PARENTS' BY JOHN EVERETT MILLAIS - PERMISSION OF THE TATE

Two Friends

FORD MADOX BROWN AND DANTE GABRIEL ROSSETTI

Although Ford Madox Brown was never a member of the Pre-Raphaelite Brotherhood he is acknowledged as a leading influence upon it. He always adhered to 'realist' principles, hence his insistence on an accurate landscape even if these were only backgrounds to his early historical pictures. This ties in with the Brotherhood's declared aim of a new naturalism free from inherited conventions.

Brown was born on the sixteenth of July 1821 and was therefore a few years older than Rossetti, Hunt and Millais and consequently is often referred to as a father figure to the younger artists. He was born in Calais and spent most of the first twenty years or so of his life abroad, a reason for his lifelong problems with spelling. His early years were blighted by the deaths of both his mother and sister from tuberculosis (or consumption, as it was then known). This continental upbringing however gave him an atypical artistic grounding in places such as Bruges, Ghent and Paris and in his teens he became aware of the German painters called The Nazarenes whom he also visited. This group of artists included Friedrich Overbeck and Peter Cornelius and their work showed an interest in the medieval way of life to the extent that they often dressed in clothes appropriate for the Middle Ages. They also painted religious frescoes and paintings working as a group in imitation of a medieval colony. Their work and ideas were later to influence and inspire the Pre-Raphaelites.

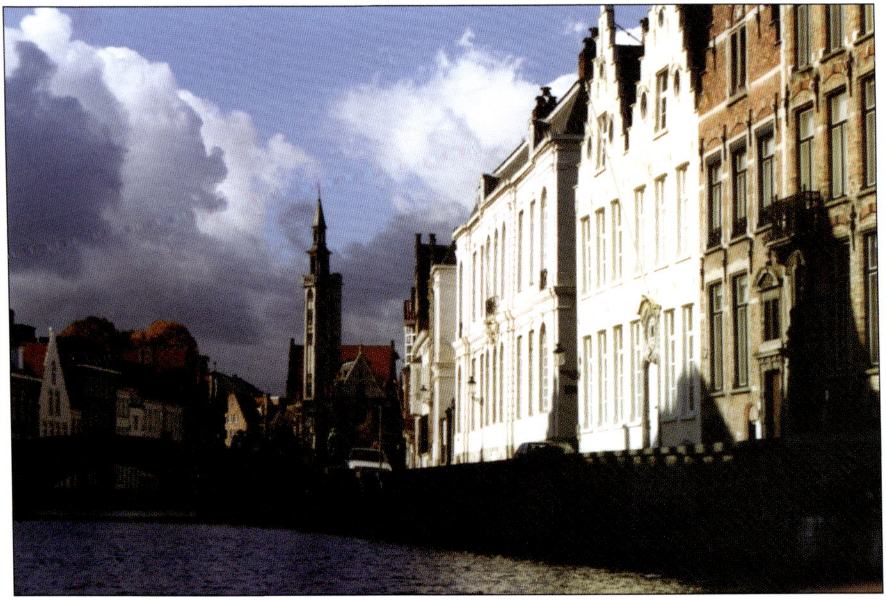

BRUGES TODAY - PHOTO BY AUTHOR

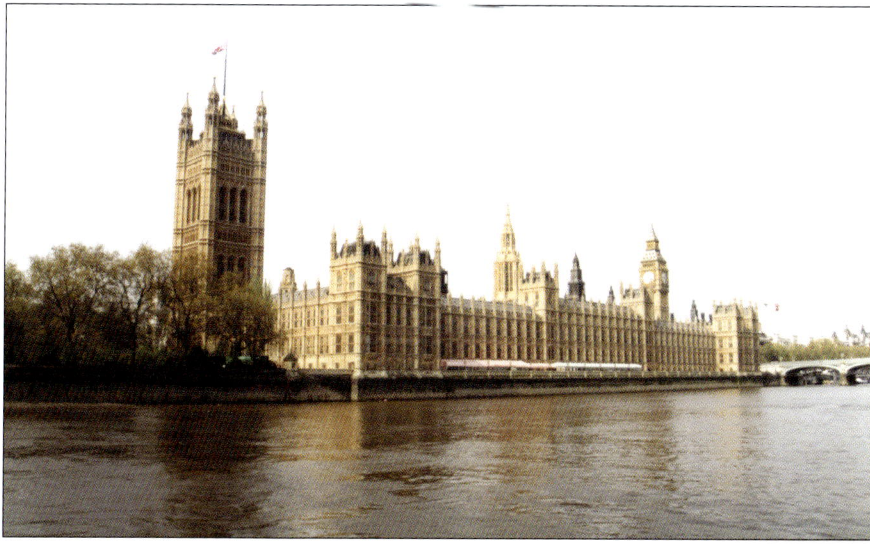

HOUSES OF PARLIAMENT - PHOTO BY AUTHOR

In April 1841 Brown married his first cousin Elisabeth Bromley in **Meopham**, Kent but they initially continued to live abroad and their daughter Lucy was born in Paris in 1943. Later they settled in London and Brown submitted a number of (unsuccessful) cartoons for the competitions to produce murals for the new Houses of Parliament. In the autumn of 1845 he and Elisabeth stayed in Italy because of his wife's poor health and it was there that he started to plan his first multi-figured easel painting *Chaucer at the Court of Edward III* (Art Gallery of New South Wales, Sydney). Sadly his wife died of tuberculosis a year later and Brown placed his daughter Lucy with his sister-in-law who had a school in **Gravesend** whilst he threw himself into his work in London.

As he travelled back from **Gravesend** to London in November 1847 he thought up the idea for his next large historical oil - *Wycliffe reading his Translation of the New Testament* (Bradford Art Galleries and Museums - a shortened version of the original title). In addition he commenced a diary at about this time which records his day-to-day struggles with hated authority figures and poverty as well as his visits to his beloved daughter. Money at this time (and throughout his life) was a constant worry for Brown although his choice of historical subjects probably didn't help his work to sell.

A few months later Brown had his first meeting with Dante Gabriel Rossetti. The latter had begun to view and admire Brown's work and consequently sent him an effusive and appreciative letter suggesting that Brown might become his tutor and mentor. This communication was initially misunderstood by a suspicious Brown who needed much re-assurance from Rossetti, when they did actually meet, that the younger man was not making a fool of him. However with all doubts resolved Brown and Rossetti were to enjoy many years of close friendship.

Brown travelled over to **Shorne Ridgeway** in July 1849 and produced the work entitled *View from Shorne Ridgeway, Kent* (National Museums and Galleries of Wales). This was in fact a study for the background of the fore-mentioned *Chaucer* picture which Brown only started actually painting that year. The picture shows an imaginary scene in

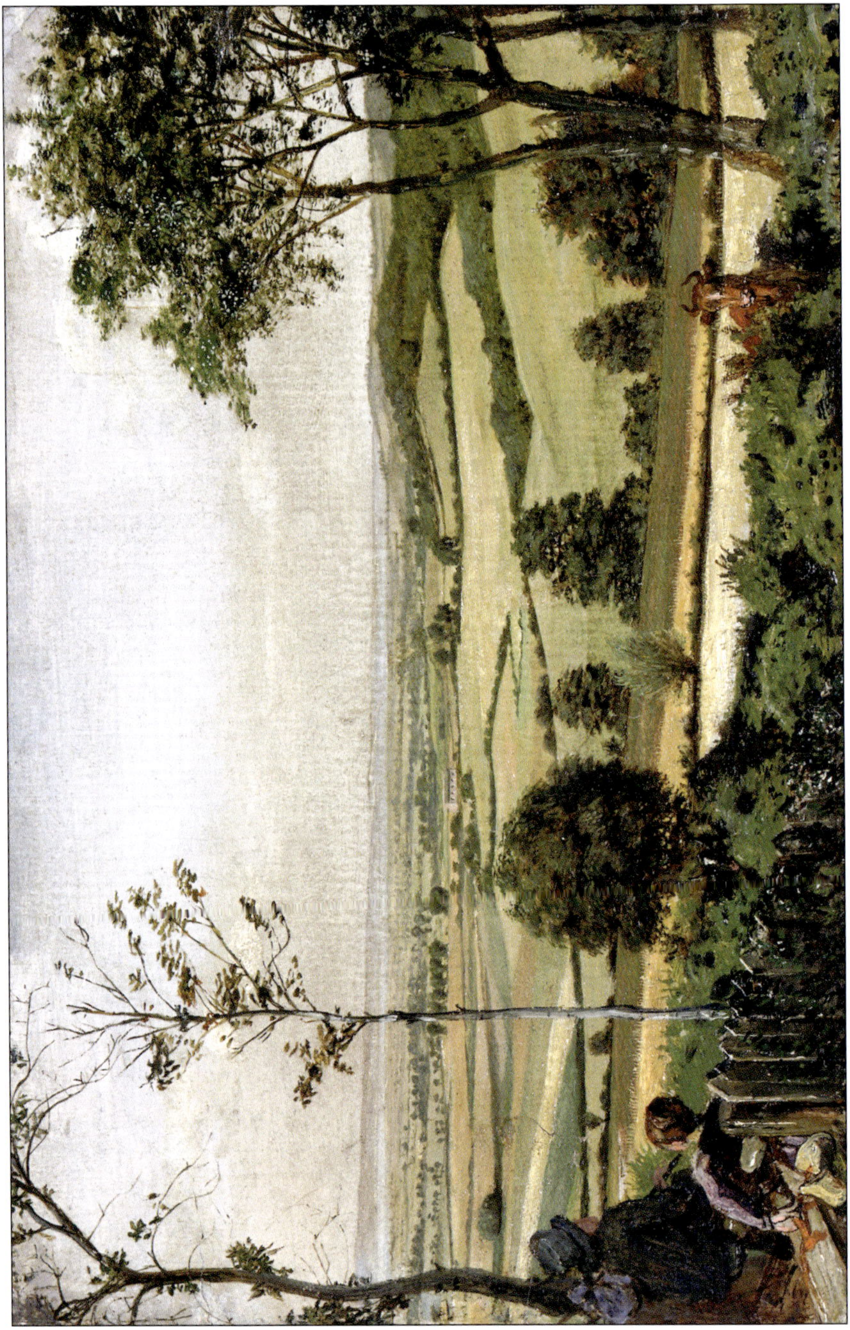

'VIEW FROM SHORNE RIDGEWAY, KENT' BY FORD MADOX BROWN - PERMISSION OF NATIONAL MUSEUM WALES. AMGUEDDFA CYMRY

which the poet Geoffrey Chaucer reads aloud to the King (Edward III) and his court. The supposed date of the scene is 1375 and it also shows the King's wife Joanna, who was called 'the Fair Maid of Kent'. In the study the landscape is shown in reverse without the ploughing taking place that appears in *Chaucer*. Brown knew this part of the county because of his regular visits to Lucy at **Gravesend** and it was there that he had accommodation whilst he worked on this study for three days, two of which were unfortunately windy.

In September of the same year Brown stayed for two weeks at **Margate** with Lucy and produced a fine portrait of his six-year-old daughter after three sittings lasting a total of nine hours.

During 1850 Brown was asked to contribute to *The Germ*, the short lived journal (it ran to only four issues) of the Pre-Raphaelite Brotherhood. The same year saw Rossetti producing his first ink drawing of Lizzie Siddal (*A Parable of Love*) to whom he had recently become acquainted.

Another event occurred in the autumn of that year when Rossetti accompanied his friends Holman Hunt and Frederic George Stephens (both original members of the Brotherhood) to **Knole Park** near **Sevenoaks** for some joint working together. This was to prove to be the first of three significant visits to Kent for Rossetti which were all at times of differing crises. On this occasion the problem was related to his painting, in particular to the difficulties of painting landscape in the outdoors. Hunt described how Rossetti was coping with the challenge:

'I ran up occasionally to see him, and found him nearly always engaged in a mortal quarrel with some particular leaf which would perversely shake about and get torn off its branch when he was half way in its representation. Having been served thus repeatedly, he would put up with no more such treatment, and left canvas, box, and easel for the man to collect when at dusk the barrow came for my picture, he stalking back to the lodgings to write and to try designs.'

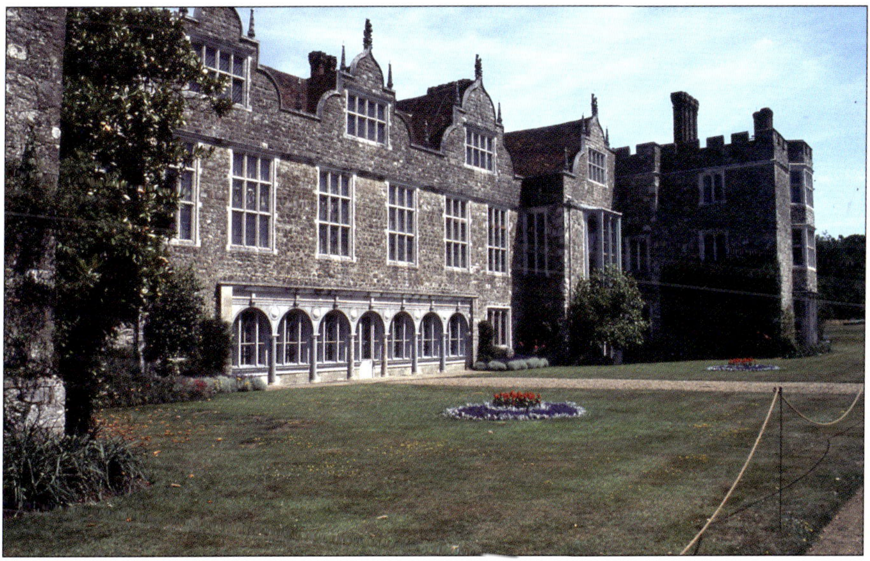

KNOLE - PHOTO BY KIND PERMISSION OF THE NATIONAL TRUST

Rossetti's initial idea had been to paint an out-of-doors picture with a subject taken from his hero, the medieval poet Dante. The picture that Hunt was working on was the Shakespearean subject *Valentine Rescuing Sylvia from Proteus* (Birmingham City Museum and Art Gallery) which although dominated by the principal figures has a highly detailed background taken directly from the landscape seen at **Knole**. Rossetti's efforts were not totally in vain however as he later used his uncompleted canvas from the trip for his familiar *The Bower Meadow* (Manchester City Art Gallery) adding four figures of women to the foreground. There is subsequently little in the way of landscape in Rossetti's oeuvre perhaps suggesting the appalling weather he experienced at **Knole** made a deep impression on him not easily forgotten.

Later the same year Madox Brown had a child called Cathy from his relationship with Emma Hill. Emma had been modelling for Brown and it seems to have been the case that the boundaries between artist /model and artist/lover became somewhat blurred. The liaison probably began in the spring of 1849 and had been kept very quiet but had provided Brown with a distraction from his grief at the loss of Elisabeth. It had also temporarily distracted him from his art, he had even had a week's holiday with Emma at **Ramsgate** in September 1849.

Brown and Rossetti were now sharing studios at Newman Street in London, both men struggling with their art and finances. Their companionship and mutual support at this time cemented their lifelong friendship. It was there that Brown started his next major work entitled *The Pretty Baa-Lambs* (Birmingham City Museum and Art Gallery) which importantly depicted figures that were shown in natural outdoor light rather than being completed in a studio setting. The countryside shown in the background was once again based on his *View from Shorne Ridgeway* but much more loosely. The picture is arguably the first truly Pre-Raphaelite painting and was not generally well received at the time and there was a good deal of confusion over its meaning. Brown himself denied there were any symbolic messages in the work but this would have been unusual for the time when the public where adept at and expectant of unravelling these.

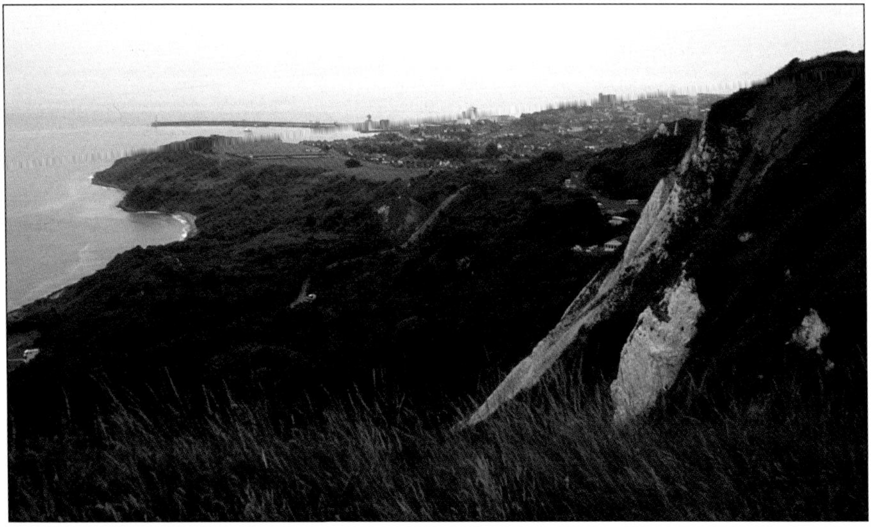

COASTAL SCENE NEAR DOVER - PHOTO BY AUTHOR

It signalled Brown's move from the shared studios to an address in Hampstead, an area that would provide him with new stimuli. From his window on the High Street, Brown could see The Hermitage, an attractive house that Rossetti was staying at in nearby Highgate. Gabriel was in the company of Edward Bateman, a designer for the Great Exhibition who was soon to leave for Australia.

Whilst Emma and baby Cathy were spending the summer of 1853 in **Dover**, following their marriage on the fifth of April (when Gabriel was a witness, although the wedding was not announced so as not to draw attention to baby Cathy), Brown worked on his next picture. This painting now ranks as one of his most interesting Pre-Raphaelite works. Its title is *The Last of England* (Birmingham City Museum and Art Gallery) and has as its subject the theme of emigration. This was very much a social issue of the time with many poor people and families choosing to seek an uncertain future in Australia. In fact one of the seven founding members of the Brotherhood, the sculptor Thomas Woolner, in the company of Bateman, had done just that on the fifteenth of July 1852 when talk of the discovery of gold in Australia was widespread. It is possible that Brown saw them off from **Gravesend** and that this event inspired the painting. The picture has both Brown and his wife-to-be Emma as models as well as a backdrop of the **Dover** cliffs similar to those used in his work *King Lear* (Tate Britain) that he had begun in 1848. This earlier work is based on Shakespeare's play and is set in Cordelia's tent in the French camp at **Dover** and it is quite possible that it originates in a sketch that Brown completed in the vicinity of that town. Rossetti appears in the picture as the jester.

In *The Last of England* there is an autobiographical element as Brown and Emma stare blankly in front of them emanating a sense of disbelief and desperation but also perhaps hope. This could well have been a reflection of Brown's mood at the time when he was depressed by the lack of appreciation for his work and on a more practical note by a chronic lack of money. He had even considered emigrating to India himself. At a wider level its subject shows an important social concern of the time with people from both the working and middle classes being forced to consider a new but undetermined future. It is clear in Brown's painting that the vessel has a mixed set of passengers who will have to spend a considerable period of time in close proximity to one another.

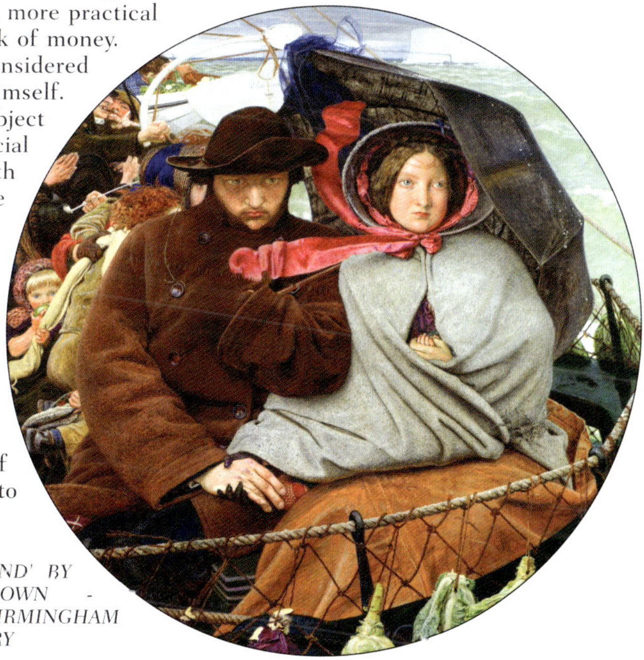

THE LAST OF ENGLAND' BY FORD MADOX BROWN - PERMISSION OF BIRMINGHAM MUSEUM & ART GALLERY

Brown spent a lot of his time on the work employing the Pre-Raphaelite technique of using a wet white background in order to obtain fresh bright colours. He spent four weeks alone working on the red ribbons attached to Emma's bonnet and his wife also had to do without her shawl for much of the winter as Brown was using it in his studio. Ironically a quick sale of *The Last of England* would ease some of Brown's financial worries and also encouraged Emma and him to remain in Britain.

Whilst Woolner was away Rossetti missed his company despite regular communication between the two, and Gabriel negatively compared his own lack of success to his friend's heroic adventures on the other side of the globe.

This rich period of Brown's painting also includes the commencement of another familiar picture *Work* (Manchester City Art Gallery) begun in 1852 and also featuring Emma, although he did not fully complete this until much later. Despite the inspired nature of his work at this time it was still not generally selling well and finances were always difficult particularly until the end of the decade.

The year 1854 saw an increasing closeness and intimacy between Rossetti and Lizzie Siddal and together they invited Brown and Emma to Blackfriars where Rossetti had set up home. Unfortunately what could have been a pleasant meeting for the foursome did not take place due to the long distance between their respective addresses and Emma's new pregnancy. Soon afterwards Rossetti and Lizzie would spend time together in Hastings where he would produce some wonderful emotive sketches of the woman with whom he was now infatuated. She was as always having periods of ill health and on one occasion Brown described her as *'looking thinner and more deathlike and more beautiful and more ragged than ever'*.

Rossetti's progress as an artist at this time was slow and because of this his moods were inevitably up and down as described by Brown again- *'after he has talked as much as his strength will bear, he becomes spiteful and crusty, denying everything'* and *'grows*

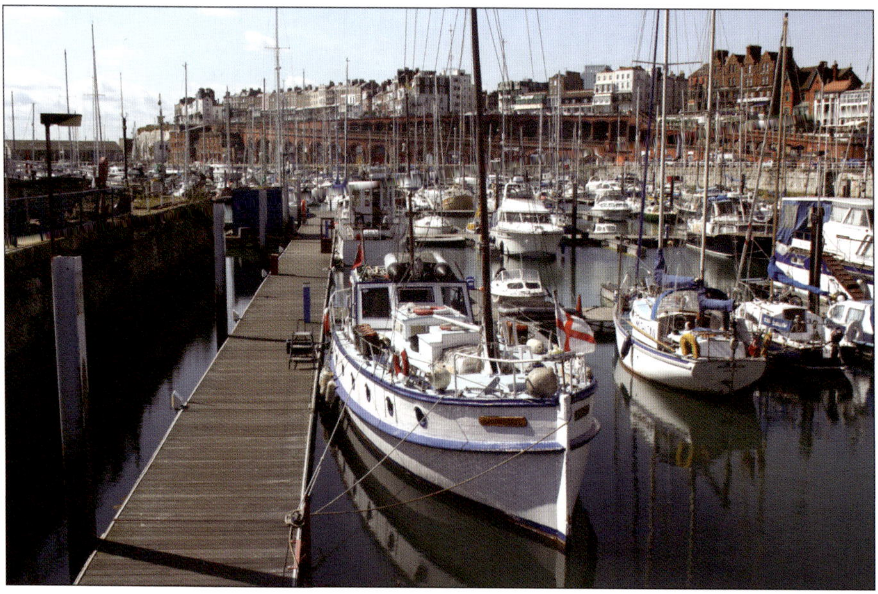

RAMSGATE - PHOTO BY BRIAN WISE

bitterly sarcastic in his way, but never quite unpleasant nor even unbearable'.

At another time Rossetti claimed that Emma encouraged Lizzie against him although he often insisted the Browns, with their new baby Oliver (known as Nolly), stayed over at Blackfriars despite the rather uncomfortable conditions. Another example seems to suggest that Emma was rather mischievous - she proposed a little holiday for her and Lizzie at **Ramsgate** and told Lizzie to borrow money for it from her husband. When Rossetti discovered the plan he was less than pleased, resulting in quarrels all round. Lizzie's motivations for going along with Emma's divisive ideas were probably connected to Gabriel's ambivalent ideas about marriage (in 1856 he was now twenty-eight) and because he had been seen with Annie Miller, another model for the Pre-Raphaelites.

He had other distractions, it was also the year he met Burne-Jones and William Morris and encouraged them to follow their artistic careers. Perhaps as a result of this Rossetti's own career began moving forward more positively and he received his first major commission - for an altarpiece in Llandaff Cathedral near Cardiff. Brown was feeling happy too - in September 1856 Emma gave birth to their second son, Arthur Gabriel.

The next year saw Brown organising an independent show for Pre-Raphaelite artists and he showed some thirty of his own works. Also, Rossetti's paintings were displayed and received generally more favourable reviews than before. The more positive mood was however broken in July when baby Arthur fell ill and died within a week. This was understandably a massive blow to Brown just at a time when his career appeared to be on the up.

The exhibition acted as a form of prelude to one of the most celebrated events that now constitute a part of Pre-Raphaelite folklore - the painting of the Oxford Union murals. Rossetti was invited by a Dublin born architect Benjamin Woodward to complete the murals for the new library in the Oxford Union Debating Society. He was accompanied by friends and artists such as Morris, Burne-Jones, Spencer Stanhope and Arthur Hughes. Brown declined (probably still reeling from his younger son's death) but Rossetti wrote to him describing the unique feeling of camaraderie present - *'it is really very jolly work in itself, but really one is mad to do such things'.* It probably took his mind off Lizzie with whom he had once again quarrelled and who was staying in Sheffield with a cousin.

Artistically Rossetti was entering a watershed period - he would soon produce the first of his many sensuous pictures of women for which he is now most remembered. These bust-length pictures of beautiful women probably reflect his growing intimacy with the model Fanny Cornforth who appears in many of the works. Rossetti was also increasing his social contacts meeting for the first time painters such as Henry Holiday and Frederick Sandys.

Meanwhile, Gabriel and Lizzie had effectively not seen one another for about twenty months. Lizzie summoned him to Hastings in 1860 when she was again very ill. So ill in fact that Emma wanted to come down for the proposed wedding although her main role was likely to have been as a nurse - in the event she did not make the journey and the marriage was conducted with no friends or family present. After their honeymoon they arranged to see the Browns on their return.

Both Rossetti and Ford Madox Brown were founder members of Morris Marshall Faulkner & Company a year later in 1861. The Firm, as it was known, was set up initially as a result of being unable to obtain furniture that was of reasonable quality and decently designed. As the Company expanded Rossetti and Brown, along with its other main contributors - Morris and Burne-Jones, began to make designs in fields that included furniture, fabrics and, particularly at the beginning, stained glass.

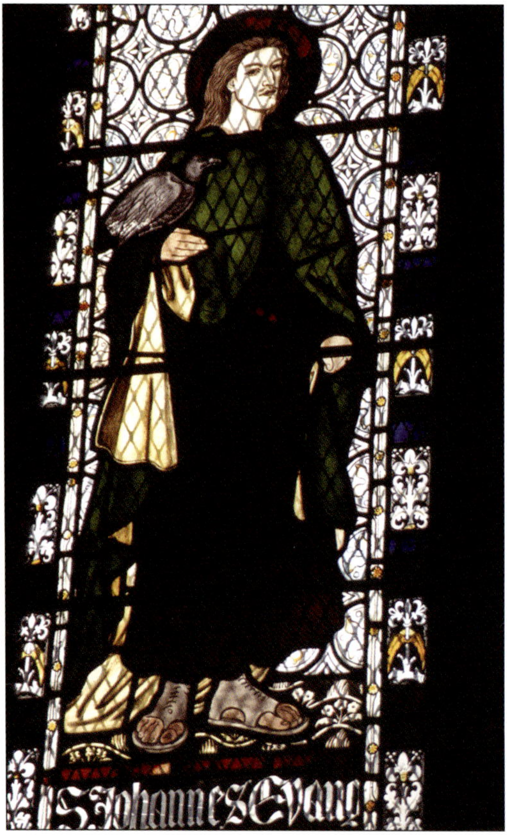

WINDOW OF ST. JOHN THE EVANGELIST DESIGNED BY MADOX BROWN IN LANGTON GREEN CHURCH - PHOTO BY AUTHOR

At the start of the year Lizzie was pregnant along with both Georgiana Burne-Jones and Janey Morris. She may well have had a rare sense of social inclusion within the close circle of Gabriel's friends and partners. A few weeks later there was a party at the **Red House** to celebrate the birth of William and Janey's daughter Jenny. At this occasion Gabriel was very quiet and possibly depressed, perhaps thinking about how their lives as young couples were already changing. He could also have been apprehensive about Lizzie's forthcoming labour. The pregnancy continued well until the middle of April when Lizzie's baby appeared to stop moving. Despite some optimism that things would still turn out okay the baby was stillborn on the second day of May. Lizzie never really recovered from this dreadful experience and began to take increasingly larger quantities of the drug laudanum.

In the early hours of the eleventh of February 1862 Brown was awakened by a distressed Gabriel at his door and both men rushed along to Blackfriars where more than one doctor had been attempting to help Lizzie who had taken an overdose of laudanum and left a suicide note. Alas, nothing could save her and after her death Brown made the necessary arrangements for the required inquest and funeral as well as, more controversially, destroying the suicide note. This is also the point at which Gabriel famously placed the manuscript of his poems in her coffin. Brown's support of Gabriel at this time was to prove typical of his behaviour at times of future crises in Rossetti's life.

Rossetti arguably never fully recovered from the events in February of that year but in 1865 showed some of his gratitude to Brown by helping him with an exhibition of his work. This one-man show had almost a hundred of Brown's paintings on view and was a resounding success enabling Brown to be freer of financial burdens and move to a larger more central property in Bloomsbury. Here in Fitzroy Square he would hold lavish parties which were attended by the likes of artists and designers such as Whistler and Morris as well as Browning, Tennyson, Mark Twain, Liszt and Oscar Wilde. At the same time Brown took on a new pupil Marie Spartali who came from a wealthy Greek family. They grew close and there is little doubt that Brown secretly desired her but no affair developed although Emma felt her place to be threatened at the time.

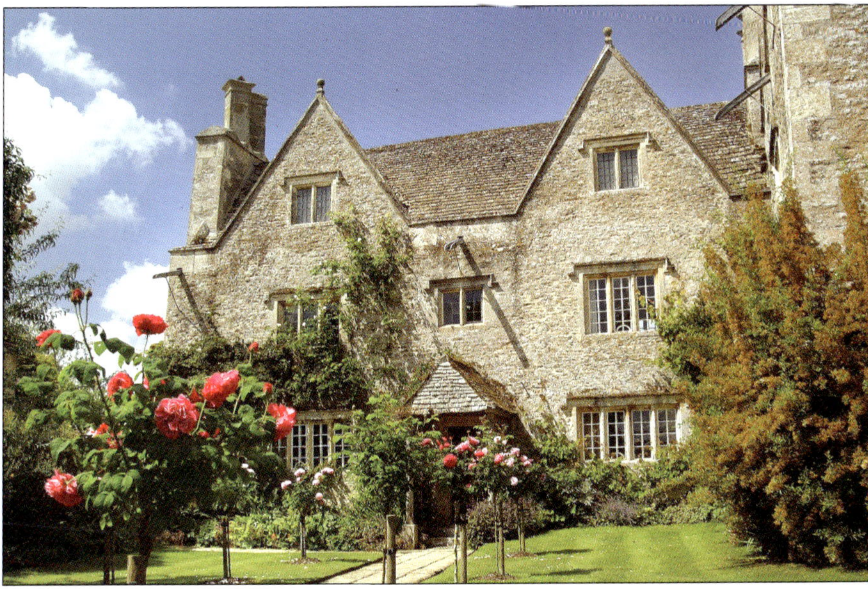

KELMSCOTT MANOR - COPYRIGHT OF THE SOCIETY OF ANTIQUARIES OF LONDON / KELMSCOTT MANOR

During this period William and Janey left the **Red House** for Queen Square in London in order to be closer to their work in the Firm. Gabriel had been living at his new home, Tudor House, at number sixteen Cheyne Walk, Chelsea, for the past three years and it was there that he commissioned some photographs of Jane Morris. This and his commencement of a number of drawings of Jane indicate their growing intimacy at this time.

The year 1869 marks for many people the moral low point of Rossetti's whole life. Although the facts differ in accounts of the incident there is little doubt that Gabriel arranged for Lizzie's coffin to be disinterred so that he could retrieve his poetry and publish it the year after to favourable reviews.

The relationship between him and Jane became even closer after Rossetti and William Morris took a joint tenancy on Kelmscott Manor in Oxfordshire in 1871. That summer William took himself off to Iceland leaving the illicit couple at the manor house with the Morris children, May and Jenny.

Unfortunately that same year there was criticism of Rossetti's poetry published in the *Contemporary Review* by a Robert Buchanan writing under the name of Thomas Maitland. The article was entitled 'The Fleshly School of Poetry' and it attacked Rossetti and other poets close to him, including Swinburne, for their poor morals and licentiousness. Rossetti published a reply in the *Athenaeum* late in the year but his health declined and he suffered a mental breakdown and became more reclusive. He began to see less of his older friends but Madox Brown proved once again to be a great ally.

In September 1873 the Browns gave a big party to celebrate twenty-two-year-old Cathy's wedding to Franz Hueffer, a German musicologist and critic. In addition, Cathy gave birth to Brown's first grandchild in December - a son, Ford Madox Hueffer, later to be the writer, Ford Madox Ford. The latter months of that year could be considered the last truly happy ones for Brown particularly as Lucy also announced her engagement to William Michael Rossetti.

The next year would bring increasing tensions with Burne-Jones and then a tragedy - the death of Nolly after suffering from a liver complaint and gout which later developed into septicemia. This was shortly after the Browns had been on holiday in **Margate** during the summer. Nolly held on to life during a long decline but died on the fifth of November.

Gabriel began to improve at Kelmscott and began to work on some of his most important and monumental paintings such as *Proserpine* and *Astarte Syriaca* (both Manchester City Art Gallery). The latter he worked on whilst being not too far from Kent - he spent time at Aldwick Lodge at Bognor Regis in neighbouring Sussex.

Following the death of his son Brown received much support from the Manchurian artist, Frederick Shields, and it was through him that Brown got an important commission to decorate the new Manchester Town Hall. The murals that he completed took up many of Brown's later years and were his chief occupation but stand up as a brilliant coda to Brown's career.

Meanwhile, Rossetti's health was still causing concern and following an operation in 1877 he convalesced at **Herne Bay** after being accompanied there by Brown. In addition to his physical problems Gabriel may have been anxious about Jane Morris whose daughter Jenny had suffered a mental breakdown and she was with her mother in **Deal** convalescing. Initially for Brown and Rossetti there were some difficulties with a landlady but then the two painters moved to **Hunter's Forestall (Forstal)** close-by. Here they stayed for a couple of months or so in a secluded cottage. Rossetti may well have been depressed and he saw the only escape from this to be through drinking alcohol or taking more chloral, a sleeping draught to which he had become addicted. His mother and sister Christina visited him but despite this the patient managed to acquire more quantities of chloral and so had a number of relapses before his health improved. Gabriel

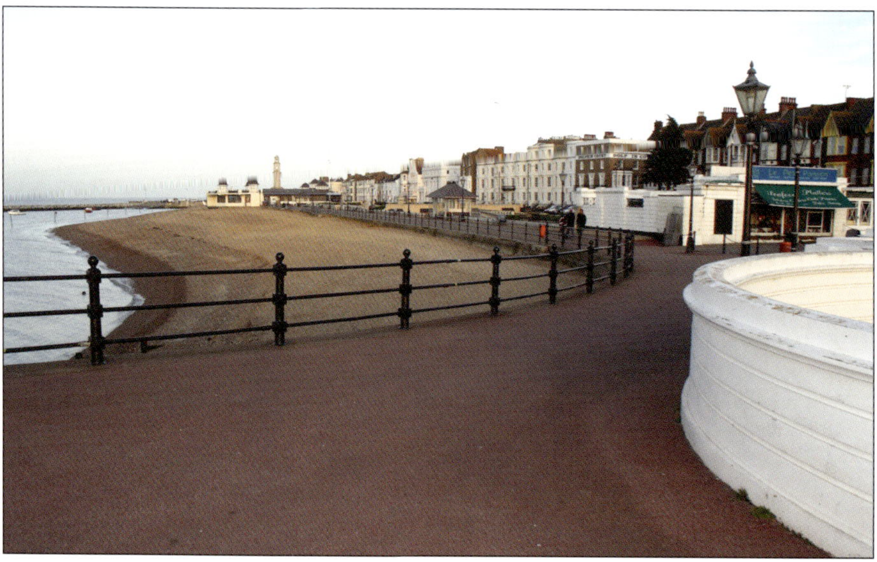

HERNE BAY - PHOTO BY BRIAN WISE

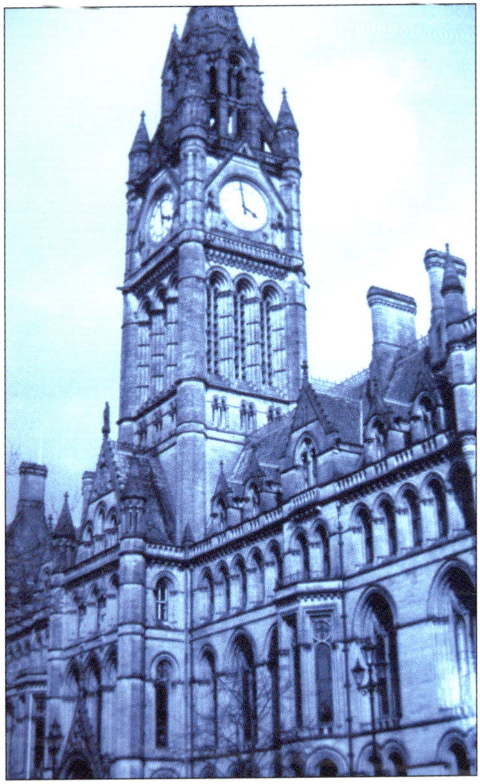

MANCHESTER TOWN HALL - PHOTO BY AUTHOR

later wrote that he was relieved to be resuming his work and he produced a charming drawing of his mother and sister whilst at the resort. Unfortunately a disagreement occurred between Brown and Gabriel over his continued, if vastly reduced, use of the chloral.

The next few years were marked by less contact between Brown and Rossetti, partly as a result of the latter's problems with drugs and health but also because geographically they were further apart. In April 1879 Brown was staying in Manchester and working in the Great Hall of the newly-completed Town Hall. He was preparing to work on the first of twelve murals depicting the history of that city. The first subject was *The Baptism of Edwin* (a copy of the cartoon for this can be seen in the house at Standen in Sussex) and this was completed by July. In September, however, he needed to return to his house at Fitzroy Square in London to care for Emma who was having increasing fits and anxiety not helped by her continued reliance on alcohol. He then returned to Manchester planning to rent a house there with Emma and also to complete further murals. In 1881 the lease of their London home was sold at last and Brown and Emma moved into a house in Crumpsall, a new suburb of Manchester. It was a brand new terraced house called Calais Cottage with views of the Derbyshire hills.

Rossetti's health was now never particularly good but he did continue to work producing a new edition of his *Poems* in 1881 as well as a book of *Ballads and Sonnets*. He was also painting a good deal but the same year saw Jane Morris model for him for the last time - their relationship had begun to cool since about five years earlier.

Rossetti continued to use large quantities of chloral which he believed to be the only form of help for his growing fears. He still felt paranoid believing there were conspiracies against him but he also had a more grounded fear of blindness and of poverty. He ruminated about his own death whilst deteriorating physically. Communication between him and Brown was at an all-time low.

Early the next year Gabriel's family, together with his physician, made a determined attempt to get him off the chloral and in this they were successful via shorter term use of morphia. It was also decided that Gabriel might again benefit from a change of scenery and John Seddon (who had been involved in earlier Pre-Raphaelite circles) offered the use of his spacious bungalow 'Westcliff 'at **Birchington-on-Sea** where for a while Gabriel

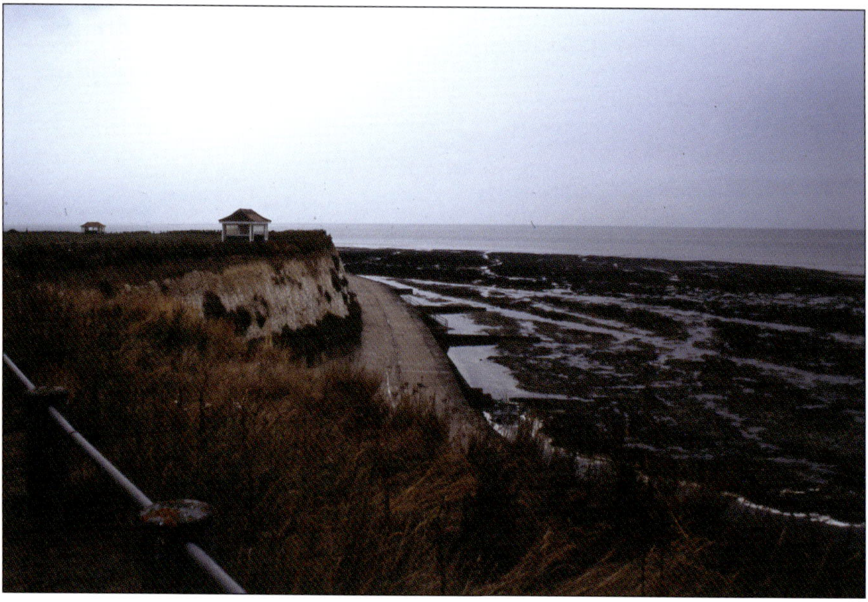

COAST AT BIRCHINGTON - PHOTO BY AUTHOR

continued to write poetry and to paint. He finished his eighth and last version of *Proserpine* and so even close to the end was still painting his beloved Jane although the image had become more conflated - she now had red hair and is perhaps a mix of Jane and Lizzie Siddal. Rossetti apparently detested the 'ugly' bungalow but his companion Hall Caine convinced him to stay, at least temporarily. Gabriel still managed the occasional walk along the nearby cliffs and was glad to see his mother and Christina when they arrived in March. Although his health was in steady decline he did experience one more positive day later in the month when he was able to go out on a fine spring day and is quoted as saying *'It is beautiful - the world and life itself. I am glad I have lived'*. His health worsened despite the arrival in April of his brother William and a kidney disease was diagnosed. He was, in addition, suffering the residual effects of an earlier stroke. Christina sat with Gabriel through the long and frightening nights. Easter came and on the Good Friday Gabriel made out his will with assistance. He died on the evening of Easter Sunday the ninth of April aged only fifty-three.

In Manchester Brown received word that Rossetti had died and wrote that *'it shot a pang to my heart as I have not felt since the acuter phase of the grief for poor Nolly -* (Rossetti was) *the warmest and truest friend anyone could have'*.

Fortunately there had been some reconciliation between the two artists the month before when Rossetti answered a letter from Brown with;

'I am very glad you have written and never loved you better than I do now'.

It was decided to bury him in **Birchington** as he had stated that he did not wish to be laid to rest at Highgate where Lizzie was buried. The discreet nature of the funeral was due to the parlous state of Gabriel's finances with a very real fear that his creditors might demand monies that had been set aside for the funeral expenses. On the day the churchyard was bright with spring flowers and the mourners included Gabriel's mother and sister Christina, William and his wife Lucy, Frederick Shields, Hall Caine, Seddon and also Frederick Stephens and another artist George Boyce. There was no Madox Brown, who was still in Manchester, or Burne-Jones who set out to attend but had to turn back from the journey through feeling unwell. Fanny Cornforth could also not attend due to being notified by William of Gabriel's death only on the morning of the funeral.

A little later Christine wrote her sonnet *Birchington Churchyard* which describes the scene and mood of the occasion:

A lowly hill which overlooks a flat,
Half sea, half country-side;
A flat-shored sea of low-voiced creeping tide
Over a chalky weedy mat.

A hill of hillocks, flowery and kept green
Round crosses raised for hope,
With many-tinted sunsets where the slope
Faces the lingering western sheen.

A lowly hope, a height that is but low,
While Time sets solemnly,
While the tide rises of Eternity,
Silent and neither swift or slow.

There was a sale of Rossetti's household effects on the fifth of July and his mother then asked Brown to design a Celtic cross for her son's headstone. When it was made she considered it to be very fine having as it did a runic bas-relief symbolising Gabriel's life and work. She also asked Shields to design a memorial window for the church. Mrs Rossetti continued to visit her son's grave in the summers of 1883 and the year after until the cross was erected in the autumn of 1884.

At the Christmas following Rossetti's death the Browns relocated to a more fashionable part of Manchester as Brown had been awarded more mural work at the Town Hall. At his new address near Victoria Park he began to socialise in style and to enjoy his celebrity. He was now quite affluent and a leading figure in Mancunian artistic circles.

In 1884 he became more friendly with William Morris due to a shared interest in social issues. A couple of years later Brown completed huge decorations for the specially constructed Jubilee building in Manchester and also had eight pictures by him exhibited in the Fine Art division of the exhibition. The

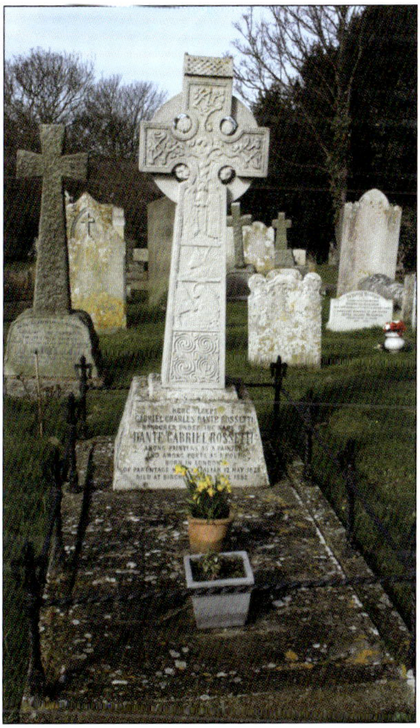

ROSSETTI'S GRAVE AT BIRCHINGTON - PHOTO BY BRIAN WISE

pictures included *Work,* one of his best paintings which had been recently acquired by the local City Art Gallery. These events mark the high point of Madox Brown's involvement with the Manchester art world for he was soon to return to London. This was mainly due to the damper climate of the north of England and the detrimental effect that this was having on his wife's fragile health. He also wanted to be nearer his daughter Cathy whose marriage to Franz Hueffer had proved to be unhappy.

In July 1887 Brown's memorial to Gabriel was unveiled on Chelsea Embankment near Rossetti's old home in Cheyne Walk and Holman Hunt gave a long speech of tribute.

A few months later Brown himself was back in London but having been away for eight years or so and having ignored his market for over thirty years he found much of the art world had forgotten him. Friends such as Walter Crane, William Morris, Arthur Hughes and Holman Hunt did celebrate his return but then two family tragedies intervened. Firstly, in January 1889, Franz Hueffer died at the age of only forty-two. Later the same year Emma, who had been bedridden since the April, died in October. Brown was knocked sideways by these events and although he was surrounded by family including grandchildren he felt desperately lonely. One of his grandchildren, Juliet, later wrote in her memoirs about her observations of Brown at this difficult time;

'He used to sit alone in the studio for hours together, doing no work at all he would wander about the house looking everywhere for her (Emma)'.

Brown continued to work painting the penultimate Manchester mural at home between April 1891 and May of the year after. He struggled with the subject *The Opening of the Bridgewater Canal* perhaps due to his mood as much as any reduction in his artistic powers. Hearing of Brown's situation Burne-Jones decided to initiate a fund for his long-term friend with a plan to raise enough money to buy one of Brown's paintings for the National Gallery.

The plan didn't work for a number of reasons but eventually Brown accepted a related commission to paint a copy of his *Wycliffe* for the gallery. Unfortunately he was never to complete this but the money raised by Burne-Jones and others was used to buy *Jesus Washing Peter's Feet* (Tate Britain)for the nation, a painting that Brown himself highly rated.

Later in 1892 Brown accepted his last big commission which provided him with an entirely new challenge. He was to design the theatrical sets and costumes for Henry Irving's new production of *King Lear.* The sets, perhaps unsurprisingly, had similarities to his own painting *King Lear (Cordelia at the Bedside of Lear)* whereby chalk cliffs were shown above a blue sea so like his earlier picture based on the white cliffs of **Dover**.

Brown now turned with increasing ill health to finishing the last of the Manchester murals *Bradshaw's Defence of Manchester AD 1642* which was initially not accepted by the authorities in the city due to its poor execution - Brown had only been able to use his left hand to paint following a stroke.

His daughter Lucy's health also caused him concern, suffering as she was from tuberculosis. On the fourth of October 1893 she left for the Riviera where she had gone before in order to avoid the English winter. This turned out to be only two days before her father's death and Brown died peacefully at home on the sixth of October where only a few days before he had been trying to complete his copy of the *Wycliffe.*

Old friends such as Georgie Burne-Jones and Arthur Hughes attended his funeral at St. Pancras cemetery as well as Holman Hunt who commented that Brown's death '*would be to me a never-ending loss*'. The ceremony was characteristically without Christian content and Brown was laid to rest by the side of his beloved Emma and their two sons.

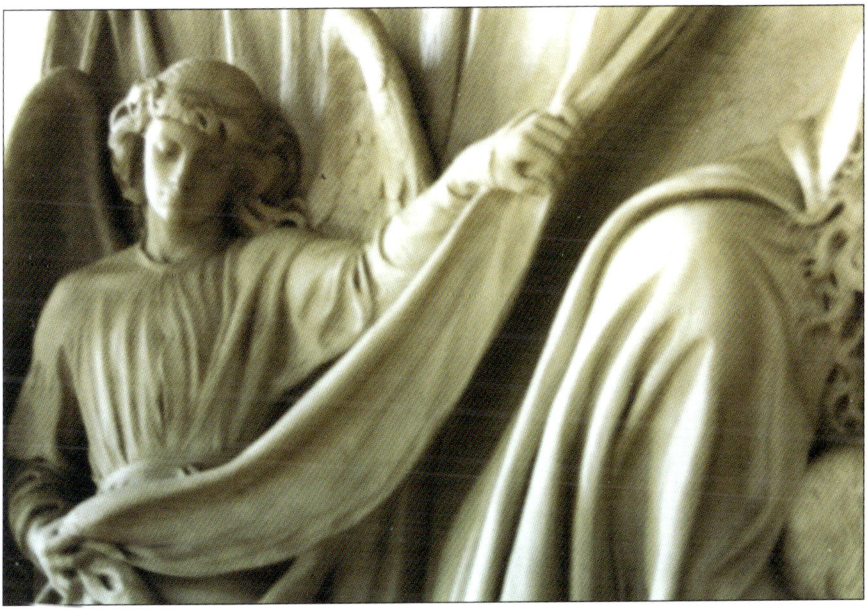

DETAIL OF SCULPTURE BY HENRY HUGH ARMSTEAD IN HYTHE CHURCH - PHOTO BY AUTHOR

The Lesser Known Story

WILLIAM MICHAEL ROSSETTI AND LUCY MADOX BROWN

Inevitably there is some overlap between this chapter and the last as they both primarily address the same two families albeit different members of them. The two stories do cross but any repetition has been kept to a minimum.

To a large extent the lives of William Michael Rossetti and Lucy Madox Brown have been overshadowed by other more familiar members of their respective families. In William's case, by his brother Gabriel and sister Christina, with Lucy eclipsed by her father Ford Madox Brown. In addition Lucy's career as an artist has not been fully acknowledged until recently as the society of her time tended to discriminate against female artists.

William Michael Rossetti was the younger brother (born 1829) of his more famous sibling Dante Gabriel but a man who achieved a good degree of success in his life as an art critic and writer. He also had a more sensible personality that enabled him to work for many years in the Tax Office thus keeping the family's finances afloat and supplying Gabriel with regular 'loans' when his 'tin' (money) was low. Much later Edith Sitwell described how William's *'saintly and sweet character'* was devoted to the members of his family, possibly to the exclusion of his own enjoyment of life. His initial ambition may well also have been to paint (he is shown wearing artistic dress in a Julia Margaret Cameron photograph of 1865) but his talent really lay elsewhere in the varied fields of his writing.

He shared a scepticism about religion with Gabriel although their two sisters Maria and Christina were very devout in their beliefs. This followed an earlier gender divide in the Rossetti household with their father Gabriele being an agnostic and mother Frances having a deep belief. Interestingly neither sister would marry and only William would have a longer term marriage. Inevitably this took place in a registry office.

In 1848 William was asked by Gabriel to join him in a secret society whose goal was to cause a revolution in art - The Pre-Raphaelite Brotherhood. Its principal members were undoubtedly Gabriel and his two friends and fellow students at the Royal Academy, John Everett Millais and William Holman Hunt. However, Gabriel wanted seven 'brothers' as he considered this to be a mystical number and so William was invited in with three other acquaintances. It should not be thought, however, that William was brought in merely to make up the numbers nor that his contribution to the Brotherhood and its journal *The Germ* was not considerable. After all in years to come he was to be the main chronicler of the Brotherhood even if he tended to play down the extent of his own involvement.

Lucy Madox Brown was born in Paris (where her father was living at the time and where he was studying Rembrandt amongst other artists in the Louvre) in July 1843. She was the only child of his first marriage to his cousin Elizabeth Bromley whom he had married two years earlier at St John's Church in the village of **Meopham** in Kent. In 1844 parents and child all moved to London although they returned to Basle and Rome in 1845-6 to see if a change of climate would help aid Elizabeth's health. She was suffering from tuberculosis and sadly she died on the fifth of July 1846. Lucy and her father came back to Britain and she was placed with his sister-in-law by marriage, Helen

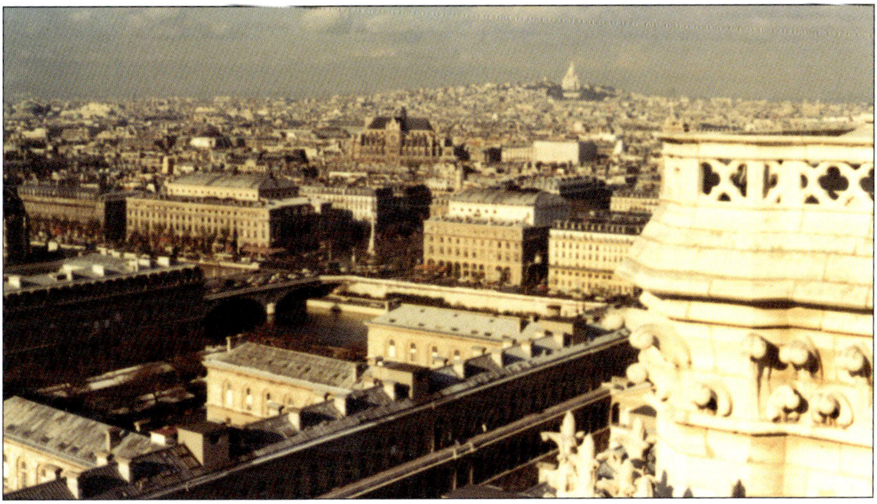

MODERN PARIS - PHOTO BY AUTHOR

Bromley and her family at **Meopham** as Ford Madox Brown was financially unable to provide a home for her. The widowed Helen lived at Melliker Farm near the village where Lucy was visited by her much missed father. Lucy also attended her aunt's school at nearby **Gravesend** in a rented house by the name of Milton Lodge. It seems Helen and Lucy were able to provide support for one another to help them through their own individual experiences of grief.

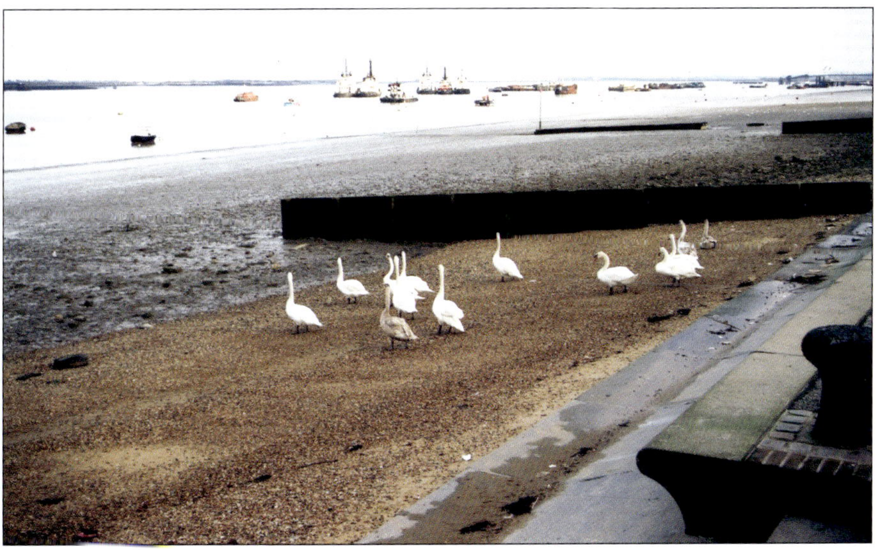

GRAVESEND - PHOTO BY BRIAN WISE

In 1853 Ford Madox Brown married Emma Hill whom he had known for about four years. They already had a three-year-old daughter called Cathy. Lucy, however, continued to have only an intermittent contact with her father usually in the school holidays. She no doubt felt excluded at times from a home where many artists came and went and where for example Emma and Lizzie Siddal would laugh, socialise and drink together.

Even when she left the school at **Gravesend** to have lessons from Maria Rossetti her father preferred her to stay with the Rossetti family. Lucy would have lunch with Maria, in what was an informal atmosphere, and perhaps visit somewhere like the Zoological Gardens in Regent's Park on occasion. Sometimes William would return from a day at the Tax Office and see Lucy although he was invariably busy with his reading, reviewing and writing.

Later there was the birth of Oliver Madox Brown for Lucy to deal with before she came to live at last with her father and Emma. Almost inevitably there was friction between Lucy and Cathy centring around their differing looks and abilities.

During the 1860s Lucy increasingly began to help in her father's studio and began to sketch and paint herself. There is, however, also evidence to show she did some painting at a younger age such as a watercolour of Melliker Farm. At the end of 1865 the Madox Brown family moved from Kentish Town to the larger and more exclusive 37 Fitzroy Square and Lucy continued to become more involved in her father's work and also that of his assistant Albert Goodwin. She even completed a picture begun by Goodwin. When Madox Brown saw his daughter's proficiency in the medium he arranged for her to attend art classes with his other two children, Cathy and Oliver.

Lucy began to have her work exhibited around 1870 and perhaps her most accomplished watercolour was shown at the Dudley Gallery in 1871. This is a work

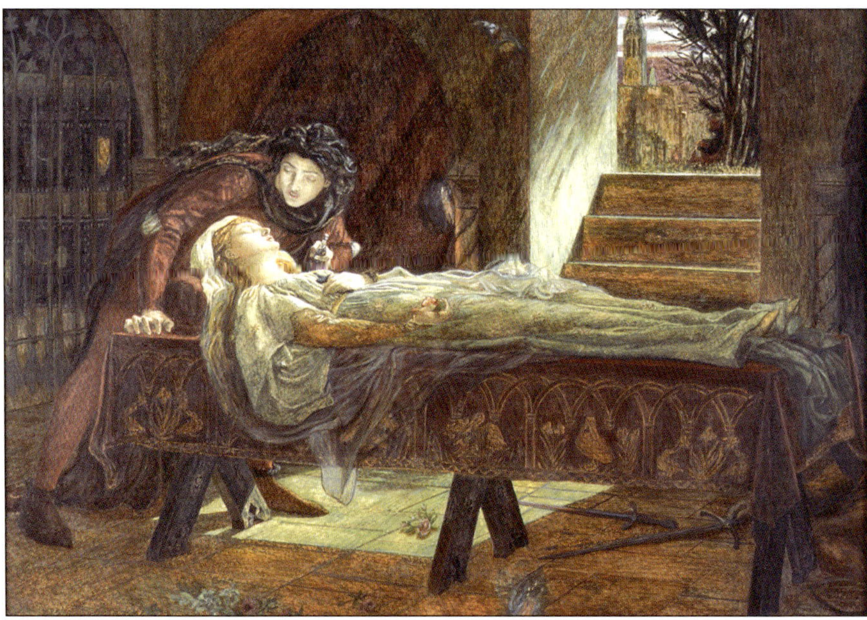

'THE TOMB SCENE FROM ROMEO AND JULIET' BY LUCY MADOX BROWN - BY KIND PERMISSION OF THE NATIONAL TRUST/WIGHTWICK MANOR

entitled *The Tomb Scene from Romeo and Juliet* (Wightwick Manor, National Trust) which may initially have been inspired by a contemporary work on the same subject by her father. However, Lucy's scene is very different but undoubtedly very detailed and Pre-Raphaelite in style. It shows the tragic moment from the play when Romeo believes wrongly that Juliet has killed herself and prepares to take poison himself. She will subsequently awake and find him dead and so too commit suicide. The picture was generally well received and Lucy produced other work on the theme of love which may have been a subject at the time that was close to her heart.

In 1873 William was feeling the need for a vacation following Gabriel and Christina having bouts of illness. He was invited to go on a trip to Italy with William Bell Scott and his wife with the addition of Alice Boyd the 'companion' of Scott. Presumably in order to avoid being a sort of chaperon and perhaps for other more important reasons he invited Lucy along for the trip. During the holiday William made up his mind to *'not again part with Lucy'* and he proposed marriage to her and was accepted. Christina wrote to Lucy from Kelmscott where she had been visiting Gabriel to offer her a *'welcome to you as my dear sister and friend'*.

The ensuing engagement appeared to bring together two families that had been quite close for a number of years. The event was only adversely affected by the continuing illness of Maria Rossetti who had a serious stomach complaint. She was at Eastbourne in Sussex at the All Saints' Hospital which was then a convalescent home run by the All Saints' Sisters of the Poor, the community Maria had joined in 1860.

Meanwhile the house at 56 Euston Square where Christina and Mrs Rossetti Senior lived was redecorated for the arrival of William and Lucy. There were going to be a number of difficulties associated with the reconstituted household some of which revolved around religious belief or the lack of it. As an obvious sign of this William and Lucy were married on the last day of March 1874 in a civil ceremony to which Maria felt unable to attend. The small group at the wedding breakfast comprised Mrs Rossetti, Christina and Gabriel with the addition of the Madox Browns and the Morrises. The atmosphere may not have been helped by a backdrop of Janey Morris still having a relationship with Gabriel at Kelmscott during this time. After the wedding William and Lucy went on honeymoon returning to Italy (amongst other countries) which they had so enjoyed the previous year. On the way they stopped at **Canterbury** en route to **Dover** and William wrote from the Fountain Inn to tell his mother *'I have not much to mention beyond what you will readily believe - my entire happiness'*.

On their return to Euston Square William and Lucy had the rooms on the top floor but this did not prevent friction forming, particularly between Christina and Lucy. This could be explained by their difference in ages as well as their changed circumstances (Lucy had gone from paying lodger in her days as a pupil of Maria's to a sister-in-law) in addition to their very different religious beliefs.

Lucy gave birth to her first child on the twentieth of September 1875 - a daughter they named Olivia after her father's son Oliver(but known as Nolly) who tragically had died the year before aged only 19. William and Lucy were to have further children - Arthur (born 1877), Helen (1879) and the twins Michael and Mary in 1881.

In April 1876 Lucy was at **Broadstairs** with her first baby keenly reading Dickens but missing her husband. It was the practice in Victorian times for wives who could afford it, to spend periods of the spring and summer by the sea but William could only occasionally join Lucy due to his work commitments. Whilst there she produced charming watercolours of the town.

However, the situation at Euston Square was even more on an edge with extra

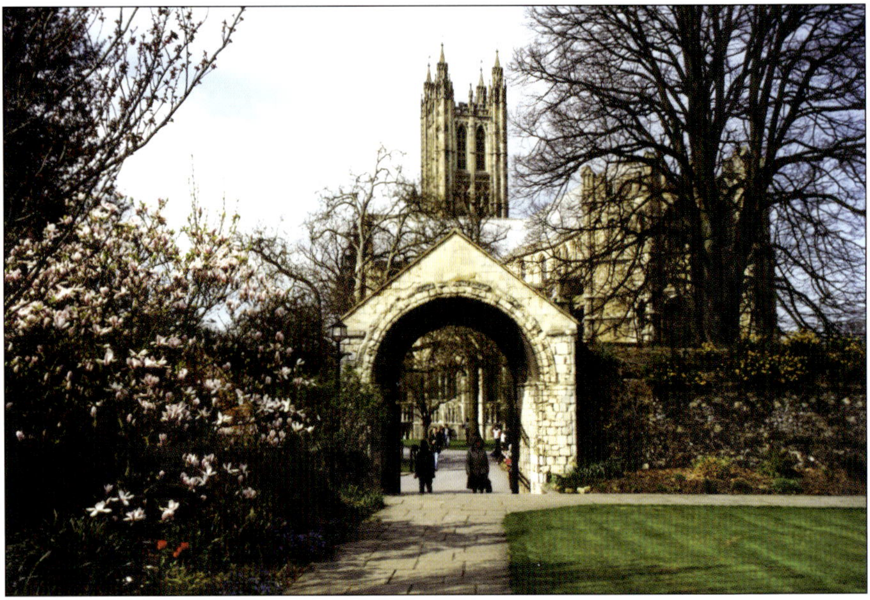

CANTERBURY - PHOTO BY BRIAN WISE

pressure on space with the arrival of a baby. Eventually the pressure became too great and Christina announced that she and her mother would be moving out of the accommodation that William had leased since 1867. From Eastbourne, where she was continuing to visit her sick sister, Christina wrote to Lucy hoping *'that when twin roofs shelter us and when faults that I regret are no longer your daily trial, that we may regain some of that liking which we had as friends, and which I should wish to be only the more tender and warm now that we are sisters. Don't please despair of my doing better'*. Alas Maria was not to recover (having cancer) and she died on the twenty-fourth of November 1876 at the age of forty-nine soon after Christina and her mother found new lodgings at 30 Torrington Square.

Understandably, Christmas that year was a miserable experience for all concerned and soon afterwards William became increasingly concerned at Gabriel's state of health. He would need to reduce his intake of the sleeping drug chloral. Time went past but on the seventeenth of August 1877 a relieved brother saw Gabriel leave for a recuperative break by the sea at **Herne Bay** accompanied by Ford Madox Brown.

William had continued to keep his monotonous job at the Tax Office because it provided his growing family with a reasonable income although he did apply for an administrative post at the National Gallery but to no avail. Thus he persevered with the job he disliked as well as writing some art criticism which itself did not excite him as it used to in his youth.

Some change from his routine was provided by the famous Whistler-Ruskin court case (where the former sued the latter for comments made about one of his paintings). Whistler asked William (in the absence of many others unwilling) to support him, which William just about did but with great embarrassment particularly as Ruskin had given the Pre-Raphaelites so much help in their early days when their work was savaged by critics. Whistler won the case but was only given an award of one farthing and became effectively bankrupt.

Shortly afterwards William had his own court case to deal with in which he was accused of libel because of remarks that he had made in the journal *The Athenaeum*. This led to a decline in his work as an art and literary critic.

Now in her mid-thirties his wife Lucy was very much a mother coping with her five children all under six. Her time to produce works of art was very limited. She and the children rarely saw Gabriel (who was now reclusive) and becoming more unwell.

Gabriel was persuaded in February 1882 to recuperate at **Birchington-on-Sea** but he did not improve and died at Easter. William was present for the final moments when Gabriel was barely conscious due to his failing liver and kidneys. He managed however to help Gabriel change his will.

After these sad events Lucy developed a badly infected finger but valiantly continued a programme of five-mile walks whilst staying at Southend. However, less than a year after Gabriel's death Michael (one of the twins), who had never been healthy, became worse suddenly and died not yet two years of age.

By the summer of 1883 Lucy had recovered enough from these tragic events to have a holiday with Cathy at **Hythe** and they enjoyed each other's company. This was against the background of all the sad occurrences and their own disagreements in the past.

Christina and William spent many months tidying up aspects of Gabriel's estate including the paying off of a number of debts with William collating diary entries and other paperwork for a biography of his brother. Lucy continued to cause him concern by having more bouts of 'bronchitis' and so taking to her bed. She spent the early part of 1886 in Italy to order to attempt to improve her health whilst the winter in England was severe leading almost certainly to Mrs Rossetti Senior's decline in health and death at the age of 86.

Lucy's own health continued to be poor and her doctor suggested more and more that she should have convalescent breaks abroad so in November of the same year she left

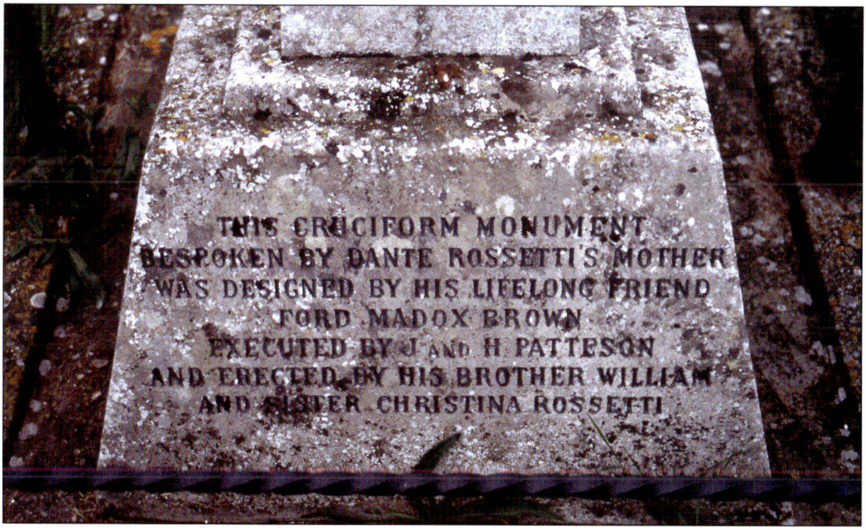

DETAIL OF ROSSETTI'S GRAVESTONE AT BIRCHINGTON - PHOTO BY AUTHOR

with her two elder children, Olive and Arthur for San Remo, an Italian winter resort. The town had been loved by Edward Lear in his later years and he was to die there on the twenty-ninth of January 1888.

Despite William's work commitments he was able to visit his wife and children for short periods of time although his work responsibilities were changing. He always regretted not visiting his old friend Lear in the last year of his life when he saw Lucy in early 1887.

At home William was asked by the Inland Revenue to visit stately homes and other properties in order to estimate a value on paintings outlined in probate matters. This provided him with an enjoyable aspect to his long-term employment against a background of worsening family health.

Lucy was in fact suffering from tuberculosis which was such a killer in Victorian times although it was often not mentioned by doctors as if not talking about the disease would somehow make it go away. But by 1893 the doctor attending Lucy felt no option but to start using the term as her condition reached its inevitable conclusion. Her end may well have been hastened by the sudden death that year of her father Ford Madox Brown although this event was relayed to her with great delicacy by William.

On the nineteenth of March 1894 William received a telegram from Olive to say that her mother's health was rapidly declining and he was at Lucy's side when she died in San Remo on the morning of the twelfth of April 1894. Within six months of one another William had lost a wife to whom he had been devoted (but who had recently become more distant) and a father figure (Madox Brown) who had supported and advised him on many aspects of his professional life. William was to live a further twenty-five years greatly outliving his sister Christina who died distressingly the same year as Lucy. He spent the greater part of his remaining time attending to the needs of his four children and enjoying his life with them. Of course he also spent much time chronicling the times of the Brotherhood and defending them from criticism and in 1895 completed a major biographical work on his brother. When he died aged eighty-nine the newspapers announced the death of the *'last of the famous Pre-Raphaelites'*.

The Great War had only recently come to an end and William in his last years must have been only too aware of how much his world had changed from the heady early days of the Brotherhood.

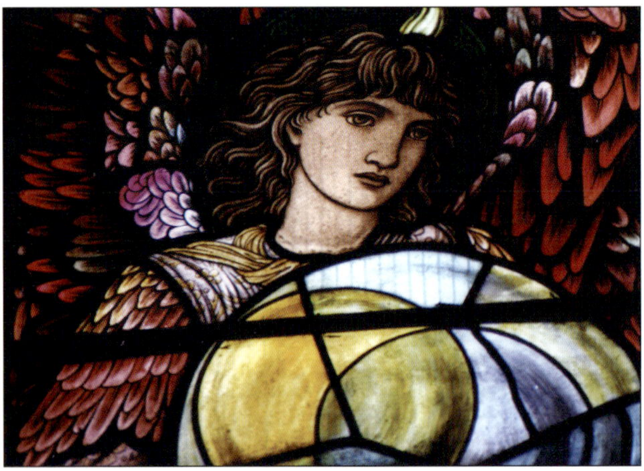

DETAIL OF THE MORRIS WINDOW IN SHOREHAM CHURCH - PHOTO BY AUTHOR

William Holman Hunt and Gad's Hill Place

Gad's Hill was the home of Charles Dickens from 1857 until 1870. Its location is at Higham a couple of miles west from Rochester. Although originally a comparatively small Regency house it was a place that Dickens had for many years wanted to own. He had told his father about this dream and there is a quote from Dickens to this effect in the outside porch. When Dickens eventually acquired the house he was by then a successful author and he had the finances to extensively enlarge the property. It is now used by a school which means a degree of hard wear for the building. Of particular interest inside are the wooden panels on the staircase painted by Dickens' daughter Kate who married Charley Collins (the brother of writer Wilkie of *The Woman in White* fame) and later celebrated the event at Gad's Hill. This occurred in July 1860 by which time Charley was no longer a painter influenced by the Pre-Raphaelites but had become a journalist. In this line of work he had had a number of pieces published in *Household Words,* a periodical which was edited by Dickens, and he thus grew closer to the novelist and his family. Charley visited Gad's Hill frequently and eventually proposed to Kate who (despite her superior social position) somewhat surprisingly accepted him. Holman Hunt was the best man for the wedding and was overjoyed that he *'should be a guest at this magical writer's table on one of the most personal and sacred events of his* (Dickens) *life'*. The weather was good and after the service the guests played games on the lawn and Hunt

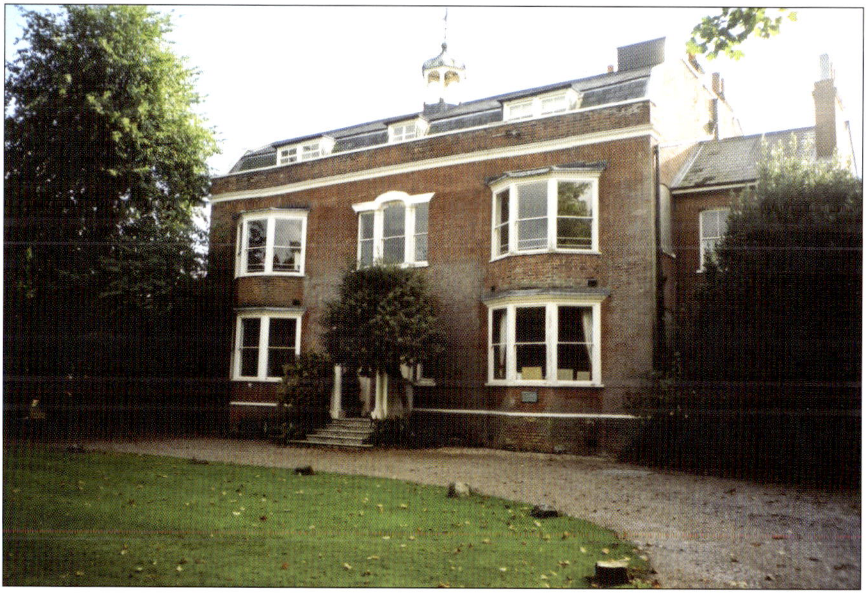

GAD'S HILL PLACE - PHOTO BY AUTHOR

found himself admiring the beauty of the new bride. He also found himself close to a painting of the Sphinx by David Roberts and a conversation took place about the picture between Hunt and Dickens. Hunt had himself spent considerable time painting the same subject whilst in the Holy Land and because of this noticed that the sun in Roberts' work was setting in the south. This he might have accepted as artistic licence but knew that it made no sense in regard to the legend of the Sphinx whose head should always be looking towards the rising sun. Dickens defended the painting saying that it was still an admirable poetical conception all the same. After the wedding breakfast Hunt went for a drive about Rochester and visited the castle with, amongst others, the mother of the bridegroom. Later all the guests attended a band rendition at Chatham.

In the library there is a print based on the painting by Luke Fildes showing that room and completed on the artist's visit to the house just after Dickens' death. The amusing titles that Dickens supplied for the false bookends attached to the library door should also be seen. In front of the house by the driveway is the tunnel built for Dickens to go under the main road and connect with The Wilderness on the other side. It was there that his Swiss Chalet was located (now in the Dickens Museum at Rochester) and where he wrote books such as *A Tale of Two Cities* and *Great Expectations*.

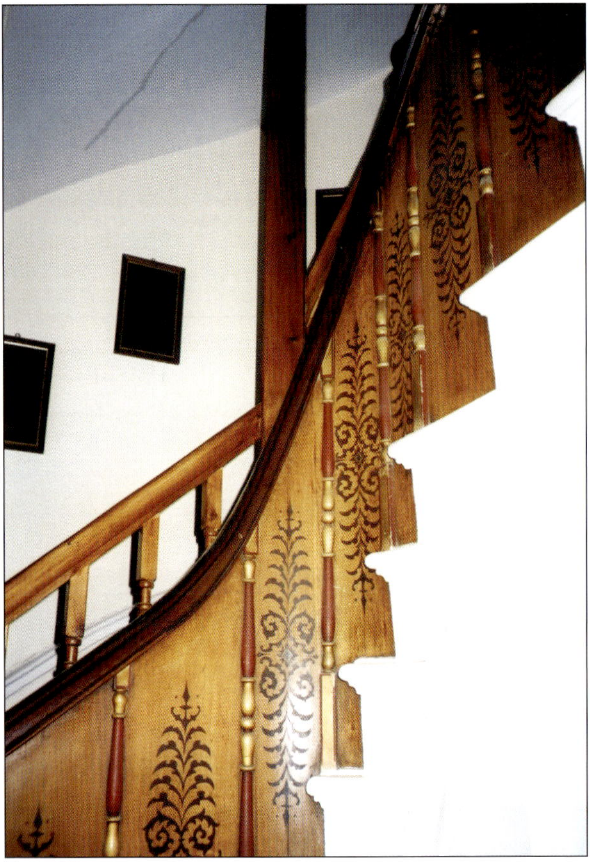

Quite recently extra ugly but essential supports have been put in the building and these are very visible in the entrance hall. The visitor can see a number of ground floor rooms and the experience is enhanced by the guide's reflections and by photographs showing the rooms in Dickens' day.

The house is open for guided tours on the first Sunday of every month from April to October.

PART OF KATE DICKENS' DECORATION OF THE STAIRS AT GAD'S HILL - PHOTO BY AUTHOR

John Everett Millais and his brother William

AT HAYES COMMON

Within the older boundaries of Kent but now officially in Greater London lies Hayes Common which has two claims to Pre-Raphaelite fame. Firstly it was the location for paintings by John Everett Millais and his brother William. Secondly it has a Philip Webb house which although a private residence still exists very much as it was completed by Webb in 1873.

The first picture in question is *The Proscribed Royalist, 1651* (Private Collection) painted between 1852-3. It was commissioned by the Hon. Secretary of the Art Union of London, Lewis Pocock. He was also a collector having already acquired a sketch of Hunt's *Valentine Rescuing Sylvia from Proteus* (see opening chapter). The subject of the Millais work comes from the Bellini opera I Puritani which Millais may well have seen performed at Covent Garden before commencing the painting. The picture shows a pair of lovers from opposite sides during the Civil War. The two figures shown are Elvira who is a Roundhead and hiding in a giant oak tree, behind is Arturo, a Cavalier. This scene has a similarity with the legend of Charles II who supposedly evaded the Roundheads by the same form of concealment. Whilst painting the picture Millais stayed at the George Inn at Hayes close to Bromley and some of the time he was accompanied by his brother William. It was William who later recounted a story of how the landlord, Mr Vidler, was upset on one occasion by the brothers ridiculing the artistic merits of his signboard showing St George killing the Dragon. Later, after a storm, the offending sign was destroyed so the Millais brothers completed a replacement sign painting one side each. Mr Vidler was still not convinced that this was as good as the original but apparently changed his mind when people came to his inn to view the sign after it became known who had painted it. Millais visited a Mr. Hamilton who was rector of Beddington near Croydon during this period and also visited his cousin George Hodgkinson and his wife Emily at their house at Waddon also near to Croydon. The ancient oak that he used for the painting was at nearby West Wickham Common and the location is also described as being on Coney Hall Hill (in the biography of his father by J. G. Millais). The particular tree achieved some fame during the latter half of the nineteenth century when it was known not surprisingly as The Millais Oak. It is now no longer to be found. The figures in the painting were added later with the model for the girl being Anne Ryan(although initially it was to have been Effie Ruskin), and Arthur Hughes sat for the Cavalier.

William Millais painted an oil at the same location and it also shows the same oak tree. The work *Hayes Common* (Yale Center for British Art) has the same degree of Pre-Raphaelite detail as his brother's picture and there is every reason to think it was completed at the same time being dated 1853. It does not have a historical subject but is a fairly conventional landscape with a child walking on the bank close to the old tree. William was John's elder brother and he was encouraged by John to paint landscapes. This initially occurred in the summer of 1850 in Jersey where the family home was situated. This gives William quite a claim to fame - he would be the first artist to attempt to paint a landscape using Pre-Raphaelite techniques. Whilst William never became a professional artist he did continue to paint for most of his life preferring the medium of watercolour. *Hayes Common* stands as one of his largest and most accomplished works.

Hayes has changed much in its character since the mid-nineteenth century but The Oast House by Philip Webb is relatively unscathed. It is one of his delightful small houses in the country, in this case designed for the aristocratic Lord Sackville Cecil. Unfortunately, Webb fell out with his client before construction was complete probably because Cecil tried to take over the directing of the work force. Webb subsequently refused payment for his work but the discord isn't apparent in the building completed in 1873. The exterior has his frequently-used hipped roofs and giant chimneys. There is also an abundance of locally-found materials evident including ragstone, red brick, tiles and oak gables and panels. As usual Webb made the most of the uniqueness of the site keeping as many of the fruit trees as possible from the old orchard that existed by the side of two cottages prior to building work taking place. The land prior to 1773 had formed part of the Hayes Common. Inside, the house had a dining room, study, drawing room, hall and kitchen but also a laboratory basement for Cecil's various experiments. There are also several outbuildings some of which now form separate residences.

The Oast House is a private house.

William Morris and Red House

In the summer of 1858 William Morris and his friends Philip Webb and Charles Faulkner decided to have a boating holiday down the river Seine in France. It was during this trip that a conversation first took place that led to the building of Red House.

Morris had to this point led a busy life full of developing interests in which a number of important decisions had already been made. Whilst a student at Oxford he had begun to write poetry and become interested in medieval stories. He had also met Burne-Jones who would become a lifelong friend. Together they had come to a decision not to go into the clergy but to take up painting (Burne-Jones) and architecture (Morris). This decision followed an informative trip to view the cathedrals of northern France and the receiving of advice from Dante Gabriel Rossetti whose influence they had come under.

Subsequently in January 1856 Morris was apprenticed to the office of the successful architect G. E. Street where his more immediate superior and advisor was Philip Webb. He was three years older than Morris and through him met other members of the Pre-Raphaelite circle. A self-effacing man whose needs were few Webb was nevertheless a popular figure well known for his dry sense of humour. However, after a year in the office Morris decided to leave wishing to explore less-regimented work such as painting. But the germ of an idea of building a house that would incorporate the Gothic and the romantic was planted hence that later conversation on the boat in France.

In October of 1857 at a theatre in Oxford Morris was accompanied by Burne-Jones and Rossetti. Whilst there he set eyes for the first time on Jane Burden whom he was immediately besotted with and to whom he was engaged in the spring of 1858 and would marry a year later.

He therefore felt the need and also had the money to commission from his friend Webb the building of an appropriate house for him and Janey (as he called her)to live in. But it would also function as a workshop and studio and as a place in which he could entertain his circle of friends. He found a suitable site at Upton in Northern Kent which although not ideal did tick some important boxes for Morris. For one the Pilgrims Way was nearby and he would undoubtedly have liked the idea of having that medieval route (so much associated with Chaucer) close by. He would later call his garden porch at Red House the Pilgrim's Rest. Another important factor was the recent arrival of the railway to the area so facilitating quicker access to and from the capital.

Webb quickly produced a possible plan which with a few exceptions would closely resemble the completed house. He would not take a fee for the work as he considered this to be work for a friend rather than a client. It was also his first commission and a chance to show his mettle. Building started in 1859 and during this time Morris and Janey stayed nearby in a house called Aberleigh Lodge which had just been built. Husband and wife moved into their new home in the summer of the following year. Janey was by then about four months pregnant.

The finished building harked back to the Middle Ages in spirit and so can legitimately be described as a pre-Raphaelite house. Hence its rather unusual plan with two of its main living rooms (a studio and drawing room) being on the first floor with the bedrooms. This conforms to the arrangement in a medieval house of having the solar (living room)

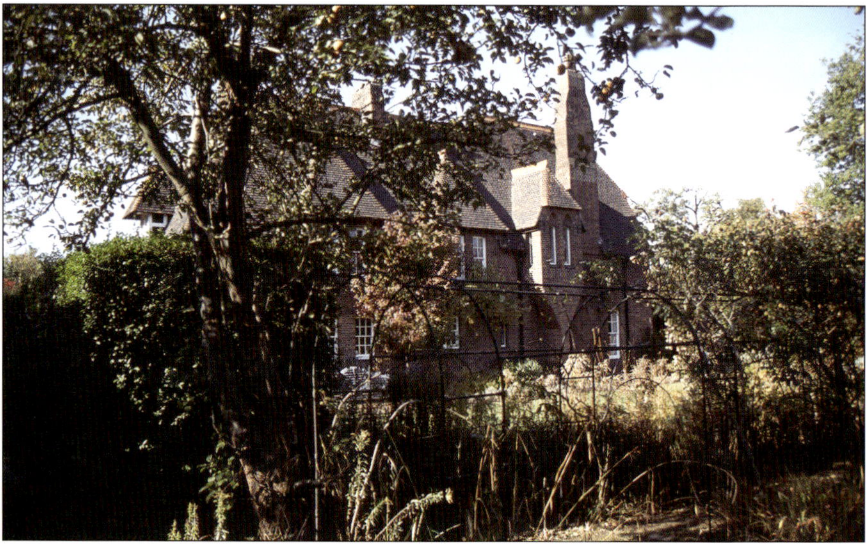

RED HOUSE FROM THE ORCHARD - PHOTO BY KIND PERMISSION OF THE NATIONAL TRUST

on an upper floor above a large hall. On the ground floor at Red House there is indeed a big hall in addition to a dining room, morning room and library. The two servant bedrooms are to be found at the end of the south wing and although smaller than the other bedrooms they were given the same amount of attention to detail by Webb as other rooms. The architect's concern for the welfare of the few servants needed is also shown by the large kitchen window (in a large room) overlooking the garden which would have provided them with a pleasant aspect whilst they were performing their various duties. Unfortunately the kitchen also received the hot afternoon sun just at a time of much activity there. The north-facing main rooms were the opposite - cold even in the summer. There were not, however, many mistakes in the design of the house (if these were indeed mistakes) especially considering it was Webb's first real opportunity to design a domestic dwelling.

Webb was much influenced by Street, his previous employer, and its roof line and Gothic arches helped the building to look ecclesiastical or even monastic. This was likely to have been Webb's intention - within its walls Morris and his friends could indulge themselves in a world far removed from the outside reality. It did make the house look a little severe although its many gables added a touch of lavishness. The interior was left plain and completely undecorated but contained Webb's Gothic staircase, brick fireplaces, some exposed roof beams and trusses and ironwork fittings.

It was in this setting that Morris and Janey, together with Burne-Jones and Georgiana (married June 1860) and Rossetti and Lizzie Siddal (married May 1860) came together to socialise. It also provided an ideal environment in which to work together on the things that jointly interested them - making Red House the most beautiful place on earth. This project was also instrumental in formulating the ideas and practical experience that would later lead to the foundation of the Firm - Morris, Marshall, Faulkner & Co.

Some of the furniture came from Morris' mother but besides this and a piano the remaining items were ordered to be made and sometimes designed by Morris himself.

He did not like any of the furniture then supplied by specialist firms. Many items were designed by Webb including various tables and chairs, a settle with canopy, a cheval mirror, candlesticks and glass tumblers, dishes and bowls. All the early furniture was plain, chunky and of low cost and was complemented by some antique pieces of armour and other metalwork. Still to be seen in the house today are a few pieces of fitted furniture such as the settles in the hall and drawing room and a sideboard in the dining room.

In that first year or so the house must have been a hive of activity with friends calling in to help with the furnishing and decoration of the house and also to socialise. The ceilings and walls were principally painted with different patterns and motifs by Morris and Janey together with Charles Faulkner. A number of other wall paintings were completed (although some of those planned never were) and work still exists by Madox Brown, Burne-Jones, Rossetti and Lizzie Siddal. Janey and her sister Bessie together with Georgie Burne-Jones and her sister Alice worked on a series of hangings and tapestries for the house that were so extensive that they remained unfinished when Morris and his family moved from the house.

From January 1861 the house became a family home with the birth of Jenny Morris and Emma Brown arrived to help with the new arrival. Jenny's christening took place in February and Peter Paul Marshall and his wife together with the poet Algernon Swinburne joined the usual group of Morris' close friends to celebrate. Georgie was also now pregnant joining Lizzie who was close to her confinement. Unfortunately, at the beginning of May, she gave birth to a stillborn daughter, an event from which she was never to recover. Her depressed feelings were probably not helped by Georgie giving birth to a son, Philip, in October. Life at Red House grew quieter not surprisingly and then in early 1862 came the sad news of Lizzie's death from a laudanum overdose. Rossetti became withdrawn and did not come for a weekend at the house again. Work continued, however, to make the house as Morris had originally envisaged it. By 1863

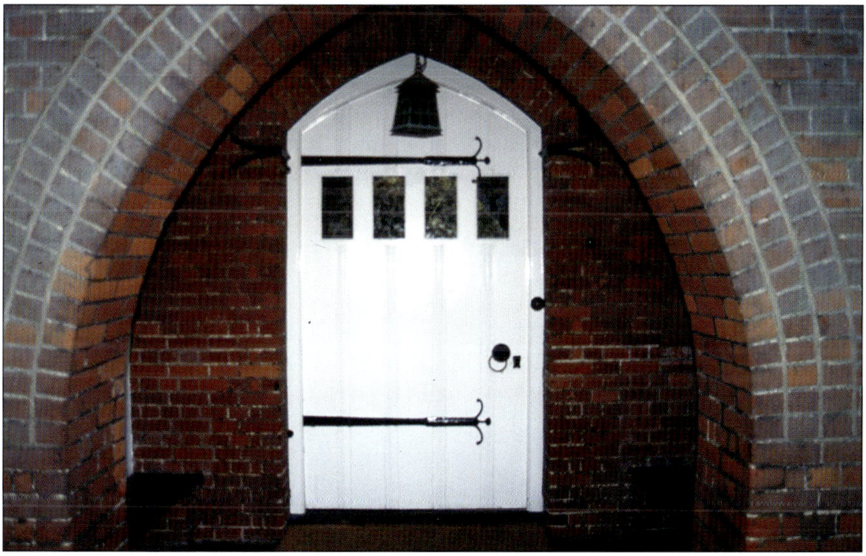

THE FRONT DOOR AT RED HOUSE - PHOTO BY KIND PERMISSION OF THE NATIONAL TRUST

the Firm was getting well established and had produced items for the prestigious International Exhibition and also contributed to the developing interior at Red Hose. Tiles and stained glass were installed with some particularly wonderful painted glass panels of farmyard birds by Philip Webb taking their place in the ground floor garden passage. Everyone was so busy that the birth of the Morris' second daughter May in March 1862 had occurred almost unnoticed.

Morris was by now commuting most days into the city where the Firm had leased premises in Red Lion Square to make and show their products. It became increasingly burdensome to do this so initially Morris devised a plan to have a workshop close to the house whilst still having a showroom in the city. There was also a plan to have Webb design an extension to the house forming an additional wing in which Burne-Jones and his family could live.

Alas at this vital moment disaster struck - Philip Burne-Jones contracted scarlet fever and as if this wasn't enough Georgie (who was pregnant again) caught the infection from her son. As a result the baby Christopher was born prematurely and died after only three weeks. This effectively ended the plan for the two families to live together and when Janey had a period of ill health Morris realised how isolated the house was from medical assistance. But it wasn't until Easter time of 1865 that Morris reluctantly decided to leave Red House. He rented a house at Queen Square which could function as a workshop and family house and put Red House up for sale.

Today the house is in the hands of the National Trust after well over a century of having private owners who all luckily cared for the house whilst introducing their own individuality. Interestingly Hall Caine, who was Rossetti's carer in the latter years of his life, came to live in Aberleigh Lodge in 1884. He knew Morris through attending meetings of the Society for the Protection of Ancient Buildings (SPAB) and much admired him. He may therefore have chosen deliberately to live close to Red House with

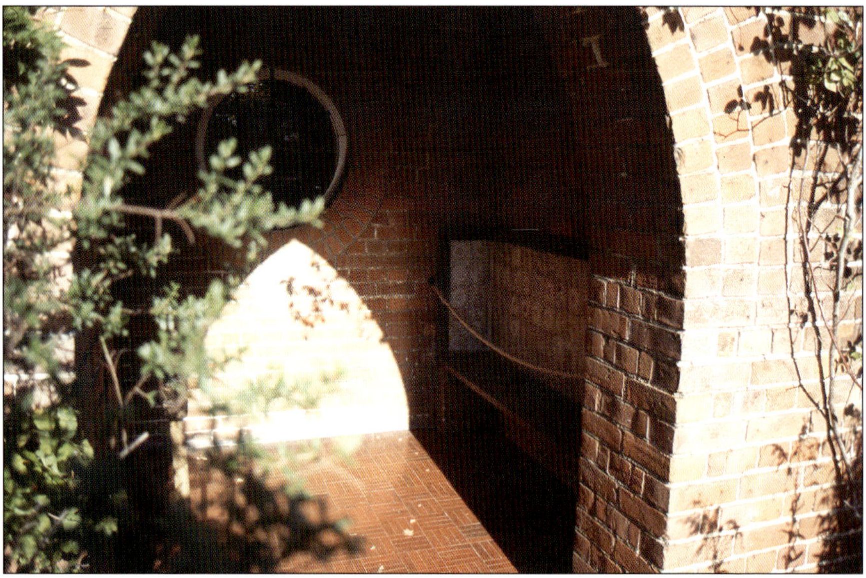

THE PILGRIM'S REST - PHOTO BY KIND PERMISSION OF THE NATIONAL TRUST

his family. Five years later Charles Holme was resident at Red House and in his time he was a buyer for Liberty's department store and also a partner with Christopher Dresser in a company dealing in Indian and Japanese wares. The house, subsequently, was decorated with many items of Oriental and exotic origin and Holme also introduced modern comforts such as electricity, heating and a bathroom upstairs. Holme was the editor of the art magazine *The Studio* which ran an article on Red House in its initial year and through the magazine younger architects such as Baillie Scott and Charles Harrison Townsend visited the house. In addition, the designer and artist Robert Anning Bell visited the house that was already growing in architectural importance. In 1905 Holme moved out to be replaced by Henry Muff (later Maufe) and his wife Maude. He was an advocate of Ruskin and his social concerns and Maude was the niece of Sir Titus Salt who built the workers' village of Saltaire in Yorkshire. Thus the house had two more sympathetic residents and they were both painted at the house by Walter Crane in 1907. Their son Edward Maufe became an architect influenced by Arts & Crafts ideals and was also responsible for the design of Guildford Cathedral.

In 1924 the house was purchased by W. Scott Godfrey who did further alterations to the property before selling it in 1927 to Alfred Horsfall who stayed there with his wife Gertrude for a further eight years. He was a later editor of *The Studio* and once again the pages of that magazine were graced by an article on Red House.

There then followed a period of uncertainty for the building with a real threat of demolition if an appropriate buyer could not be found. The National Trust became involved on two occasions but the house was not secured and a local estate agent Thomas Hills, who now owned the house, had to remain in possession. During World War II the property was occupied by the National Assistance Board when the woodwork was covered by brown paint and the garden grew overgrown. After the war the Trust became involved again but monies could not be found at this difficult time in order to buy the property. At last, in 1952, the decline in the house was stopped when the two families of Dick and Mary Toms and Ted and Doris Hollamby bought the house and moved in. Under their residency the house was gradually renovated and in 1956 the Toms left to be replaced by David and Jean Mcdonald. The three families all shared socialist principles which Morris would have approved of and the now family house continued to be restored and decorated even if it remained a cold residence in which to live. In 1964 the Hollambys became the sole inhabitants of Red House and later they introduced Morris wallpapers and fabrics into the house which although never there originally looked very much at home. When Ted Hollamby died in 1999 the Friends of Red House were already helping with the increasing number of visitors to the house but the need to finally secure the future of the building once again assumed paramount importance. Again money was the problem and for a while it looked as if the house would go back on the open market but at the last minute an anonymous benefactor donated monies so that the National Trust could finally ensure its future. When Doris Hollamby died in 2003 Red House was opened for the first season under the auspices of the National Trust.

The National Trust has a guidebook outlining the current contents of the house. It is available in the small shop at the house. The property is open from the beginning of March until the end of December from 11-4.45 Wed-Sun with last admission 45 minutes before closing. The house is closed around Christmas but open Bank Holiday Mondays. At present it is essential to book a guided tour on 020 83049878 (Tues - Sat 9.30-1.30)

PART II GAZETTEER

Tunbridge Wells together with a number of towns and villages in its immediate environs provide the interested traveller with a wealth of Pre-Raphaelite art mainly through the stained glass of their churches. For this reason I have based the first three tours in this area extending in a couple of cases to locations just north of the M25. These trails are distinct entities but occasionally almost overlap and it is quite feasible to 'mix and match' as in many cases the locations discussed are comparatively close to one another. Some of the later trails tend to be longer in distance but many have lesser known and unexpected delights to be explored.

Trail No. 1 Tunbridge Wells

AND THE GOLDEN CIRCLE

Points of Interest

(1) CHRIST CHURCH*** - Burne-Jones windows now housed in a modern building following the demolition of the original church

(2) TOWN ART GALLERY - No real Pre-Raphaelite work but a large collection of Victorian works in the Ashton Bequest.

(3) DAVID SALOMONS HOUSE - Victorian memento rooms and a painting by Simeon Solomon's brother.

(4) SPELDHURST - THE CHURCH OF ST.MARY THE VIRGIN ****- An amazing ensemble of mid-period Morris glass.

(5) BIDBOROUGH - THE CHURCH OF ST.LAWRENCE ****- Later Morris & Co. glass that fills a compact building.

(6) PENSHURST - Work by George Dewey that exhibits features important to the later Arts & Crafts movement and stained glass in the CHURCH OF ST. JOHN THE BAPTIST*** by Henry Holiday amongst others.

Optional trip to CHURCH OF ST. MARY at CHIDDINGSTONE*** with its Kempe windows.

(7) LANGTON GREEN - ALL SAINTS CHURCH *****- Important early Morris & Co. glass including Mary Magdalene window of 1862.

(8) RUSTHALL - ST.PAUL'S CHURCH ****- More Morris & Co. stained glass but with more opportunities to contrast it with other designers.

STARTING POINT: High Street, Tunbridge Wells

HOW TO GET THERE: The first location is found just south of the main railway station

FINISHING POINT: Tunbridge Wells (circular)

REFRESHMENTS: Many cafes and restaurants in Tunbridge Wells plus good pubs at Speldhurst, Chiddingstone and Langton Green. The George and Dragon pub at Speldhurst was actually used by William Morris, probably at the very beginning of 1892.

TRANSPORT: Car essential

DURATION: A long day or two, or visit parts of the trail and complete other locations at a later date

(1) CHRIST CHURCH ***is found in the High Street which forms part of the B2023 running through the town (turn right when leaving the railway station).***

The original church on this site was a white brick and stone building erected in 1836-41, the architect being R Palmer Brown. Neo-Norman in style its main interior attraction prior to its demolition was the east window. Fortunately the Morris glass was saved and can be viewed in the body of the new church on the south side. The three round-headed lights all have designs by Burne-Jones and date from 1878 although the inscription is in memory of Elizabeth Carew who died seven years earlier. The lights have a large panel with a main figure and a predella underneath showing a scene from the life of the figure above. On the left-hand side *Moses* is shown with the *Miraculous Draught of Fishes* in the panel below. The *Ascension* is in the centre and the *Baptism of Christ* is shown underneath this. Finally on the right-hand side there is the figure of *St. Paul* with *St Paul Preaching* in the panel below. Interestingly the figure of St. Paul was first used in the cathedral in Calcutta four years before its use here. ***The church is open most days.***

A little to the north up the hill that forms Mount Pleasant Road is the (2) ART GALLERY sited amongst other public buildings. It dates from 1939 as do the nearby Town Hall and Assembly Hall.

The museum and art gallery includes in its collections, perhaps not surprisingly, the largest quantity of Tunbridge Ware - those detailed wooden souvenirs made to be taken home by visitors to the town. Also of interest is the collection of Victorian pictures called the Ashton Bequest. Although not on permanent display the works are usually shown once a year more recently alongside work by contemporary artists. Included in the collection are two popular narrative paintings by Abraham Solomon (elder brother of Simeon) dating from the late 1850s and a picture entitled *The Cornfield Shelter* by John Linnell and dating from 1862. Linnell was the father-in-law of Samuel Palmer, himself a follower of Blake and an early inspiration to the Pre-Raphaelites (see section on Shoreham in the gazetteer). Also in the Bequest are some portraits by Henry O'Neil dating from the early 1860s that have some of the style of Millais and a genre scene by F.D. Hardy (see section on Cranbrook in the gazetteer). In addition you can view a domestic scene by Frederick Goodall (who later specialised in Egyptian scenes) and two evocative landscapes by Charles Leslie. The most directly inspired painting from a Pre-Raphaelite perspective would be *Approaching Night* by Henry Davis dated 1863. A London painter who exhibited regularly at the Royal Academy between 1852-1904 this work is from the period when he was much influenced by the Pre-Raphaelite artists and consequently it shows a high level of detailed observation. ***The gallery is open Monday to Saturday 9:30-5:00. Admission free.***

(There is very extensive stained glass by the firm of Heaton Butler and Bayne at the CHURCH OF ST. BARNABAS in the town.). William Morris stayed at 67 Mount Ephraim when he visited the town at the end of 1891. He may have been visiting his daughter Jenny who had several periods of ill health that year.

(3) DAVID SALOMONS HOUSE ***is to be found on the Speldhurst Road sign-posted from Southborough. Turn left when you see Broomhill Road and the entrance to the house is immediately to the right.*** The name of this road is also the earlier title for the house which was enlarged and rebuilt following its purchase by Sir David Salomons in 1829. In 1855 he became the first Jewish Lord Mayor of London and was very outspoken in Parliament attempting to obtain equal political rights for Jews and other neglected groups.

He was succeeded in 1873 by his nephew David Lionel Salomons who was also talented and outspoken but in the field of science. Amongst other pursuits he was a pioneer in photography and cinema and also invented an automatic railway signal. He added further to the already large house completing a water tower, workshops and stables and more importantly, a theatre begun in 1894 which has a rare Welte organ. He also provided the building with the early use of electricity.

Within the house which is now used as a training centre and for social functions are a couple of 'memento rooms' in which there are a number of pictures by Victorian artists. Included is a fine oil *Doubtful Future* of about 1855 by Abraham Solomon the brother of Simeon Solomon the Pre-Raphaelite painter. ***The rooms are generally open during business hours and occasionally at weekends.***

The (4) CHURCH OF ST. MARY THE VIRGIN ***is in the centre of the village of Speldhurst further along the road of the same name and then by way of Etherington Hill.***

The best way to approach the church is via the churchyard entrance to the rear where, in the spring, long rows of recently pollarded trees lead the visitor to the Victorian building. Similar trimmed trees can also be seen at the front but this way of entry presents more difficulties with car parking.

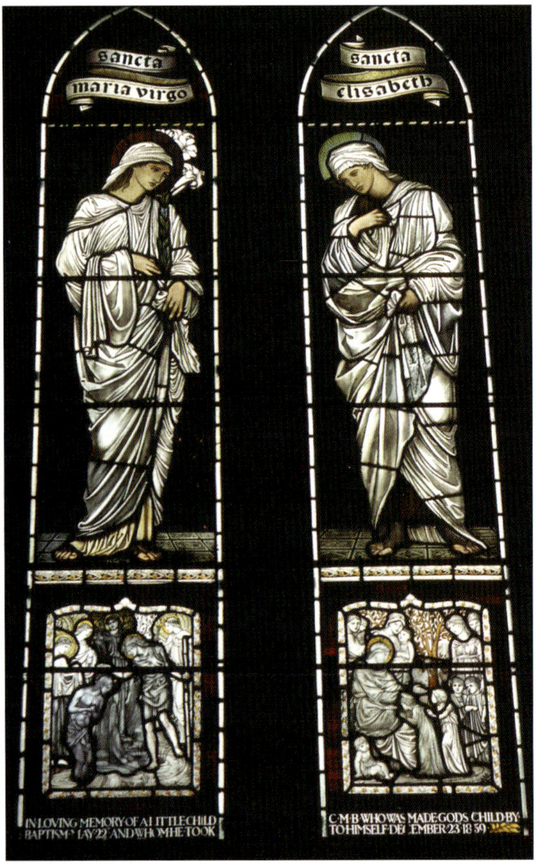

THE MARY VIRGIN AND ST. ELIZABETH WINDOW BY EDWARD BURNE - JONES AT SPELDHURST CHURCH - PHOTO BY AUTHOR

The church dates from the 1870s and the architect was John Oldrid Scott. His design needed to be a significant improvement on the building's poor predecessor which only stood for 65 years finally succumbing to dry rot. That building itself replaced a fifteenth century one that was destroyed by lightning. William Morris came here in December 1891 to see the glass that his company had installed between 1873-6. He was not impressed by the church building and described it as *'a beastly modern abortion, I suppose about 50 years old, and no doubt takes the place of some interesting old building'*. He wasn't entirely correct with the last part of this statement but his opinion of the nearby pub was much more positive and probably helped to lift his mood.

An initial glimpse at the interior may be a little disorientating full as it is with Morris glass which can be explored chronologically. Start with the west window of the north aisle and a tall two-lighted window showing six angels with various musical instruments. This dates from 1873 soon after the construction of the building and is known locally as the Window of Praise. All the figures are by Morris with only the lozenge above being a Burne-Jones design. The six Morris designs were all originally used elsewhere from 1867-1871 at places such as Liverpool (Tuebrook), Furneaux Pelham in Hertfordshire and Llandaff Cathedral.

Moving up the north aisle the next window has the same date with its designs of *St Ursula* and *St Nicholas* by Burne-Jones. The patron Saints of Children have this location in the church as this was where the Sunday School would meet.

In date order the next window to look at is the easternmost one on the north wall with the figures of the Saints *Gregory* and *Augustine*. In this case the former figure is perhaps the more interesting as this is the first and last use of this particular Burne-Jones design with its dove on the shoulder of *St Gregory*. That said it was used in a reversed form as late as 1948 at Leek in Staffordshire after the purchase of Morris & Co's glass department by Duncan W. Dearle. *St. Augustine* is by Morris.

Next for examination is the westernmost window of the south aisle with its depiction of the *Virgin Mary* to whom the church is dedicated. Below is a small panel showing *Christ's Baptism* and next door *St Elizabeth* with another panel, this time showing *Christ blessing the Children*. They are all to designs by Burne-Jones and there is an entry in his account book dated the thirtieth of November 1874 - '*Saints Mary and Elizabeth for Speldhurst nave £15 each - £30*'.

Advancing to the easternmost window in the same aisle there are the figures of *St. Matthew* and *Mark* from 1875. They each have a panel beneath which are respectively an *Annunciation* and a *Nativity* both in grisaille. Both the figures were initially used at Jesus College Cambridge only a year or so before. Returning to the middle window there are the two other Evangelists with smaller panels of the *Doctors in the Temple* beneath *St Luke* and *Christ in the Carpenter's Shop* under *St. John*. These figures and the two described before them clearly show the influence

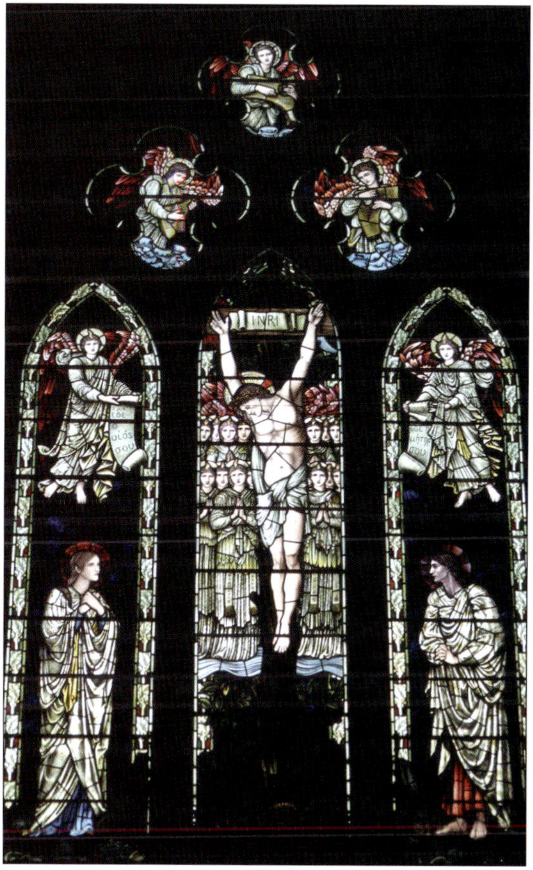

THE MAIN EAST WINDOW IN SPELDHURST CHURCH - PHOTO BY AUTHOR

of the work of Michelangelo on Burne-Jones' designs.

It is now necessary to move into the chancel where Scott's recessed windows and arches provide a suitable backdrop to yet further Morris glass. The window on the south side and second from the east is certainly one of the more interesting with its dominant grey-brown and green colours. On the left the subject is the *Cleansing of Naaman* and adjacent another *Baptism of Christ*. Naaman was the man cured of leprosy and in *Christ's Baptism* can be seen the figure of St. John the Baptist with his hair shirt. This combination of the two scenes had been used once previously at Cheddleton in Staffordshire some ten years previously in 1865 and was never repeated again.

Continuing to look at the glass in its order of installation the next window involves a move over to the east end of the north aisle. Six early English Saints are shown between the organ pipes. These figures with their pale grisaille-work backgrounds are the work of Burne-Jones and date from 1876. The designer's account book has the following note; *'Speldhurst vestry west - 6 figures, St Helena £8, 5 others, St Alban, Walberga, Oswald, etc. £40'* (the figure of St. Helena is on the top right).

Before finally coming to the main east window there is one remaining window to be discussed in the middle of the north aisle. Having the later date of 1898 it depicts on the left *Queen Bertha* and adjacent *King Ethelbert*. This window appears to have been planned about nineteen years earlier and a cartoon for the design is in the collection of Birmingham Museum and Art Gallery. The figures of the first Christian monarchs of Kent are the work of Burne-Jones and the window is in memory of Baden-Powell the grandfather of the founder of the Scout movement.

Finally we come to the main east window and its central *Christ on the Cross* accompanied by the *Virgin Mary* on the left and *St John* opposite. The very pink flesh colours with off-white draperies and red wings of the angels have always been a bit controversial. Pevsner described the window as *'disastrously alien'* and *'conventional and the flesh a repulsive pink'*. It dates from seven years after Burne-Jones' death in 1898 and all the figures had been used in different combinations in a number of other churches earlier. A later local example being that the *Virgin Mary* was used in its original reversed format (but as *Mary Magdalene*) at Edenbridge in 1909. The two windows either side of it are by the contemporary glass firm Clayton & Bell and provide a contrast or relief from the Morris glass depending on your point of view. There is a window by C E. Kempe in the south aisle showing the Saints *Michael* and *Gabriel* and dating from 1878. ***The church is open most days.***

To reach the (5) CHURCH OF ST. LAWRENCE at Bidborough ***go north along Barden Road and turn right at its junction with the B2176.The village is sign-posted to the right off the B2176 which runs along a ridge hereabouts and from which there are fine views to the north.*** The church itself is built on high ground and has its own lovely views to the east and west. The sandstone building is Norman in origin but had a 'restoration' in 1876-7 when the south aisle was constructed and the chancel largely rebuilt. Once inside it is quickly evident that the church is quite compact and this undoubtedly adds to the intense feeling created by the many Morris windows present. The main east window is not of particular interest to the subject of this book (it was executed by Clayton & Bell) but immediately to its left is a Morris window from 1924 which shows a figure representing *Faith* on the left with *Hope* adjacent. Rather than depict the figures with their virtues inscribed above them in Latin, they are entwined in long scrolls. These two Burne-Jones designs were first used at Christ Church Cathedral in Oxford in 1871. Moving to the right and into the south aisle there is probably the finest window in the church fitted as it is amidst this impressive grouping of later Morris

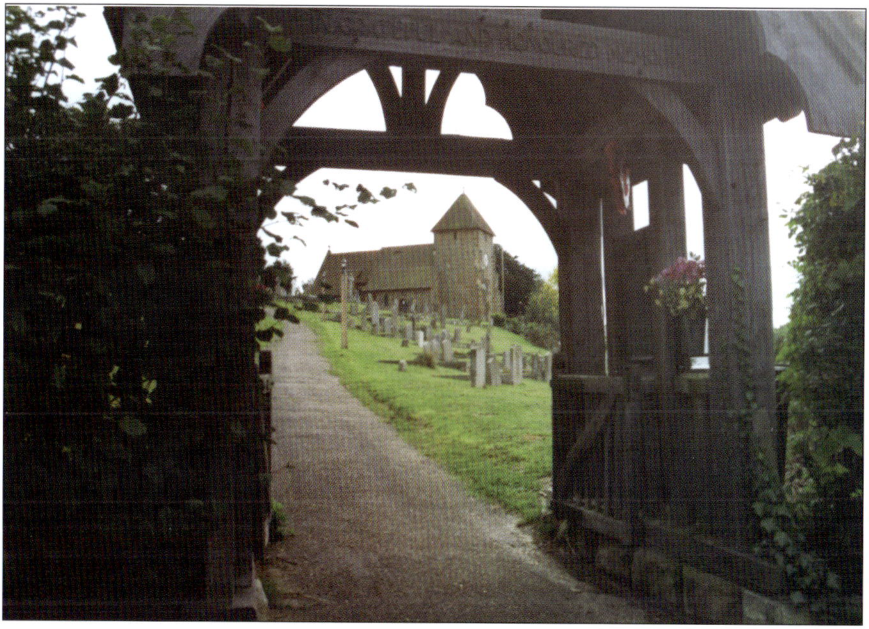

BIDBOROUGH CHURCH FROM THE LYCHGATE - PHOTO BY AUTHOR

glass. The window shows *St. Paul Preaching* and is also to a design by Burne-Jones. It dates from 1909, the design being first used at Morton Church in 1891. There are angels and a dove in the tracery above and a sketch for this window tells us that differently designed angels with scrolls were originally considered.

Moving in a clockwise direction the next adjacent window depicts the symbolic figures of *Generosity* and *Love*. The left figure is in fact based on a Burne-Jones design for *St Martin* with the *Love* figure being originally conceived as *Humility*. It shares the same date of installation as the *St Paul* window just discussed but the designs for the two figures date from 1880 and 1883 respectively. *Generosity* (or *St. Martin*) was first used at Brampton church in Cumbria which was Philip Webb's only ecclesiastical commission.

The next piece of Morris glass is a small lancet to the left showing the *Virgin and Child* and dating from 1925. Passing another large window by Clayton & Bell there is yet more Morris glass this time in the form of *St George* and *Abraham* as two Roman soldiers. It dates from six years after the end of World War I and commemorates the men of the village who gave their lives in that conflict. In order to take a picture it is necessary to avoid the swinging pendulum in front!

The Morris windows in the church are completed by two designs by John Henry Dearle who took over as the chief designer following Burne-Jones' death in 1898 and one other by the great master himself. The north aisle's west window is by Dearle and called *Christ as Youth* and it dates from 1925. More Dearle glass is in the chancel on the north side with another allegorical figure *Purity* from 1924. General opinion is that Dearle's designs are overall competent but that they show him to have few distinctive inspirations of his own. In between there is the small window in the east corner of the little north aisle showing Burne-Jones' design of *St Lawrence* and from whom the church has its dedication (1925). This leaves but one window in the north aisle which although similar in feel to the Morris glass is not from that workshop. It has a figure not too dissimilar to Holman Hunt's *Light of the World* and is by James Powell & Sons, being completed in 1897. Powell supplied coloured glass to Morris in 1861 when he and his friends first began to produce stained glass in larger quantities. Powell also made table glass. ***The church is open most days.***

Retrace your steps to go back along the B2176 and follow this directly to Penshurst where the church is found on the right-hand side.

Before entering the (6) CHURCH OF ST. JOHN THE BAPTIST it is rewarding to take a look at the weather-boarded cottages facing the churchyard. Although it is hard to tell when looking at these buildings today, they were in fact extended by George Dewey from 1848 to 1850 coincidentally the time of the formation of the Pre-Raphaelite Brotherhood. His work was part of the Vernacular Revival in which Philip Webb was to play an important part. The idea behind this movement in architecture was to create buildings which although modern used the best elements of our building history. Because of the skill used in applying modern materials in a respectful fashion it is now difficult to tell Dewey's work from that built hundreds of years before. This concern for the appearance and modification of old styles to new buildings had this early flourish in Penshurst and would lead later to the distinctive buildings associated with the Arts and Crafts movement, a local example being Standen in West Sussex.

The main Pre-Raphaelite interest in the church is the two clerestory windows high up on the south side of the chancel. These date from 1884 and were designed by Henry Holiday, a lifelong admirer and friend of Burne-Jones although by this date his style was a mix of Pre-Raphaelite and Neo-classical. At the time Holiday was chief designer at James Powell & Sons and there is further glass by this company in the north aisle although by a different designer.

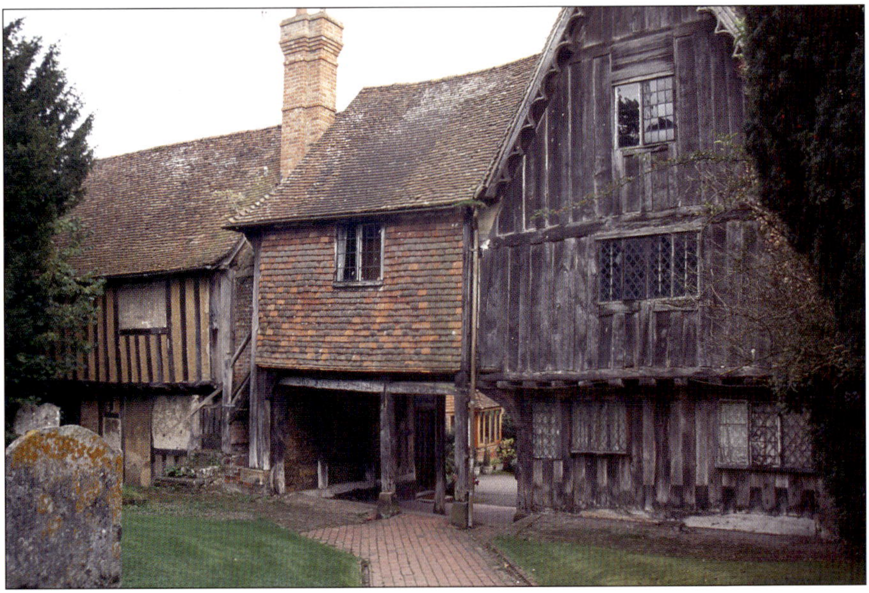

COTTAGES BY GEORGE DEWEY AT PENSHURST - PHOTO BY AUTHOR

The partnership of Bodley and Garner produced the screen between the chancel and the nave, G.F. Bodley providing the newly-formed firm of Morris, Marshall, Faulkner & Co. with some of their early important church commissions in the 1860s. Before leaving the church be sure to view the large Victorian plaque on the north wall to Henry, first Viscount Hardinge and the impressive pulpit. ***The church is open most days.***

ALSO

At this point it is possible to make a visit to the church at Chiddingstone by following the sign-posted local byroads.

The delightful village of Chiddingstone has featured in many period films and dramas because of its mainly unspoilt sixteenth and seventeenth century timber-framed buildings. At its centre is the CHURCH OF ST. MARY which receives more visitors than many other churches in this area due to the popularity of the village with tourists. Inside there are a few features that are contemporary with the Pre-Raphaelites. The rather dull east window showing the *Crucifixion* and *King David* is by Kempe and dated 1898. His wheat-sheaf monogram can be seen in the quarry glass on the right hand side. Kempe's detailed figures and use of blue-green and ruby colours on occasion have led to comparisons being made with artists more usually associated with Pre-Raphaelite art. There is an example of the later glass by Kempe & Tower (C. E. Kempe & Co. Ltd.) in the north aisle with its monogram of a wheat-sheaf with a castle in its centre and this commemorates a victim of the Great War. At the west end on the south side of the church is a window designed by Christopher Whall's daughter Veronica (showing the *Virgin Mary*) completed in 1929 and there is Powell glass from 1919 nearby. Perhaps the most impressive artefact from the Victorian era is the reredos completed by the industrious Gothic Revivalist architect George Edmund Street in 1866 although the author of the church guide seems glad he did not go on to install seating and a proposed elaborate screen. William Morris and Philip Webb both spent time training to be architects in Street's office in the 1850s. As you leave you have an opportunity to view a 'vinegar' bible so called because of its misprint of 'the parable of the vinegar' (instead of vineyard) which was in use until 1860. ***The church is open most days.***

Retrace your way back to Penshurst. Follow the B2188 southwards from the village and then turn left at its junction with the A264 to find the church at Langton Green on the left-hand side by the green.

(7) ALL SAINTS CHURCH is built of local sandstone and dates from 1862-3. Involved in the building's planning were members of the Powell family who had a house at Speldhurst. They were relatives of the same family who produced stained glass and mosaics as James Powell & Sons in their Whitefriars factory. The architect of the church was the industrious and prestigious George Gilbert Scott and originally the building had no aisles. Consequently when it was enlarged beginning in 1889 and subsequently in 1901 and 1904 the stained-glass windows on occasion needed to be relocated. So it was that some of its Morris glass was moved from the east window to the west window of the south aisle with a window on the south side of the chancel eventually finding a home in the vestry and another in a church in Cambridgeshire. Its present interior is enriched by superior Victorian stained glass and mosaic work such as on the canopied reredos in a setting truly contemporary to it.

Unusually, let's begin to look at the interior by initially ignoring the Morris glass. The main east window is a late work by Kempe and replaced 5 lancets of Morris glass distributed elsewhere in the building. It really is first class and surprisingly so in view of its late date (1904). Its subject is the *Jesse Tree* (which spreads across the entire window) and it has a very deep green hue to it but one which is not in any sense oppressive.

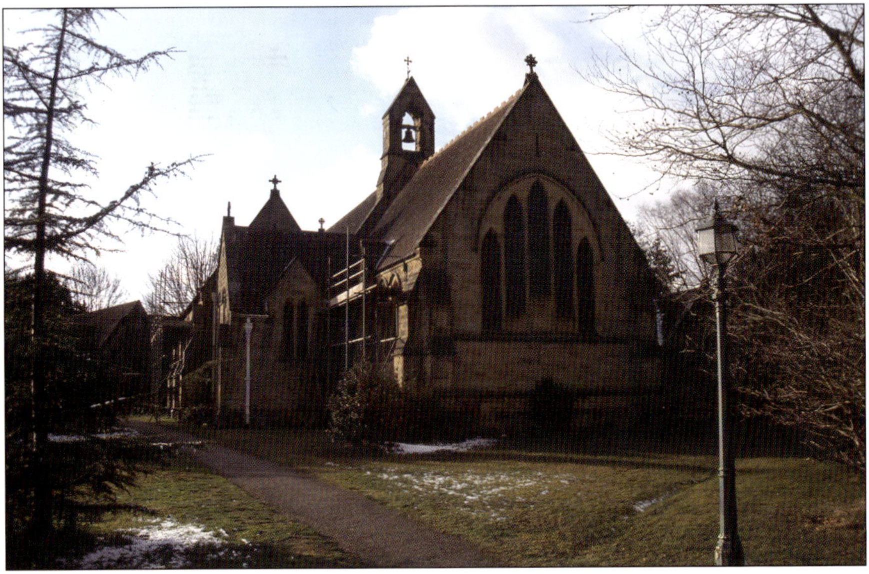

LANGTON GREEN CHURCH - PHOTO BY AUTHOR

Kempe had many local connections and it is perhaps his sense of community with the area and its inhabitants that made him raise his game on this occasion. His motif of the wheat-sheaf can be seen in the extreme left light.

Not wishing to delay any longer let's now explore the Morris glass some of which is importantly early. Chronologically the earliest of all is the window moved to the vestry ***(this may well be locked if there is no-one else in the church)*** and this depicts *St Mary Magdalene* to a design by William Morris. The figure (in a patterned pink robe with blue sleeves) dates from 1862 and only a year after the foundation of 'the Firm'. The next two windows in chronological order date from 1863 and these show *St. Alban* and *St. Stephen* and they are found in the choir area. They were both designed by Burne-Jones although the Gothic canopies which are similar in style to the *Magdalene* window were designed by Philip Webb.

Just a little later in time are windows at the west end of the church. Two lancets are crowned by a mandorla window showing *Christ in Glory with a Choir of Harping Angels*. This is undoubtedly a Burne-Jones design but there is some confusion over who designed the figures of *Jeremiah* and *Isaiah* (on the left) and *Ezekiel* and *Daniel* (on the right). It may be that the two uppermost figures are in fact Burne-Jones but the designer for the other two is even less certain. The Firm were responsible for other windows showing the same characters and these include work by Morris and Rossetti but the designs at Langton do not appear elsewhere in exactly the same format.

They date from 1865-6 as do the last of the Morris windows to be found at the west end of the south aisle. These were originally located as the side lights on the first main east window and three designers are represented. Burne-Jones completed *St Mark*, a design he also used at Bradford Cathedral whilst Ford Madox Brown designed the figures of *St John the Evangelist* and *St Matthew*. Both of these he had previously used at Bradford and reused later at Gosforth in Northumberland. The figure of *St Luke* was designed by William Morris and all four designs appear side by side in the second tier of the side lights in the large east window of Bradford Cathedral dating from 1864.

We finish now with the Powell glass which is also largely Pre-Raphaelite in inspiration perhaps particularly the windows in the north aisle showing the saints *Michael* and *Gabriel*. They are the work of Henry Holiday and date from 1885. The dedication includes a reference to Charles Powell from nearby Speldhurst. The windows depicting *St Lois* and *St Phoebe* are also by Powell as is the one with *The Blessed Virgin Mary* adjacent to *Saint Simeon* in the baptistery with its square marble font. Both windows have nice grisaille predellas beneath the main forms and were finished in 1903. On both sides of the chancel are further Powell windows depicting differing angels and completed a year earlier. In addition there is work by H. Walter Lonsdale (who worked with William Burges on occasion) showing *Faith* and *Hope* in the north aisle and dating from 1897. Yet another window of great interest is found at the east end of the south side of the chancel - here is a rare window by the artist Gerald Moira who exhibited at the Art and Crafts Exhibition Society from time to time and is better known for his book illustrations and mural decoration. The two lights show the *Feeding of the Five Thousand* and date from 1914. For those interested in another Victorian company's work the glass showing *Moses* and *John the Baptist* is by Clayton & Bell (1870).

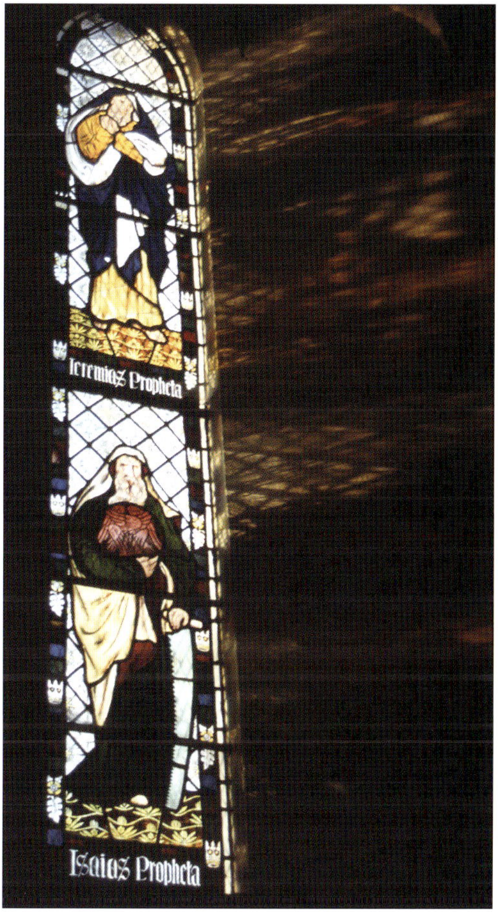

THE JEREMIAH AND ISAIAH WINDOW IN LANGTON GREEN CHURCH - PHOTO BY AUTHOR

It is worth mentioning that before the insertion of the Kempe glass this church was even more endowed with Morris glass although the clear south aisle windows always provided the church with some natural light. The three centre lights of the original east window can now be seen at St Mary's, Doddington in Cambridgeshire and include a fine *Christ on the Cross* by Rossetti. Either side of it are *St Peter* (by Morris) and *St Paul* (by Ford Madox Brown) both against a blue background. They are fine examples of early Morris glass but perhaps we should not mourn their loss too much for surely Langton has enough fantastic and important windows which now harmonise with the work of a number of their important contemporaries.

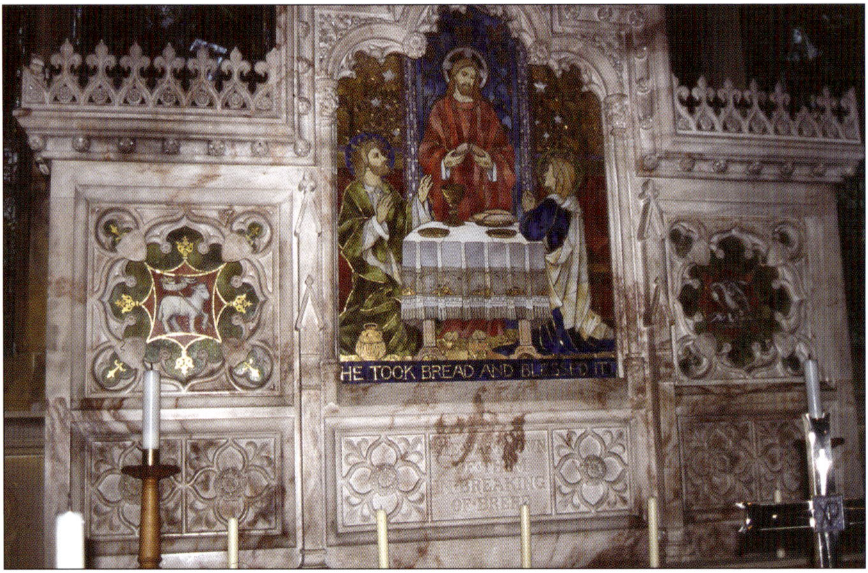

THE REREDOS IN LANGTON GREEN CHURCH - PHOTO BY AUTHOR

The church is often locked but usually open on Wednesdays (11-12) and Saturdays (9:30-10:30). At other times the keys can often be obtained at the vicarage by the green.

The final port of call on this trail is Rusthall which is further along the A264 in the direction of Tunbridge Wells where the church is found relatively hidden on the right-hand side of the road near but not in the village. Look for it just after the Tea Garden Lane turnoff.

The (8) CHURCH OF ST. PAUL is a good example of an early Victorian parish church in the Early English style. It was built in locally-quarried sandstone by the architect Henry Isaac Stevens who hailed from Derby in conjunction with his brother Nehemiah Edward Stevens who lived locally. The building was consecrated on the fourteenth of August 1850 and it cost £5200, a not inconsiderable figure for the time. In 1864 the same architect with a different partner added the north aisle and extended the northern transept. More alterations occurred in 1875 when the vestry was added and in 1913 when both the nave and aisle were extended westwards by one bay and the entrance porch added.

The interior seems very large for a building in a relatively isolated position but its various extensions are evidence of its once swelling congregation.

There is a charming water-colour on the south wall of the nave showing the interior prior to any adaptations in 1850. This is by Charles Tattershall Dodd Snr. who was a drawing master at nearby Tonbridge School (the location of sculpture by Henry Wilson and glass by Christopher Whall) and there is a large collection of his work in the Town Hall.

Moving on to look at the stained glass, the large east window (1855) is by Thomas Ward, later of the firm of Ward & Hughes. Adjacent to it on the south side of the chancel is a figure of *St Paul* executed by Powell in 1935 and inscribed with their monograph of

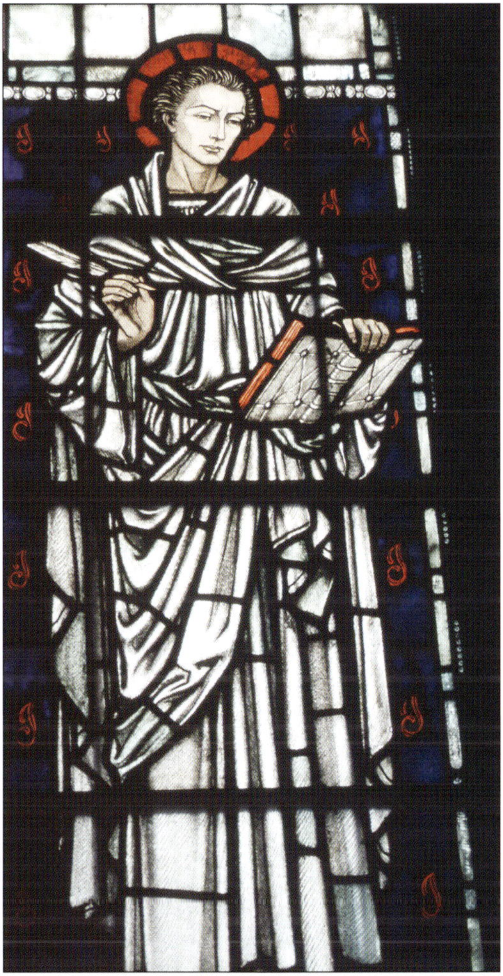

WINDOW DESIGNED BY MARTIN TRAVERS IN RUSTHALL CHURCH - PHOTO BY AUTHOR

a white friar. Throughout the building there is other glasswork by William Wailes and Henry Hughes and above the new chapel at the west end of the north aisle a Clayton & Bell window (1866)placed between two lights by the company of Heaton Butler & Bayne (1886). Of a more Pre-Raphaelite style is the window on the south wall next to the pulpit by the company of Jones & Willis and showing *St Barnabas* (1914). This could, on an initial look, be seen to be a window by Powell or even one by Morris & Co. Also of interest is the window showing *St John the Evangelist* on the same wall and farthest to the west by Martin Travers (1917), a follower of Christopher Whall who was in turn inspired early on by William Morris.

The actual Morris window is to be found on the north wall of the chancel, a single light showing *St. Paul* and dating from 1903. It is a Burne-Jones design that was first used at Ashton-under-Lyne in 1892 and also appears in the guise of the allegorical figure of *Knowledge* in the south aisle of St. Stephen's church at nearby Tonbridge.

Whilst in the area of the sanctuary the carved reredos of Portland stone is worth a look, it was erected in 1869 and replaced 'tablets' of the *Ten Commandments* which can now be seen at the west end of the north aisle. The abundance of stone and marble fittings throughout the church is typically Victorian and undoubtedly one of its strengths. The church is also reputed to have the largest bell in the whole of Kent with the exception of those at Canterbury. ***The church is open on Sunday afternoons throughout the summer and by arrangement.***

To return to Tunbridge Wells continue along the A264 in the same direction as before to the Pantiles area of the town.

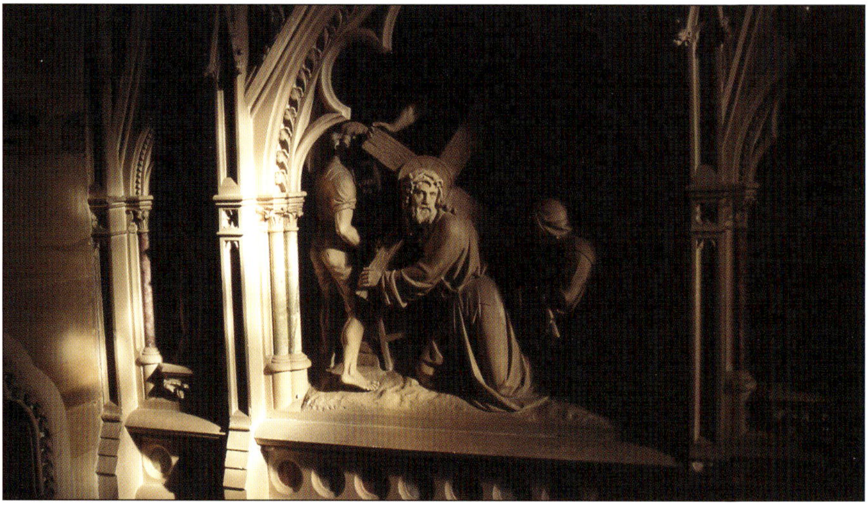

PART OF THE REREDOS AT RUSTHALL - PHOTO BY AUTHOR

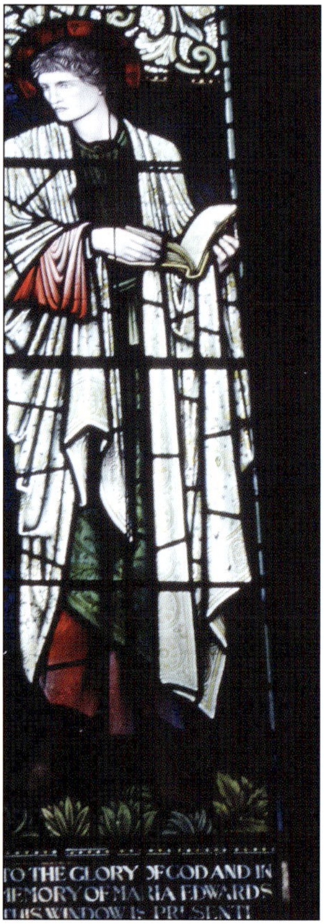

WINDOW OF ST. PAUL BY MORRIS & CO. IN RUSTHALL CHURCH - PHOTO BY AUTHOR

Trail No. 2 Edenbridge and Sevenoaks

Points of Interest

(1) EDENBRIDGE - CHURCH OF ST. PETER AND ST. PAUL ***- Late Morris glass and a fine window by Herbert Bryans

(2) CROCKHAM HILL - CHURCH OF THE HOLY TRINITY ***- Wooden screen by George Jack and monument to Octavia Hill

(3 WESTERHAM - CHURCH OF ST. MARY THE VIRGIN ****- Morris glass and further windows by Henry Holiday

(4) DOWN HOUSE - The home of Charles Darwin

(5 HALSTEAD - CHURCH OF ST. MARGARET ***- Late Morris stained glass then an opportunity to see MORANTS COURT - Site for a John Brett painting

(6) COMBE BANK - Home to an exceptional decorative scheme by Walter Crane

(7) FOUR ELMS - CHURCH OF ST. PAUL *****- A little known Arts & Crafts showpiece

Also: HOW GREEN HOUSE

STARTING POINT: Edenbridge is on the extreme west of the county a little to the north of East Grinstead

HOW TO GET THERE: The B2028 runs through the town.

FINISHING POINT: Edenbridge (circular)

REFRESHMENTS: Pubs and cafes at Edenbridge and Westerham and a tea-shop at Down House

TRANSPORT: Car essential

DURATION: One day

The (1) PARISH CHURCH OF ST. PETER AND ST. PAUL in Edenbridge ***lies a little to the east of the long High Street in the centre of the town. It is well sign-posted.*** The building dates from early Norman times and throughout the centuries has seen periods of great prosperity but also decline. As you enter the church there is a very good example of the early years with the fine late Norman font and its fifteenth century oak cover.

If you walk down the nave you can see in front of you a Morris window in what is now the Martyn Chapel. Rather confusingly the chancel and east window now lie to the north of it and we shall return to these later. The chapel is large due to it originally being two chapels that became one in order to house the tomb of Sir Richard Martyn and his wife in 1499. The remains of the tomb are now on the south wall of the chapel.

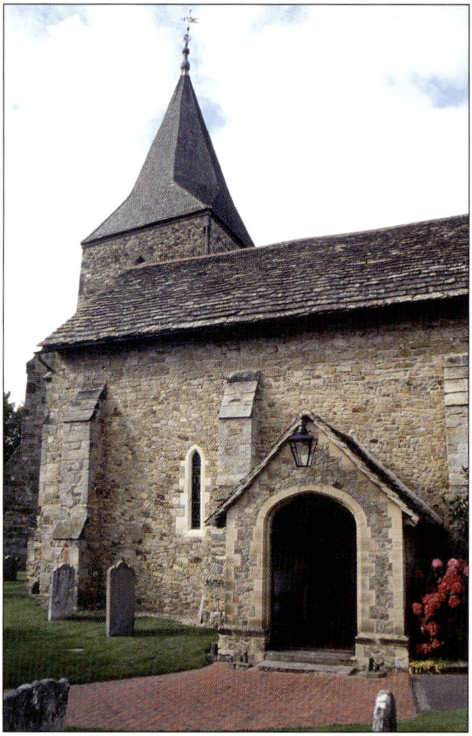

EDENBRIDGE CHURCH - PHOTO BY AUTHOR

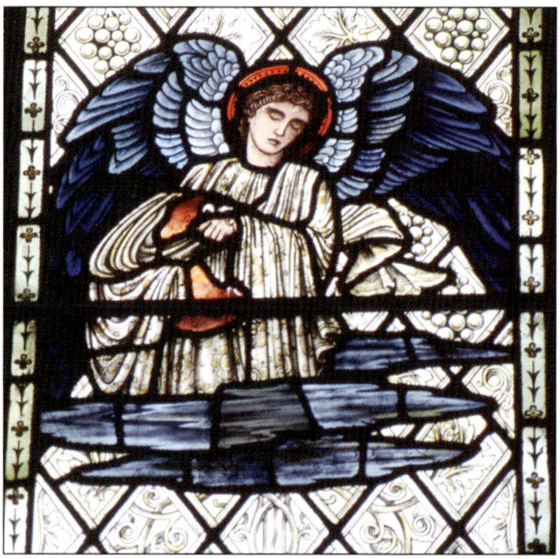

DETAIL OF AN ANGEL IN THE MORRIS WINDOW AT EDENBRIDGE - PHOTO BY AUTHOR

The Perpendicular window here has Morris & Co. glass dating from 1909. It shows *Christ on a Cross* that is a living tree, the branches of which extend into the tops of all five lights. On the left-hand side are the figures of the *Centurion* and the *Virgin Mary* with *Mary Magdalene* and *St John the Evangelist* on the right. All the designs are by Burne-Jones and had been used before in a number of different churches. The figure of *Christ* was used just two years previously at Hawarden church near the home of the Prime Minister, Gladstone. The figure of *Mary Magdalene* was adapted from a design for the *Virgin Mary* but clearly a different one to the figure on the left. There are some charming angels, seraphims and minstrels in the tracery at the top of the window.

Interestingly this window was intended for Crockham Hill church as a three-light but never installed there and later converted to a five-light by the addition of the two outer figures. Due to the backgrounds of quarries the window lets in a good deal of light although perhaps this reduces its impact.

The present appearance of the chancel's east window is owed to Sir Gilbert Scott who in 1848 objected to a replacement window and thus the original tracery was put back. The very dark glass in mainly blues and greens is by Herbert Bryans, a great admirer of C.E. Kempe and his running dog monogram can be seen at the bottom. Before leaving you may wish to view the Victorian glass in memory of William Gray who was the station-master at the town's station for many years. There is also a good example of very recent stained glass with the Millennium west window. ***The church is open most days.***

Follow the B2026 north where the village of Crockham Hill is situated at a high point on a sandstone ridge

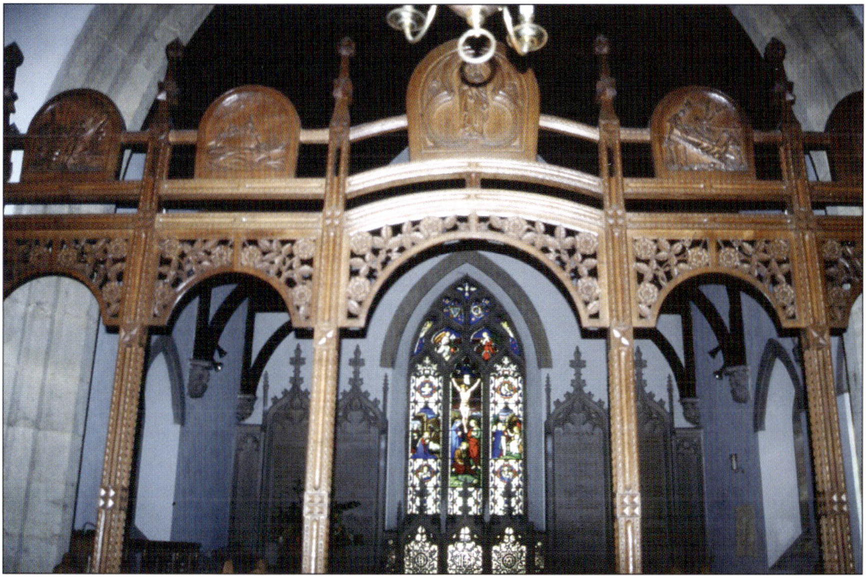

THE SCREEN BY GEORGE JACK AT CROCKHAM HILL CHURCH - PHOTO BY AUTHOR

and consequently there are fine views to the south. These are thought to have been painted by Samuel Palmer, the visionary landscape artist whose work was seen and appreciated by Rossetti, Hunt and Millais. In order to take advantage of the prospect a number of wealthy middle class clients had large houses built for them in the late nineteenth century by architects working in a style similar to Norman Shaw.

Once again it is the local church that provides a connection to the Pre-Raphaelites. The (2)CHURCH OF THE HOLY TRINITY ***is found by following a lane to the right (the church is sign-posted) shortly after entering the village from the south.*** The architect of this building (constructed as it was of the local sandstone in 1842) is unknown but his patron was Charles Warde of nearby Squerryes Court. Inside the main source of interest is the emotive monument to Octavia Hill in the north-east corner of the chancel which shows the co-founder of the National Trust as an old woman in a shawl. It was sculpted by Dora Abbott. Octavia Hill was a long-term friend of John Ruskin who gave the social reformer drawing lessons as well as money in order for her to upgrade slum dwellings. She spent many years in the village which she loved and her grave can be seen outside by the large yew tree close to the entrance path.

Other items of interest worth looking out for throughout the interior include the chancel screen which Pevsner describes as a *'weedy Gimsonish affair'* suggesting it is rather a pallid version of the work of Ernest Gimson, the designer much influenced by William Morris and the Arts and Crafts Movement. In fact the screen is the work of George Jack (who earlier taught carving at the Central School of Arts & Crafts) and serves as a memorial to the men of the village who took part in the First World War. It dates from 1920 and has scenes from the war in its upper panels.

The window dedicated to E.B. Shand and dated 1882 on the south side of the nave is particularly golden hued when the sun is behind it and betrays much Morris inspiration. This can be seen in the fruit on the trees (right light) and the movement evident in the angel to the left. It was produced by James Powell and Sons. ***The church is open most days.***

Follow the the same B2026 northwards to Westerham.

The town has some fine countryside surrounding it which is perhaps surprising in view of the close proximity of London and the busy M25 motorway. The jewellery designer John Paul Cooper, who was a contributor to the Arts & Crafts Exhibition Society, lived hereabouts from 1911 until 1933 in a house he designed called Betsom's Hill. The town also has many connections with Churchill who lived close-by at Chartwell and whose bronze seated figure graces The Green in the centre of the town. Nearby the large solid looking (3) CHURCH OF ST.MARY THE VIRGIN with its distinctive three east gables was the subject of two Victorian 'restorations' in 1854 and 1882. It has both north and south aisles and a fantastic wooden spiral staircase for access to the tower. Amongst its more famous artefacts such as a hanging sanctuary lamp given by the Churchills are some Pre-Raphaelite inspired windows. The most obvious of these is the Morris & Co glass at the west end of the north aisle. Although even on a bright day it can appear rather dark it is a satisfying composition showing a Nativity across its three lights. Interestingly although the two side lights were first used at Allerton near Liverpool the central light with its *Virgin and Child* beneath a thatched conical shelter comes from the *Star of Bethlehem* tapestry design. There are no canopies present in this landscape design which enables the star-studded night sky to extend to the upper tracery of each light. It dates from 1909 and comes originally from the hand of Burne-Jones. It is dedicated (on a tablet close-by) to the memory of the local hero Major-General James Wolfe.

Elsewhere in the church are two Kempe windows opposite one another at the east end of both aisles. The *Crucifixion* dates from 1888 and *The Resurrection* from two years later. They are fairly average. Much more Pre-Raphaelite is the curious window at the east end of the south wall. With its unusual wide blue, gold and white borders it faithfully resembles early Morris glass in the way the figures are drawn. This is also noticeable in the wonderful angels shown in the quatrefoils above. The date is the same as early Morris

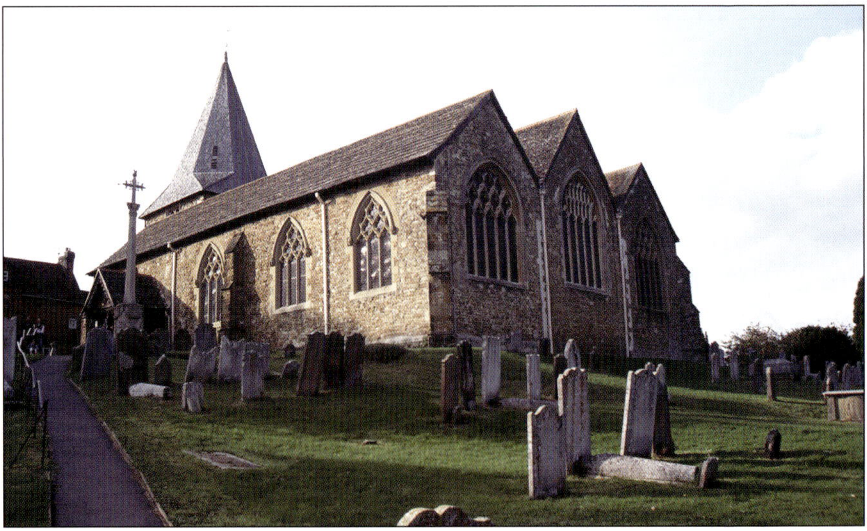

WESTERHAM CHURCH - PHOTO BY AUTHOR

glass (1864) but the designer is Henry Holiday whilst working for Powell and obviously much influenced by Morris and his friends.

In order to see how Holiday's art developed walk to the main east window which is also by him and produced in conjunction with the same glass company. The style here is overtly classical which was much in favour in its year of manufacture (1883) with the success of painters such as Albert Moore. Beneath the window is a nice part-mosaic reredos.

You may also wish to view another Powell window in the centre of the south wall which is like the similarly coloured Holiday window but less typical of the Powell workshop. This one is less successful perhaps because it is more conventional and was designed by Casolani in 1867. It does have amazing colouring, however, particularly seen in the Gothic arches towards the bottom. ***The church is open most days.***

To find Downe village leave Westerham by going north on the A233 over the M25 and after passing Biggin Hill look for signs to Downe.

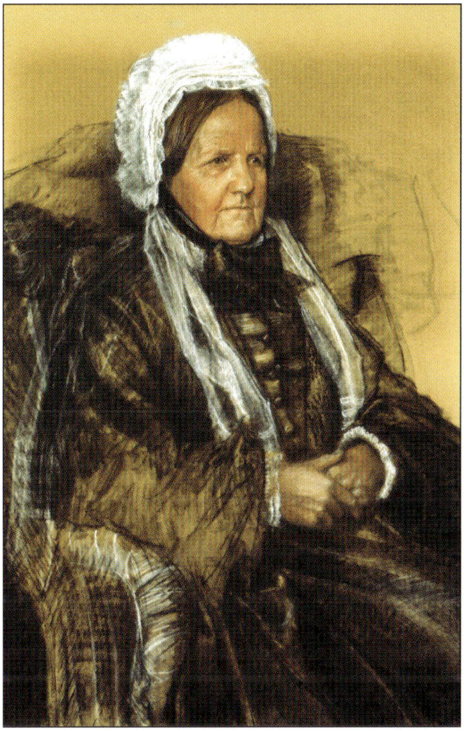

PORTRAIT OF EMMA DARWIN BY CHARLES FAIRFAX MURRAY © English Heritage Photo Library

(4)DOWN HOUSE (sign-posted and now administered by English Heritage) was the home of Charles Darwin from 1842 until his death forty years later. It was in this house that he devised and wrote many of his most successful books including *The Origin of Species*. It contains a number of pictures by Albert Goodwin including a couple of watercolours of the house dating from the 1880s. Perhaps the most significant picture by an associate of the Pre-Raphaelites is to be found in the Drawing Room. This is a large oil by Charles Fairfax Murray of Emma Darwin (nee Wedgewood) dating from the mid-1880s after the death of her husband. This was commissioned by two of Darwin's sons, Horace and George, along with pictures of other members of the family. Fairfax Murray is sometimes referred to as the 'unknown Pre-Raphaelite'. He was a man of many parts, at various times assuming the role of artist, connoisseur or art dealer/collector, and a friend to Ruskin, Morris and the Rossetti family as well as Burne-Jones to whom he was also a studio assistant. He had come to know the Darwin family through John Henry Middleton, an archaeologist and scholar at Cambridge University.

Down House is open Feb-April Wed-Sun 10-4, April to mid-July Wed-Sun and B/H10-6, mid-July-Aug daily 10-6,Sept Wed-Sun 10-6,Oct Wed-Sun 10-4.

To get to Halstead head right as you leave the house along Luxted Road and then follow signposts to Cudham and Knockholt. After entering the village of Halstead the church can be found by turning right at the crossroads.

The (5) CHURCH OF ST. MARGARET was originally a burial chapel of 1854 but then the two aisles and the nave were added in 1880-1. Thus the church was enlarged in order to cater for the spiritual needs of an increased congregation grown at times when workers descended on the area for employment during the strawberry picking season. The building replaced an earlier one on the site and is largely flint with some red brick dressings and a low sweeping roof. Inside the building it takes time to adapt to the low light levels caused principally by a preponderance of stained glass. The most significant being the Morris & Co. glass in the north aisle. This shows two armoured figures and has the inscription *The Souls of the Righteous are in the Hands of God.* The work dates from 1909 and the figures are *St. Martin* on the left with *St George* adjacent. They are both to Burne-Jones' designs first being used at Philip Webb's church at Brampton in 1880 with the glass-painters in the Morris workshop on this occasion identified as Messrs. Potts, Howard and Knight. Other significant glass is to be found in the west window (by Powell and designed by Casolani in 1867) and in a south window of the chancel that shows the *Annunciation* (by Kempe in 1898 with his wheat-sheaf motif). ***The church is open most days.***

Leave Halstead by Otford Lane to join the A224 and turn right. This road goes close to the motorway and at the first roundabout go straight ahead on the B2211 where the building that appears on your right is Morants Court Farm. To the left MORANTS COURT ***can be seen although it now occupies an unenviable position on the other side of, but almost adjacent to, the M25 where it has its junction with the A21.***

This comparatively modest building was the subject of two pictures produced by John Brett in spring of 1864 when its surroundings must have been considerably more ideal. Brett entered the Royal Academy in 1853 where he came into contact with the ideas of

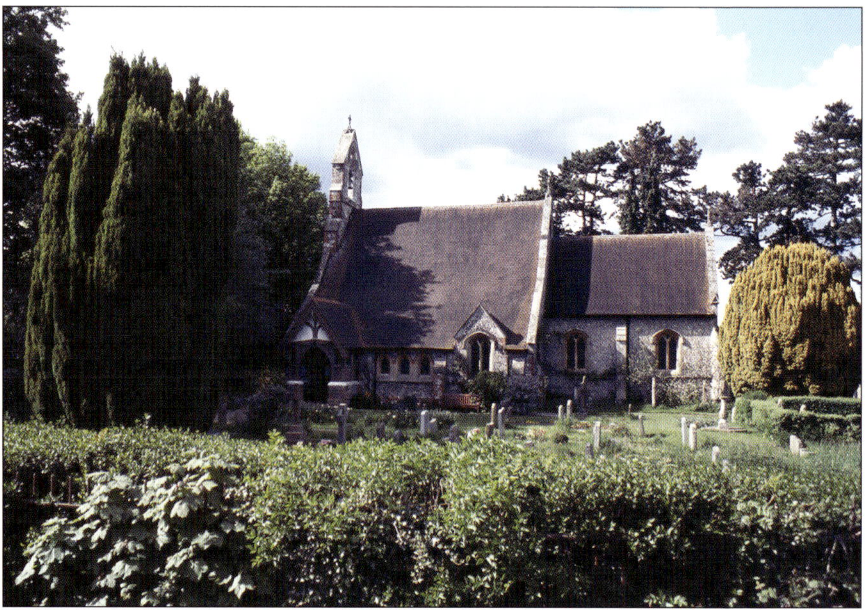

HALSTEAD CHURCH - PHOTO BY AUTHOR

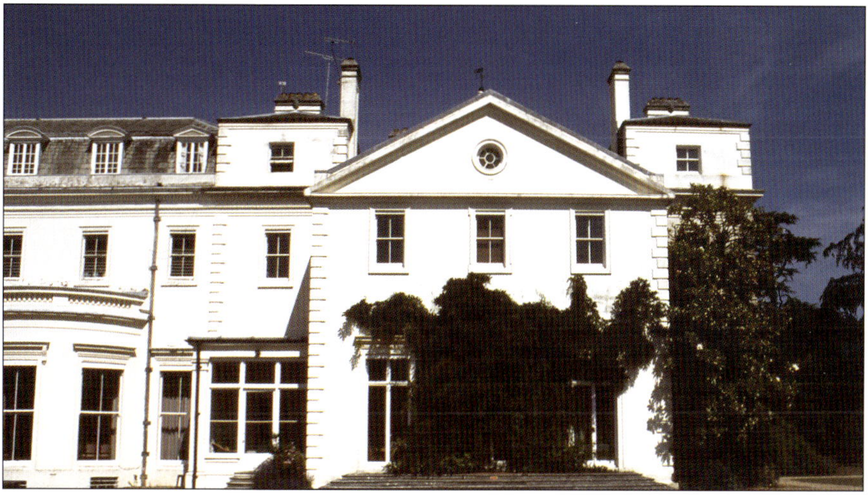

EXTERIOR OF THE SALOON AT COMBE BANK - PHOTO BY AUTHOR

Ruskin and the Pre-Raphaelites. His earlier work drew great praise from Ruskin and just prior to coming to Kent to paint this house he had stayed in Florence in order to complete his highly detailed vista of the city entitled *'Florence from Bellosguardo'* (Tate Britain).

Morants Court in May (Private Collection-illustrated in *The Pre-Raphaelite Landscape* by Staley) was painted for £100. It shows the farmhouse and surrounding buildings in a rural setting with cows and calves in the foreground. Its companion picture cannot presently be located but showed the house from a different viewpoint. The painting belongs to a time in Brett's career when, perhaps to save labour, he no longer completed his pictures with the same exacting levels of detail that had been present in his earlier works and which were of course a central characteristic of the first Pre-Raphaelite landscapes. In this work the house is well detailed but the foreground is looser and there is little in terms of a background to the main subject. The differing amounts of detail tend to give the picture a dream-like quality.

Continue south along the B2211 in the direction of Sundridge and upon arriving in the village look for a sharp right-hand turn called Combe Bank Drive which leads to the school of the same name.

The main house at (6) COMBE BANK is found by following signs to the reception for the senior school. Although massively extended to the north on a number of occasions it is still relatively easy to make out the original Palladian house which is a square two-storeyed block with turrets at each corner. It was built in the early eighteenth century and has on the west side a pedimented main block that extends outwards and houses the saloon. Before becoming a girls school the building played host to a convent but in the late nineteenth century was home to Dr. William Spottiswoode, a scientist and mathematician who was also an elected President of the Royal Society. Here he would entertain such notabilities as Oscar Wilde and eminent fellow scientists such as Darwin and Huxley. The main room of the house that he used for this purpose was the fore-mentioned saloon which Spottiswoode had decorated appropriately but also lavishly. The artist that he chose for this grand scheme was Walter Crane in c.1879-80. He is probably best known today as an illustrator to children's books but also completed a number of

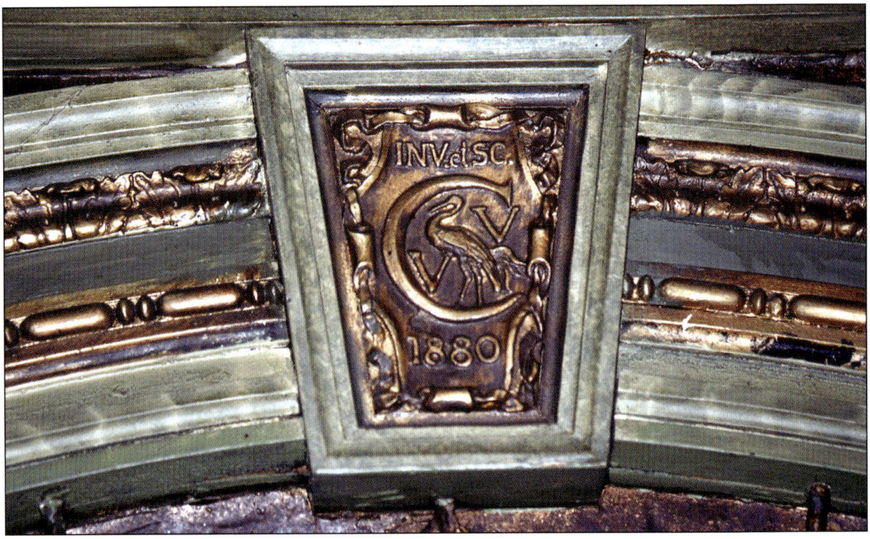

WALTER CRANE'S INSIGNIA - PHOTO BY AUTHOR

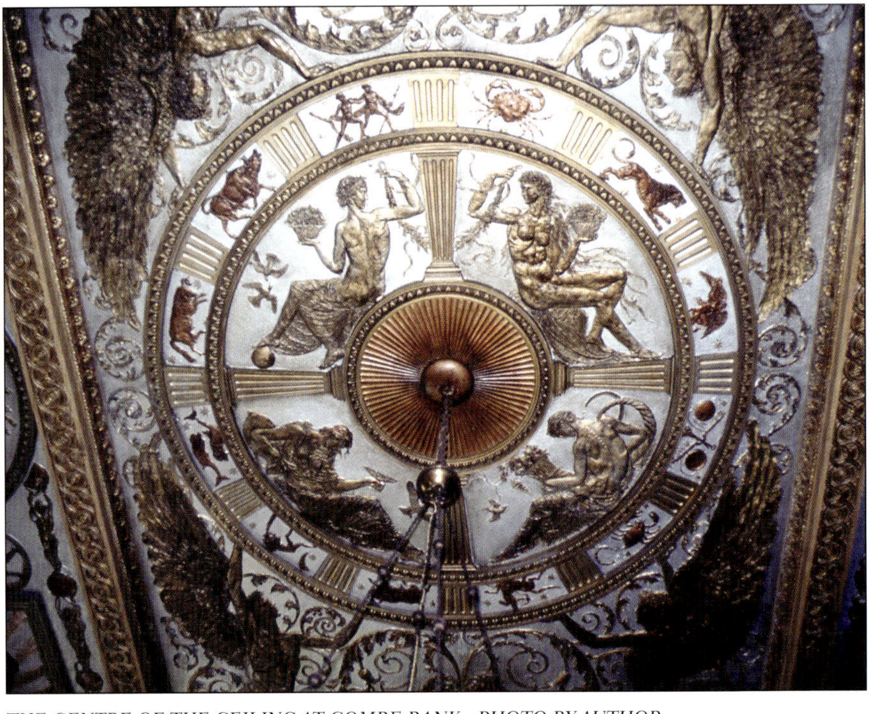

THE CENTRE OF THE CEILING AT COMBE BANK - PHOTO BY AUTHOR

oil paintings (sometimes in a late Burne-Jones style) and important decorative schemes.

When one enters the saloon the contrast to the mid-eighteenth century pastel-shaded decoration in the entrance area (that includes door pediments, niches and swags) could not be greater. Gold and greens dominate this magnificent space and your eyes rise after glimpsing the glorious fireplace to the full-blown tour-de-force that is the ceiling. The initial inspiration for the scheme can be seen along the frieze where early sixteenth century Italian panels which show putti carrying fruits etc. are supplemented by Crane's own thinner figures. Below the walls are covered in a gold-embossed paper and the doors and window shutters have more of his elongated figures. One of the doors has figures representing the Senses whilst another has figures symbolising intellectual pursuits with a middle door welcoming guests and bidding them farewell.

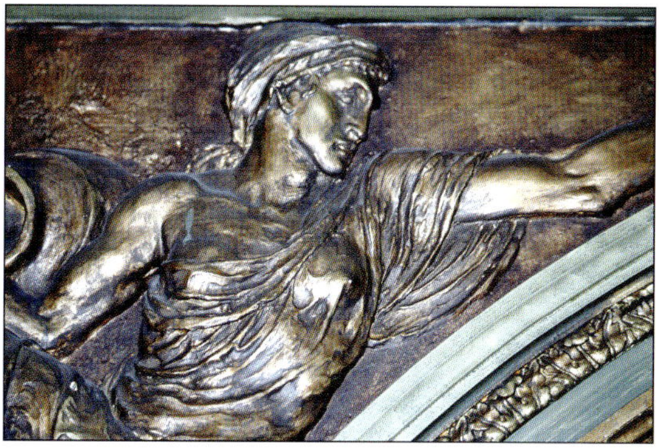

DETAIL OF CEILING DECORATION - PHOTO BY AUTHOR

The fireplace has a relief of the *Fates* with a thread running through their fingers until it is cut thus symbolising the ending of a mortal life. The chimney-piece has pilasters on each side and includes an inscription and the artist's monograph with a date of 1880.

The ceiling is really rather complex in its use of iconography. In the centre is the sun and seasons with the signs of the *Zodiac* supported by four enormous winged figures. Smaller figures representing the *Hours* with hour-glasses intertwined with the snake of time around them are nearby as are figures showing *Morning, Noon, Evening* and *Night*. The four large panels in the corners have figures to show the planets *Venus, Mars, Neptune* and *Uranus* with *Jupiter, Saturn, Mercury* and the *Moon* in circular panels at the centre of each side and ends.

The overall scheme has survived remarkably well and does succeed in uniting the ancient world with the modern scientific, exemplified by the small panel on one of the window shutters with a nude classical figure looking through a telescope.

The saloon decoration may have more in common with the Classical Revival in Victorian art than the Pre-Raphaelites despite the presence of figures similar to those of Burne-Jones after Michelangelo. This cannot however be so readily said about the small sketch for a stained-glass window by Crane found on the wall in the staircase area just outside the saloon. This small work showing *St Cecilia* is charming and has some very Pre-Raphaelite elongated angels in its backdrop. It is uncertain how the sketch came to the house but no doubt its appearance here may well relate to the friendship between Crane and Spottiswoode. ***The saloon can be visited by appointment.***

A little to the south of the crossroads between the A25 and the B2211 is the CHURCH OF ST. MARY THE VIRGIN at Sundridge which has windows by Powell, Kempe, Clayton & Bell and Heaton Butler & Bayne but access is difficult and the author has been unable to verify this.

To proceed to Four Elms head along the A25 in the direction of Sevenoaks and

take a right turn along the B2042 to the village. Then turn left on the B2027 where the church is soon seen on the left-hand side.

The (7) CHURCH OF ST. PAUL is an unexpected sight just outside the centre of the village of Four Elms. It lies a little back from the busy road which separates it from the cricket ground where in the last war a bomb landed causing the destruction of some stained-glass windows in the church. The building was constructed in 1880 and is externally very satisfying with its prominent rose window above the apse of the baptistery even though its 'crazy paving' styled sandstone is rather eccentric. The architect was E.T. Hall who also partly designed the prestigious shop for Liberty's in London, the company so associated with the retailing of Arts & Crafts merchandise. Inside the church appears quite spacious with light coming through the seven small windows in the apse which would originally have been filled with glass by Clayton & Bell as were all the other windows. The bomb landing on the cricket ground put paid to the apse glass as well as some other windows. However, the increased light shows to advantage the delightful rounded font with its four angels and inscription carved on the outside of the bowl. Moving to the nave there are nice mosaic (opus sectile) tablets on both walls by Powell and Company. The glass is less distinctive but there are rare and excellent examples of design work by George Jack including the carved oak screen and lectern. The screen has fine leaf detailing at its top and Joseph Armitage was responsible for much of the main carving of this screen The lectern was made in 1929 for Jack by Laurence Turner who had a workshop specialising in architectural decoration. There are further plaques in this area and a well-designed pulpit with an inscription.

Perhaps the church's finest fitting is seen in the chancel being a reredos of Torquay marble which gleams white and has simple fine lines. This is a Lethaby design and was started by the sculptor Thomas Stirling Lee who died in 1915 whereupon Henry Alfred Pegram was called on in order to complete this wonderful piece of work. There is an original framed drawing by Pegram on the north wall which is a sketch for one of the kings shown on the reredos (the *Adoration of the Magi*). This is dedicated to Rachel

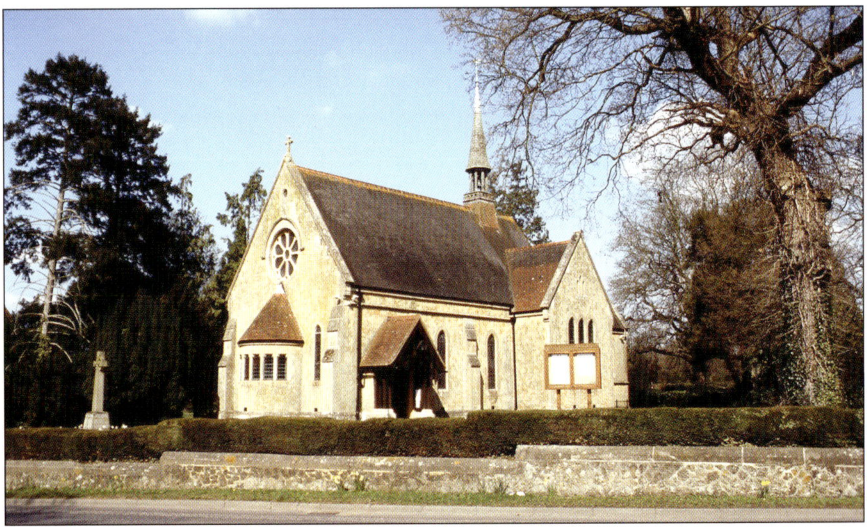

FOUR ELMS CHURCH - PHOTO BY AUTHOR

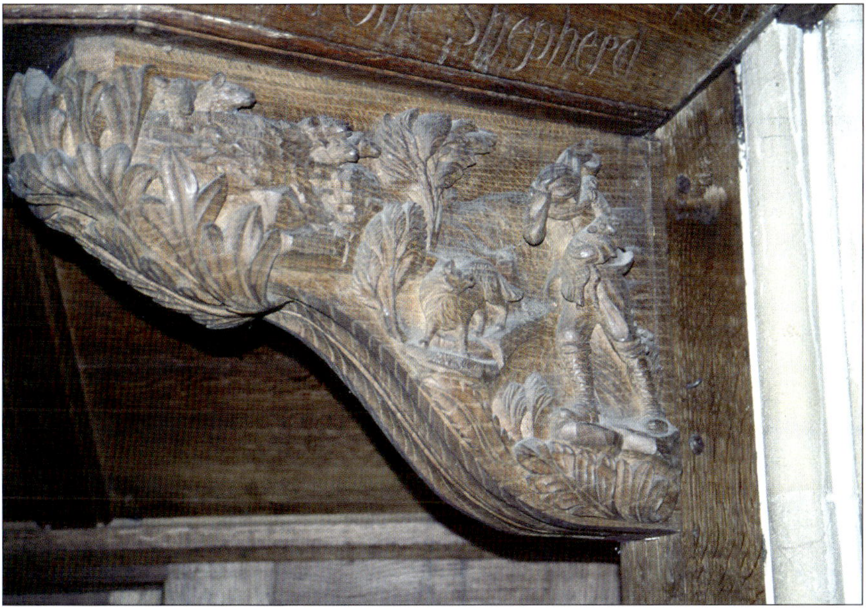

EXAMPLE OF THE CARVING OF GEORGE JACK IN FOUR ELMS CHURCH - PHOTO BY AUTHOR

Faudel-Phillips who was involved with the Arts & Crafts movement and who commissioned the sculpture in memory of her mother.

The more unusual Clayton & Bell glass in the chancel has one window showing the *Light of the World* although its design is far removed from Holman Hunt's picture of the same name.

On the opposite side of the chancel is the organ which has a case specified by Jack to be *'all in English oak clean from the tool'* and lower down there is exquisite carving on both brackets by Jack himself and depicting *The Good Shepherd*. The sheep shown appear in some precarious positions as if they are going to fall at any moment. It is likely that Lethaby advised the church committee on the decoration of the building resulting in an interior completed by this rich mix of Arts & Crafts practitioners. In addition to those already discussed the metalworker John Paul Cooper was also involved. All in all a lovely and little known interior which even has some Morris-designed fabric on a table just in case his astounding popularity in furnishings should be forgotten. ***The church is often locked but the keys can be accessed via the churchwardens.***

Return to Edenbridge or take an optional diversion to HOW GREEN. ***If you wish to do this leave the church and head east along the B2027 in the direction of Leigh. Go right along How Green Lane and a mile or so you will arrive at How Green.***

The house of the same name is the work of the architect Robert Weir Schultz. It was built to a butterfly plan in 1904-5. This plan was used in order to catch the best amount of sunlight but led to complexities in regard to the internal design. At How Green the design was successful and very much in the style of Norman Shaw and Lutyens with plaster-work by the Arts & Crafts designer Ernest Gimson in the original dining room. ***The house is now divided into privately-owned flats.***

Trail No. 3 Tonbridge Circular

Points of Interest

(1) TONBRIDGE - CHURCH OF ST.STEPHEN ***- An opportunity to look at Morris glass designed by John Henry Dearle

(2) HILDENBOROUGH - CHURCH OF ST JOHN THE EVANGELIST ***- A wide naved building with good glass by Morris, Powell and others.

(3) KNOLE - HOUSE AND GROUNDS - Historical associations to the Pre-Raphaelites

(4) SEVENOAKS - CELEBRATED BAILLIE-SCOTT HOUSE,CHURCH OF ST. NICHOLAS**AND LIME TREE WALK - Or an art house, some beautiful Powell glass and an early attempt at social housing.

(5) RIVERHEAD -CHURCH OF ST.MARY THE VIRGIN***- A wonderful chancel with mosaic and tiling work

(6) KEMSING - CHURCH OF ST. MARY*** - Sculpture by Henry Wilson

(7) SHOREHAM - CHURCH OF ST. PETER AND ST.PAUL ***AND THE HOUSE OF SAMUEL PALMER - Includes Morris glass in the church

(8) SEAL CHART - CHURCH OF ST. LAWRENCE **- Glass by Henry Holiday in a less visited church

(9) IGHTHAM MOTE - Haunt of Henry James, Sargent and Burne-Jones amongst others

Also: MATFIELD** and BRENCHLEY*** churches to the south-east.

STARTING POINT: A little to the south of Tonbridge town centre

HOW TO GET THERE: The train station is just to the north of the first location

FINISHING POINT: Tonbridge (circular)

REFRESHMENTS: Tonbridge and Sevenoaks have many cafes and pubs and there are also good pubs at Kemsing, Shoreham and Brenchley. Also National Trust restaurants at Ightham and Knole

TRANSPORT: Car essential

DURATION: Full day but if the visitor wishes to visit Knole and Ightham at length extra time may be required and will need to be mindful of NT opening hours.

(1) ST. STEPHEN'S CHURCH ***is found in Quarry Hill Road and is easily visible to drivers coming into Tonbridge from the south on the A26 where its impressive spire appears on the left-hand side.***

The architect here was Ewan Christian and the building dates from 1851-4 at a time when there was a growing population of mainly railway workers, following the arrival of that form of transport in the town. The north aisle was added in 1866 but the interior remained quite plain until the insertion of important late Morris & Co. glass beginning in 1910. This ensemble provides us with an opportunity to look at a series of designs by John Henry Dearle who took up the position of chief designer for Morris & Co. following the deaths of Morris and Burne-Jones. ***To explore the glass in chronological order is worthwhile but does necessitate moving about the church a little more.***

We begin at the west window in the north aisle with its three lights and tracery. It shows *The Maries at the Empty Sepulchre* across the whole width of the window and has a starlit sky above. It is from a Dearle design completed well after the deaths of his two mentors. The subject was in fact used by Morris for one of his early windows in St Michael and All Angels Church in Brighton in 1862. This Dearle design was first used here and later repeated in Australia and a number of other churches in Britain. It takes much of its inspiration from the later more pictorial work of Burne-Jones and like other windows in the church is strikingly modern.

The west window in the nave has five lancets showing the archangels and is of the same date and has a Dearle design *Christ Ascending* in the centre. The figures on the left are *St Michael* and *St. Gabriel* with *St Raphael* and *St. Uriel* on the right side. These are all to Burne-Jones' designs, the last one *(Uriel)* being adapted from his figure of *Joshua*. Interestingly the figures of *Michael, Gabriel* and *Raphael* were first used at Rottingdean in nearby Sussex in 1893.

Moving to the west window of the south aisle the two lights show *Christ and the Woman of Samaria* (1910) against a landscape background and are again from a Burne-Jones design.

In the centre of the opposite aisle is Dearle's *Road to Emmaus* of 1911 which is a simpler design than his *Maries at the Empty Sepulchre* and arguably the better for it. The left light depicts two apostles with the town shown in the background.

From the same year is the east window on the wall of the same aisle, a *Resurrection* by Dearle but based reasonably closely on a Burne-Jones window at Allerton near Liverpool.

The most westerly window on the same wall shares the same date and completes Dearle's original designs for the church and shows the *Agony in the Garden*. The limitation of a two-light window is overcome with some inspiration with the *Angel of Martyrdom* high up in the right hand light and a low *Christ* complimenting this on the opposite side.

Dating from 1912 are the allegorical figures of *Fortitude* and *Courage* found left of centre in the south aisle. They are both based on Burne-Jones' designs as are the figures of *Devotion* and *Charity* found nearby but dating from a year later. The westernmost window of the same aisle completes these figures depicting the Virtues with *Knowledge* and *Wisdom* from 1913 based on Burne-Jones' original designs for *St Paul* and *Solomon* respectively.

The final window is found (not surprisingly) by going to the other end of the aisle where Burne-Jones' *Adoration of the Magi* has been adapted from designs previously used at Hawarden and Westerham. This window depicts the *Virgin and Child* under a thatched shelter itself derived from the designer's *Star of Bethlehem* tapestry.

Much has been written of the decline in the quality of work produced by Morris & Co. after the deaths of its founders and largely there is little denying that overall this is the case. However at Tonbridge there is an almost unique opportunity in this part of Britain to assess for yourself whether Dearle's designs have merit. They were designed just prior to the Great War following which the taste for this style of work would change forever. It may well be that the Company never responded to this change of fashion and artistic climate but here in this church the best windows appear now to be good of their type and surpass much work done at the time.

(The CHURCH OF ST. SAVIOUR in the town has stained glass by Powell in five windows dating from 1907-31.)

Head northwards passing through the town and then turn left on the B245/London Road. Follow this to Hildenborough where the church is found on the right-hand side.

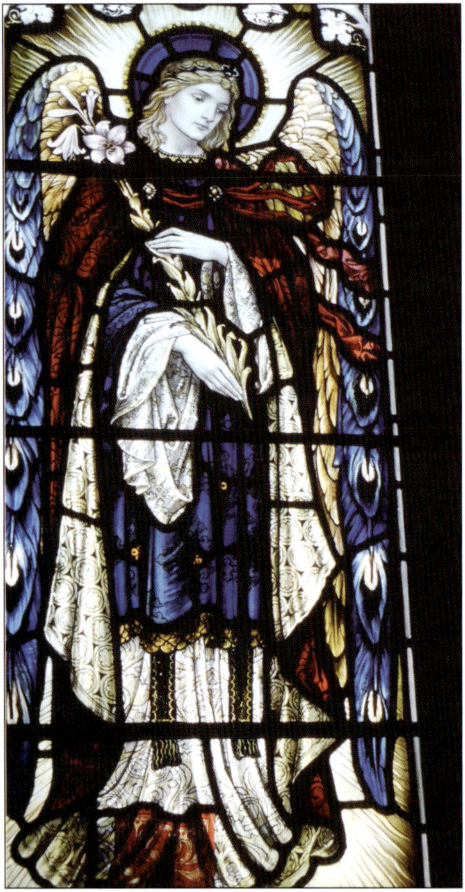

WINDOW DESIGN BY POWELL IN HILDENBOROUGH CHURCH - PHOTO BY AUTHOR

In a way the (2) CHURCH OF ST. JOHN THE EVANGELIST is like a reversed Tardis (the fictional form of transport for Dr. Who) whereby its interior initially seems too small for its external appearance. However it does have its compensations with the satisfying mix of materials particularly evident in the sanctuary. Here the carved sandstone blends admirably with the marble finish of columns and murals amidst some fine woodwork. The church was built in 1843-4 and is the work of the appropriately named Ewan Christian and is the first of many other ecclesiastical commissions. The interior has a distinctive arched-braced roof seemingly rising from lowly positioned stone corbels. The wide nave enables a large congregation to view the proceedings taking place in the apse-shaped sanctuary.

There is a good degree of stained glass which significantly reduces the available light in the sanctuary or chancel area. But even this helps to lend a welcome degree of atmosphere to this special space. The windows here date from 1898 and are the work of James Powell & Sons who also produced the memorial plaques dotted around the interior such as the one to Charles Fitch Kemp by the entrance door. The four smaller windows running below the main lights are particularly satisfying with their depictions of angels (1900). From left to right we have the *Angels of the Renunciation, Nativity,* the *Passion* and finally of the *Resurrection*. The main lights show the *New Testament Saints* (left), the *Adoration of the Risen Christ* (centre) and the *Saints of the Early English Church* (right light).

Powell were also responsible for the series of nine windows on either side of the nave which were installed from 1900-11. They are considerably lighter in tone which may well have been a consideration of the parishioners at the time.

The central west window has the *Patron Saints of England, Scotland and Ireland* (but not Wales) and was produced by Herbert Bryans in 1908. His running dog logo can be seen and this is also present in the nearby St Raphael window dating from a year later. The similar *St Gabriel* window is in fact distinctly later (1921) and also by Bryans although it does not bear the logo. The bulls-eye window above shows *St Michael* and has the same origin and dates from 1909.

Pre-Raphaelite styling is not evident in much of the Powell glass but more direct examples are to be seen in small windows in both the transepts. This is work by Morris & Co., the earlier window being the one in the north transept. This shows an *Angel with a scroll* and dates from 1876. It was probably adapted from a William Morris design that he used for a mural on the ceiling of Jesus College Chapel in Cambridge. It is interesting therefore as it does not appear to have been used before or after as a design in stained glass. On the south side is *St John the Evangelist* (to whom the church is dedicated) a Burne-Jones design that was first used in glass at the same college in Cambridge in1873. This version dates from 1881, six years after it was used at nearby Speldhurst church. Both windows are modest but delightful with the north window having the edge because of its uniqueness.

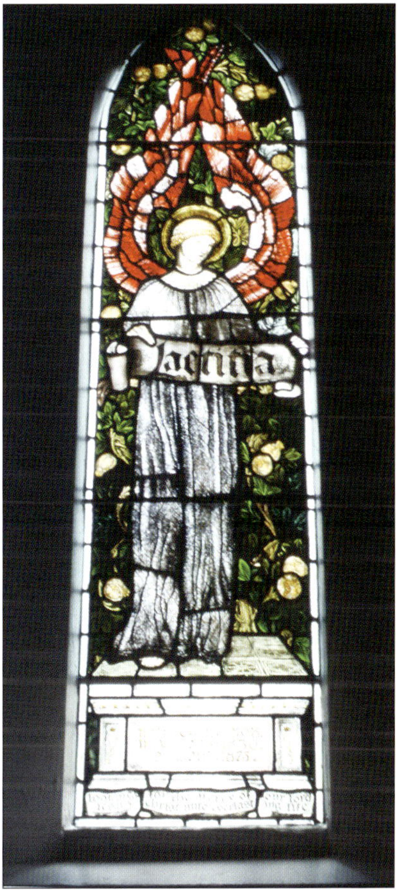

MORRIS WINDOW SHOWING LAETITIA (ANGEL WITH SCROLL) AT HILDENBOROUGH - PHOTO BY AUTHOR

Before leaving you should look at the Clayton & Bell window next to the entrance door with its more medieval styling.

Now head northwards along the B245 Tonbridge Road which becomes the A225 and as you enter the southern end of Sevenoaks town go right along a sign-posted drive to (3) KNOLE.

It is one of the largest private houses in the country and has over three hundred rooms. Building commenced in 1456 under Thomas Bourchier, Archbishop of Canterbury, but it was greatly added to in 1603 by Thomas Sackville the first Earl of

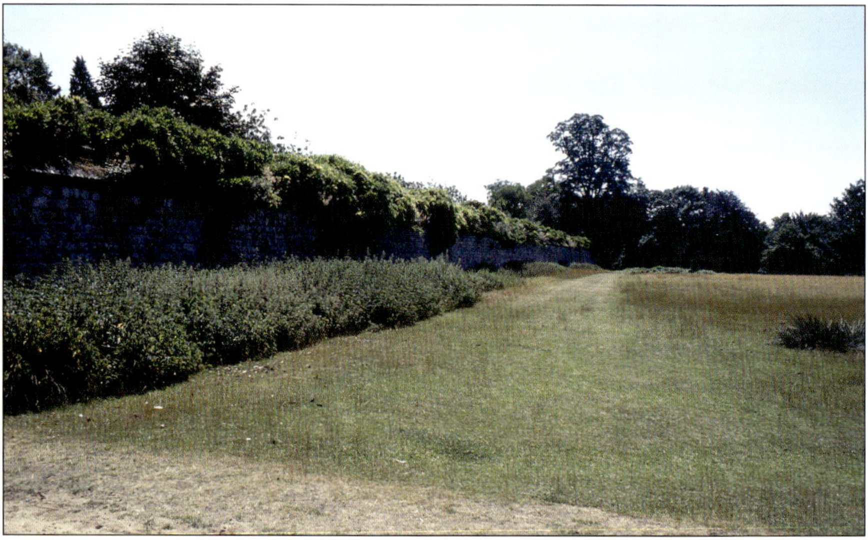

PART OF THE ESTATE AT KNOLE - PHOTO BY KIND PERMISSION OF THE NATIONAL TRUST

Dorset. Its exterior is more akin to a college or institution and Virginia Woolf (whose friend Vita Sackville-West spent some of her childhood in the house) described it as *'more like a village than a house'*. Portraits of the Sackville family by the likes of Reynolds and Gainsborough grace the rooms although artists of more interest to the reader of this book used its magnificent interiors and expansive park as the inspiration for their pictures.

In late October 1850 Holman Hunt started work on what was to be the background for one of his most important early works in the grounds of Knole Park. The picture *Valentine Rescuing Sylvia from Proteus* is taken from Shakespeare's *Two Gentlemen of Verona* where the setting is the Forest of Mantua for which Knole approximates. It was the first time that Hunt used extensively the 'wet white ground' method of oil painting in order to get greater luminosity in his colours.

This method of applying the ground fresh each day would form the basis for the Pre-Raphaelite techniques that make their earlier pictures in particular so distinctive. The painting is dominated by four figures but Hunt also gives as much importance to the detail of the foreground and background, a tenet so daring and revolutionary to his pictures of this time.

In a letter of late October to John Lucas Tupper a sculptor and former fellow student, Hunt draws himself sheltering from the rain at Knole and surrounded by deer. He had in fact been joined there by Frederick Stephens and Rossetti and much to their annoyance the bad weather continued. Hunt's background took longer than he expected and he still needed to complete some aspects of the foreground(such as leaves) in his studio on his return. Rossetti used his hard won landscape as the background for his later work *The Bower Meadow.*

Stephen's *The Proposal* (Tate Britain)was completed at the same time and shows the Marquis and Griselda from Chaucer's *The Clerk's Tale (Canterbury Tales)*. The background shown is from the kitchen of the rural lodgings that Stephens shared with

Hunt and Rossetti near Knole. It provides a rare example of his painting before he largely gave it up to concentrate on being an art critic.

Twelve years later Millais and his wife Effie made the trip to Knole where she was to be his model for Madeleine, the heroine of Keats' poem *The Eve of St Agnes.* Millais completed both oil and water-colour versions(Collection of The Queen Mother, V&A) of Madeleine standing in the room where the bed is kept that James I is reputed to have slept on. He shows her undressing near the bed where in the poem she is being secretly observed by her lover Porphyro. Millais spent three cold nights there in December 1862 trying to perfect his treatment of the moonbeams falling across her bodice. However he had to resort to using a bull's eye lantern as the light coming through the window from the moon was not as strong as that described by Keats in his poem.

Visiting the room today it is quite difficult to imagine the scene as the room has had to be fitted with protective transparent screens in order to help preserve the delicate fabrics and furniture within it. ***The house is open March - October between 12-4 on Wednesday - Sunday.***

As you leave the house drive you may wish to visit the (4a) CHURCH OF ST. NICHOLAS where there is an interesting Powell window on the north wall of the nave which although somewhat faded is the best in the building. It shows *Gideon* and *Jonathan* and dates from 1879. There is another Powell window showing the *Resurrection* in the chancel this time dating from 1913 and further glass in the south aisle of the nave depicting *Bourchier, Morton and Cranmer* (1910). The window by W. F. Dixon in the tower is rather Pre-Raphaelite inspired but partly obscured by a modern porch structure. There is also much glass by Kempe but not the finest and a memorial on the west wall to that ubiquitous architect and restorer of the church T.G.Jackson.

(There is stained glass designed by Jackson and produced by Powell at the CHURCH OF ST. GEORGE at Sevenoaks Weald)

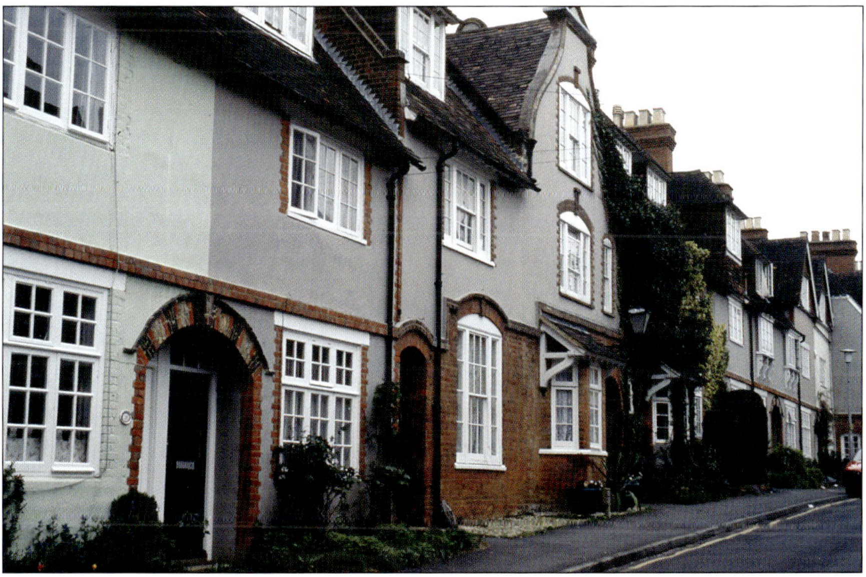

LIME TREE WALK IN SEVENOAKS - PHOTO BY AUTHOR

Continue into the main town by either foot or car taking the A224 London Road where (4b) LIME TREE WALK ***is soon seen on the left-hand side.***

Sir Thomas Graham Jackson crops up again here as the architect of these cottages in the 'Queen Anne' style. They were built in 1878-9 and Jackson's client was his own father who was a solicitor interested in the plight of the working classes who wished to see them housed in well-designed buildings in the centre of town close to their place of work. The plan was also to reverse the movement of workmen and their families out of towns because they were supplanted by the rising middle classes. Even the style of the cottages was one associated with the more moneyed. Today the buildings continue to be very pleasing to the eye and no doubt Morris and Ruskin would have approved of the socialist ideas behind the plan which assumes that all classes have the sensibility to appreciate the quality of their surroundings.

(4c) SEAL HOLLOW HOUSE ***is in Quaker Close off Bayham Road. To get there continue northwards on the A224 but turn right at its junction with the B2020 St. Botolph's Road. Turn left at the A225 and then immediately right along Vine Court Road which leads into Bayham Road. Follow this down almost to its end where Quaker Close is on the right.***

The house is a good example of the work of Hugh Mackay Baillie-Scott who also built other houses in the vicinity(Whiteladies and Kilnwood). He was a contemporary of Voysey and Lutyens and with the former in particular he developed the idea of the smaller 'artistic' house. The most obvious prototype for this was Philip Webb's Red House that was designed for William Morris as early as 1859-60. Seal Hollow with its low sweeping roofs and windows that reflect the internal arrangement also exhibits the principles of the Arts & Crafts Movement. The south front has typical attention to detail with its polygonal bay with candle snuffer cap. The interior also follows the maxim of 'truth to materials' espoused by Morris with its richness of wood so lovingly turned and carved by craftsmen. Although both the garage and billiard room have been demolished and it is surrounded by later development it still settles well into its present environment.

(In later years C.R. Ashbee lived at Godden Green a little to the east of Sevenoaks. Ashbee was a designer and architect but above all a social reformer following in the steps of William Morris and John Ruskin. He started the Guild of Handicraft in London in 1888 moving it to Chipping Campden in 1902. In 1924 he moved with his wife Janet into a large Gothic house at Godden Green in which his wife had grown up and where her mother still lived. Knole is nearby and Ashbee the architect liked its close proximity. Whilst there he altered the facade of the building and had the attic storey removed. The house is now called Stormont Court. He also did some alterations to another house nearby The Hatch in 1932.)

Retrace your route back to the A224 where you should turn right. Follow this to a busy roundabout where the (5) CHURCH OF ST.MARY THE VIRGIN ***stands on a prominent site to the right. Parking for the church is found behind the building by using the A25 going east and turning right along Shoreham Lane and Church Field.***

Although Riverhead is now joined to the building sprawl of Sevenoaks it continues to exude its own personality. The church itself has a wonderful location on top of a small sandy hill. It dates from 1831when the nave was built to the plans of the prestigious Decimus Burton. Once inside we see its plain simplicity which provides a contrast to the chancel of about fifty years later. The architect for this was Sir A.W. Blomfield and within it are some wonderful Pre-Raphaelite angels forming part of the reredos. The central figure of *Christ in Majesty* of 1894 predates the rest of the decoration and is a mosaic by Salviati. Either side are groups of four angels rather echoing Burne-Jones' familiar *The*

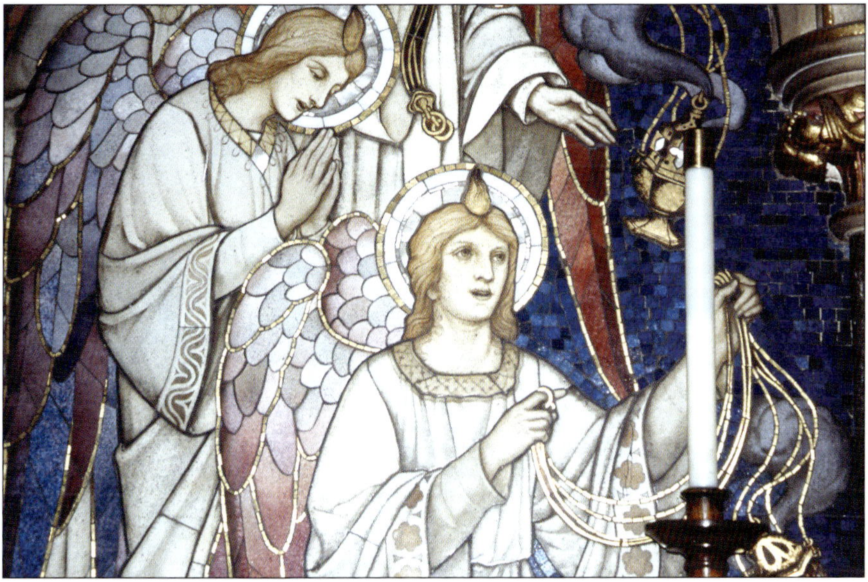

DETAIL OF ANGELS IN THE MOSAIC AT RIVERHEAD CHURCH - PHOTO BY AUTHOR

Golden Stairs (Tate Britain). They appear to be holding incense vessels and are rather charming providing as they do a contrast to the main central figure. They are from a sketch by A.F. Coakes, one of Powell's chief designers with cartoons by Charles

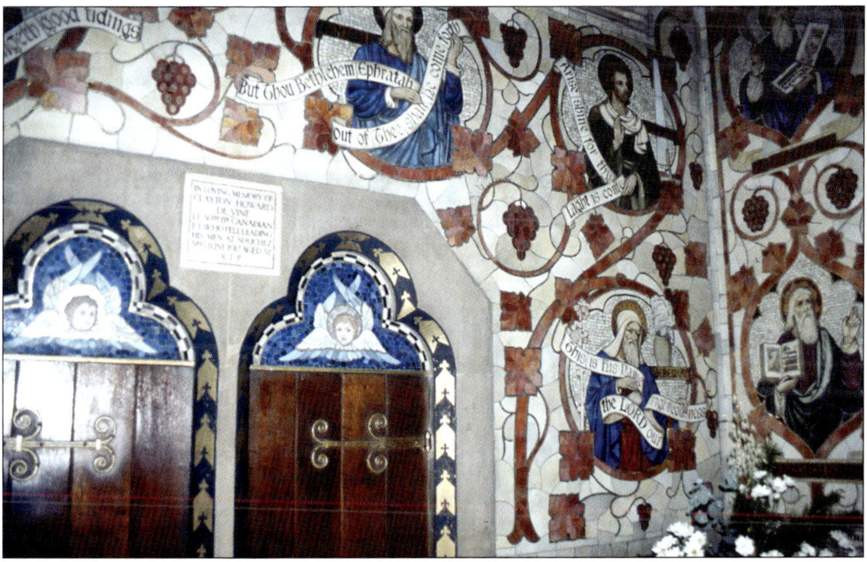

MOSAIC WORK IN THE CHANCEL AT RIVERHEAD - PHOTO BY AUTHOR

Hardgrave.There are two arches to both sides and on the right are typical Powell putti above patterned blue tiles. Opposite are two further larger putti with wooden doors below. The main decoration is in memory of Adeleve Cressy who died in 1911 but remembered for her devoted service to the Parish whilst other parts were given later by other families in memory of loved ones. For example the panels of the four Evangelists were given by members of the France families and a Clayton Howard De Vine is also remembered. There is also on the left-hand side a list of soldiers that fell in World War I. Adjacent is more tiling with the Tudor rose and fleur-de-lis. The remaining figures depict old testament prophets and were erected between 1912-16. Above all this opus sectile work are three Kempe windows dating from 1905 with a *Crucifixion* and the saints *Mary* and *John*. They are rather dark with lots of trees outside but that does add to the way that the rich decoration beneath slowly reveals itself. Also in the chancel is a window by Powell from 1912 showing a *Nativity* scene and below it the *Flight into Egypt*. ***The church is sometimes locked but access via the vicar is actively encouraged.***

A little north of the ever busy M26 lies the village of Kemsing and the (6) CHURCH OF ST. MARY. ***To reach the village head north on the A225 and turn right onto the A25 as far as Seal.*** (The CHURCH OF ST PETER AND ST PAUL in the village has stained glass by Francis Wilson Oliphant in the east window of the chancel and in the south chapel dating from the late 1850s. Oliphant was a freelance designer but worked as Pugin's second designer from 1848-50. Ashbee also repaired the tower at the church in Seal during 1913 and repaired the east window in 1939.) ***Now follow signs to Kemsing. The church is close to the local primary school.***

This pretty church with wood-shingled spire was given a north aisle by the ubiquitous Sir T. G. Jackson in 1890-1. The flints used in its construction were collected from the hill to the north of the building by local women using baskets. However, many of the church treasures exist as a result of his friend the Rev. T. C. Skarratt who initiated the decoration of the chancel largely completed by Ninian Comper in the early years of the twentieth century. Comper was also responsible for the vaguely Pre-Raphaelite war memorial at the east end of the north aisle. There are a number of his stained-glass windows with an example on the west wall having his logo of a strawberry leaf with a flower and berry.

A window from the company of James Powell & Sons depicting *St. Edith* can be seen over the porch and dates from 1893.

But the church is also home to a number of works by the Art & Crafts designer Henry Wilson who lived nearby. You come across one of his works as soon as you enter the building - a sculptural relief of the *Virgin and Child* near the font. This may well have been intended for a larger monument. Wilson was an architect and metalworker who was a member of the Art Workers' Guild and perhaps most remembered today for his church silver and unique jewellery designs. A little further down the south wall is a stained-glass window also designed by Wilson but made by Christopher Whall and his daughter. Whall was also an advocate of the Arts & Crafts Movement who early on in his career was inspired by the images of Edward Burne-Jones. The window shows the *Transfiguration* with *Moses* and *Elijah* in the lights either side. It is in memory of Mark W. Collet who died in 1905 and who owned the nearby house of St. Clere. In the north-east corner of the churchyard are further memorials to (amongst others) members of that family also by Wilson in designs associated with the Arts & Crafts Movement. Over the years they have been vandalised but the tall tapered cross in memory of the Rev. Skarratt's father is still splendid and there is a bronze relief to be seen on one of the Collet graves. ***The church is open most days.***

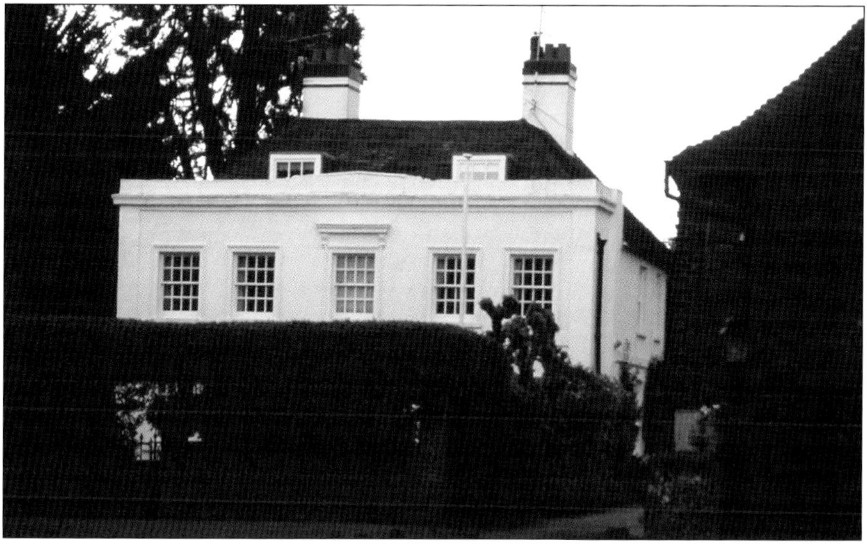

SAMUEL PALMER'S HOUSE AT SHOREHAM - PHOTO BY AUTHOR

Leave the car park and turn right at the High Street and then turn right again to go along The Landway. At the end go left along the road that runs along the Pilgrims' Way until you reach its junction with the A225 where you should turn right and then take the second left into Shoreham.

Despite its proximity to Greater London the village of Shoreham maintains its sense of remoteness. In many ways it is unchanged from the days when Samuel Palmer was a resident. This 'visionary' painter lived here from 1827 until 1833 and his early atmospheric pictures were a great form of inspiration to people such as Millais, Hunt and Rossetti. Palmer was himself inspired by the pictures and writing of William Blake and Blake visited him in the village. He was also a member of the Ancients, a group of painters that included Edward Calvert and George Richmond who had formed in about 1824. Neither Calvert or Richmond lived at Shoreham but both for a while closely shared Palmer's ideals for the group. Many of these were similar to the German Nazarenes, a revivalist group of the 1810-20s who celebrated medievalism and the paintings of the Italian, Flemish and German Primitives. Their activities included dressing in appropriate costume and producing work that was principally religious in tone. They were also very influential to the Pre-Raphaelites, Ford Madox Brown visiting them in Rome. Palmer himself dressed on occasion in suitable archaic-styled clothing and painted wonderful spiritual pictures showing biblical subjects set within the local landscape. Palmer's white Water House, where he lived with his father brother and nurse, is easily found by the bridge over the river Darent.

The (7) CHURCH OF ST. PETER AND ST. PAUL is at the east end of the village and has a delightful path lined with tall yews leading up to its porch. The porch itself is fifteenth century and formed from the single root of a massive oak tree and in 1925 C.R. Ashbee was called in to make some repairs to it. Just inside the building is a fine oil by Charles West Cope dated 1878 and entitled *The Return of Verney Lovett Cameron RN.* Cameron was a local man who became the first man to cross Africa from east to west and

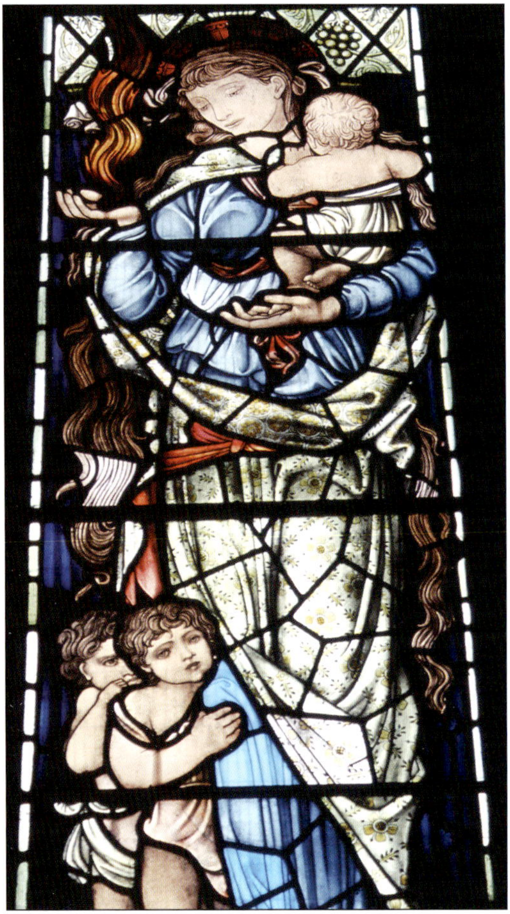

DETAIL OF THE FIGURE OF 'LOVE' DESIGNED BY BURNE - JONES IN SHOREHAM CHURCH - PHOTO BY AUTHOR

the painting shows his celebratory return to Shoreham. There are other treasures within including the eighteenth century chandeliers and the pulpit that once graced Westminster Abbey. The plain lofty interior also houses a fine decorated organ case and the remains of some medieval stained glass in the form of a pelican in the north wall. The only other stained glass to survive the heavy wartime bombing is in the south aisle and it is a Morris & Co. window designed by Burne-Jones and dating from 1903. It is in memory of the geologist Sir Joseph Prestwich who lived on the hill above the village. The design shows (from left to right) the figures representing *Joy, Creation* and *Love* and they have been adapted from allegorical figures used before elsewhere. *Joy* comes from an original *Hope*, found firstly at Christ Church, Oxford but used subsequently in many locations including Bidborough and Bishopsbourne in Kent. The middle figure comes from the *Days of Creation* series found initially at Middleton Cheney where six angels are shown but at Shoreham only the first 'day' has been used. The figure of *Love* was also first used (1870) at Christ Church in the role of *Charity*. Despite the window's late date and its position in the church we should all perhaps breathe a sigh of relief that such an harmonious window should have survived those troubled times of war. ***The church is usually open most days.***

Leave Shoreham by retracing your way along Station Road and turning right at the junction with the A225 going in the direction of Sevenoaks. On the outskirts of that town go left along the A25 through Seal before turning right on Church Road where a church soon appears on your left-hand side.

The (8) CHURCH OF ST. LAWRENCE at Seal Chart was begun by the architect C.H. Howell in 1867 and his work was completed a year later. The church was however extended in 1876 and the tower and transepts were added by F.W. Hunt twelve years later. The church was commissioned by the Wilkinson family who also used Howell to build their home, Frankfield House, which can be seen amongst trees to the north of the church. At the time they were mourning their daughter Mary who had died the previous year at St Lawrence on the Isle of Wight aged six. Parts of the building at Seal Chart resemble the church at St. Lawrence where a memorial to Mary can be seen and where coincidentally there is Morris glass.

The exterior of the church consists of two types of local stone with a light yellow stone providing the mouldings around the windows and doors. Once inside the east window attracts attention as it is placed inside stone arches in a manner reminiscent of William Burges. The figure at the top is based on a portrait of the deceased child as is the figure kneeling to Christ lower down. Despite the fact that some of the details are deteriorating and the main scenes have a somewhat unusual style, the window has an overall appearance that is early Morris inspired. This is not altogether surprising as it was designed by Henry Holiday whist working for the glass makers, Lavers, Barraud & Westlake. There are three smaller windows nearby depicting the *Mary Virgin, Rachel* and *The Good Shepherd* by the same firm and dated 1868. They all have distinctively elongated figures.

In the south transept is another memorial window to a member of the Wilkinson family with figures again taken from portraits of the daughters, Annie Clare and Mary again. This is dated 1876, two years later than the similar window in the north transept which shows boys instead of girls. This charming glass is perfectly complemented by its partner opposite. They provide an opportunity to compare these slightly later designs by Holiday (now working for the firm of James Powell & Sons) with his others in the church. Don't miss the smaller window on the east wall of the south side depicting the figure of *Charity* given by the same donor as the north transept window and dating from 1884. This is also from the Powell Company and designed by Henry Holiday. ***The church is open most days.***

Continue along Church Road in the same direction as you were previously travelling. Turn left along Stone Street Road to arrive in the village of Ivy Hatch. Keep right to go along Mote Road where the entrance to Ightham Mote arrives shortly on the left.

(It is possible to visit the CHURCH OF ST. PETER at Ightham by turning sharp left at The Plough pub in Ivy Hatch (down Ismays Road and Bates Hill) where there is a heraldic tomb behind the church. This is the work of the distinguished if a little eccentric architect and designer William Burges.)

(9) IGHTHAM MOTE is a very fine moated manor house dating from the 1330s which has seen many changes throughout its long history. Its very survival may well be due to its seclusion hidden as it is within the landscape. It has been altered and added to during its 670 years or so but only one named architect is known to have contributed to its current appearance. He was Richard Norman Shaw and although his contribution to the house is rather minor it occurs at a time (the 1870s) just before the life of the house became increasingly connected to an artistic circle that included painters and literary figures associated with the Pre-Raphaelites.

In 1880 the Selby family had been resident at the Mote for almost 300 years but the family line faltered that year and the house was rented out to General William Jackson Palmer and his family. This man was the founder of Colorado Springs (a resort in the Rocky Mountains of the United States) and he enjoyed a wide social circle. Among the friends he entertained at Ightham were Edward Burne-Jones and William Morris. The family also invited Henry James, Ellen Terry and John Singer Sargent to dinner at the Mote. In fact Sargent produced two lovely pictures here - one a portrait of General Palmer's daughter Elsie painted inside the house with the distinctive linen fold panelling

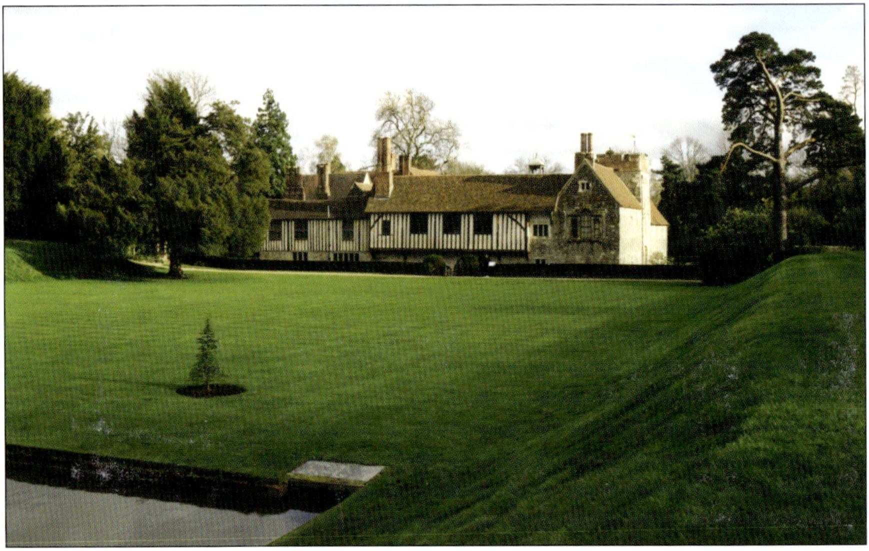

IGHTHAM MOTE - BY KIND PERMISSION OF THE NATIONAL TRUST

in the background and the other an exterior scene. This showed a group playing bowls on the lawns that included members of the Palmer family and Mrs Comyns Carr, the wife of Joseph who in 1887 initiated the building of the New Gallery in London. This was where Burne-Jones would exhibit many important paintings following a spate of disagreements at the Grosvenor Gallery. In her book *Reminiscences* Mrs. Comyns Carr wrote of her *'delightful interludes'* at Ightham with Henry James and George Meredith as well as her own children. Another occasional childhood visitor was Edward Gordon Craig, the son of Ellen Terry and the architect E. W. Godwin. There is an account of how the various children would each take a separate window seat in the house and then compete to see who could catch the most fish from the moat with their lines.

At the end of July 1889 the house was sold to Thomas Colyer-Fergusson and the Palmer family were given notice to move. Eighteen-year-old Elsie found leaving the house a difficult experience and wrote about how she wandered about after breakfast on the last day trying to say goodbye.

In 1953 following a period of uncertainty about the future of the house it was bought by an American batchelor, Charles Henry Robinson, who was also responsible for donating the house to the National Trust in 1985.

There is of course an excellent guide to the house available and I only wish to highlight some features within the house that date from the late nineteenth century or so and which readers of this book may be particularly interested in.

As you first enter the building you come into the Outer Hall which is a space created by Norman Shaw from the old buttery. This was done to cut down on draughts in the Great Hall and beneath its woven fabric on the walls is some Art Deco wallpaper. The Great Hall has the frieze and panelling that was designed by Shaw. The frieze was carved by James Forsyth who was also working with Shaw at Cragside about the same time. This large house in Northumberland has a number of Pre-Raphaelite artefacts in its collection including paintings by Evelyn De Morgan and Spencer Stanhope, sculpture by Alexander Munro and glass by Morris & Co.

Returning to Ightham one can really sense that Burne-Jones, Morris and many of its other illustrious visitors must have appreciated its unique charm. It has a long and complicated history from medieval times which can still be felt and experienced within its walls. ***The house is owned by the National Trust and is open March - October 10:30-5:30 on Mondays, Wednesday-Friday and Sundays***

Return to Tonbridge by heading south along the A227.

In the vicinity are two further churches you may wish to visit at some point. ST.LUKE'S CHURCH at Matfield was constructed between 1874-6 by Basil Champneys. It is small and made of sandstone and its timber bell turret and spire give it a rather charming exterior resembling an Arts & Crafts style. The churchyard has some nice yews that line the path to the porch and inside there are some simple but effectively designed pews with carved rosettes. In the north wall is some Powell glass dated 1916 which is in memory of a soldier who died in Mesopotamia and there is also some rather uninspired glass by Kempe & Tower (C. E. Kempe & Co. Ltd.) of *St Luke* and *St. Paul* (1923) with their wheat-sheaf and tower insignia. The chancel contains some better Kempe work in the form of a 1904 *Annunciation* and the way the lilies are used here is a nice touch. Perhaps the best window however is the main east *Nativity* of 1893 also by Kempe (although no sign of a wheat-sheaf) with a good amount of detail in the main scenes. ***The church is open most days.***

The sandstone CHURCH OF ALL SAINTS at Brenchley has an unusually wide chancel and within it on the east wall is a large Morris window of 1910. It tells the story of the *Ascension* and is the work of John Henry Dearle who was chief designer for Morris & Co at the time. Although Pevsner calls the work *'pale and poor'* on a dull day it provides virtually the only warmth in a cold interior. Its dominant blues, reds and gold and sheer scale combine to give it a good deal of impact. The design had been used once before at Troon in Scotland seven years earlier. It seems that there were other designs completed by Morris & Co. for Brenchley church including an *Adoration of the Magi* but these were not executed.

According to the church guide the north and south sanctuary windows were designed by Robert Anning Bell, a designer and sculptor often inspired by Pre-Raphaelite ideas. They date from 1899 and 1906 respectively.

The church is open most days.

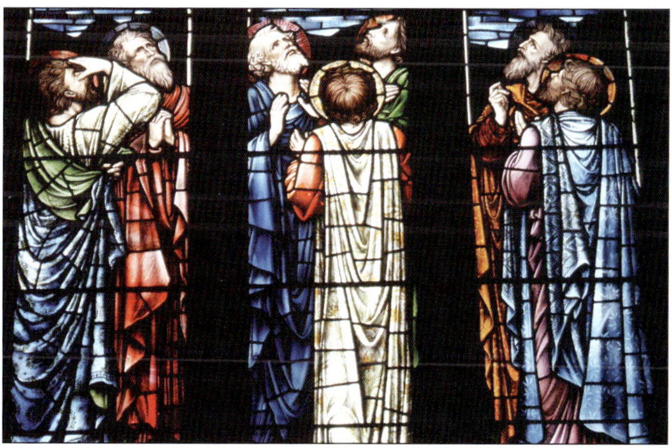

DETAIL OF THE MAIN EAST WINDOW IN BRENCHLEY CHURCH - PHOTO BY AUTHOR

Trail No. 4 Maidstone and District

Points of Interest

(1) MAIDSTONE - The BENTLIF ART GALLERY - Has many works by Albert Goodwin who was the studio assistant for a time to Ford Madox Brown. In addition there are other paintings by members of the same family.

(2) OTHAM - STONEACRE - Is the former home of Aymer Vallance the first biographer of William Morris

(3) DETLING - It was here that the parents of the artists John and Rosa Brett lived and the area provided inspiration particularly for the paintings of Rosa Brett

(4) BLUEBELL HILL - Another location used by Rosa and John Brett for their paintings.

ALSO: In the vicinity are the following:

(1) SUTTON VALENCE SCHOOL (1910-14) - By the architect Charles Holden who for a period of his life worked with Ashbee

(2) LOOSE - ALL SAINTS CHURCH**- Has glass by Kempe dated 1892.

(3) BICKNOR - CHURCH OF ST. JAMES**-Was 'restored' by Bodley in 1859-61.

STARTING POINT: St. Faith's Street, Maidstone

HOW TO GET THERE: The museum is found in the central pedestrianised area of the town close to the Fremlin Walk car park.

FINISHING POINT: Bluebell Hill

REFRESHMENTS: Many opportunities in Maidstone and there is a pub at Detling

TRANSPORT: Car essential

DURATION: A leisurely day.

(1) MAIDSTONE MUSEUM & BENTLIF ART GALLERY ***is to be found in St. Faith's Street*** and is housed in the former Chillington Manor although the building has later additions to both sides. The original manor is an early Elizabethan house with a long gallery constructed in the sixteenth century although it was heavily restored three centuries later. The art gallery area is housed in an addition of 1890 by the architect H. Bensted who was also responsible for the main staircase of 1877-8.

The gallery has an impressively large permanent collection which includes over 500 oils and 2500 water-colours and drawings. Included in the collection are about 200 water-colours by Albert Goodwin in addition to a number of oils by him and members of the same family.

Goodwin was born in the town at 1 Acton Place (now 62 Boxley Road) in 1845. He came from a large family of nine children, four of whom became artists. His elder brother

Harry is represented in the gallery's collection as is Harry's wife, Kate Malleson, with two accomplished water-colours. Another brother, Frank, has four water-colours in the collection. His work in particular has a Pre-Raphaelite inspiration and he may have become a more well-known figure had he not died at the early age of twenty-five. A further brother, William, also produced work. Albert was educated in Maidstone (at Mr Weakstead's school in Bedford Place) and after some dire experiences as a draper's apprentice he came into contact with Holman Hunt through a local printer. He then met Arthur Hughes who had married Tryphena Foord, the daughter of a local plumber in 1855. This is the same year Hughes painted one of his better known works *April Love* which was partly completed in the Maidstone garden of a Mr Cutbush who was the employer of Tryphena's father. Through his contact with Hughes, Goodwin went on to be taught by Madox Brown and hence to become acquainted with the likes of Rossetti, Morris and Ruskin. With these influences his landscapes became increasingly atmospheric and highly finished in the earlier Pre-Raphaelite style.

His work *Allington Castle* of 1866-8 was deeply poetic and was accomplished by the use of a wet white background as innovated by Holman Hunt and Millais. Under the more direct influence of Ruskin he toured Italy, France and Switzerland in the early 1870s continuing to produce detailed but subtle works. Later he painted more religious compositions but still with a Pre-Raphaelite intensity, his work eventually becoming broader but still adopting unusual viewpoints. Goodwin moved from Maidstone in about 1867 to Arundel where he was briefly married. Following his wife's early death he spent time in Hove, London and Devon before retiring to Bexhill in Sussex where he died in 1932.

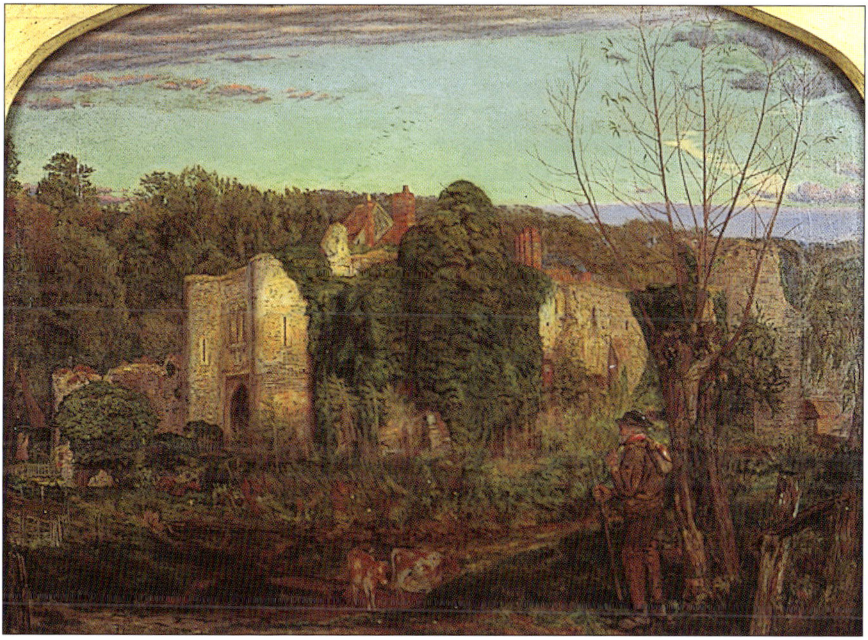

'ALLINGTON CASTLE' BY ALBERT GOODWIN. PHOTO © MAIDSTONE MUSEUM AND BENTLIF ART GALLERY

There are likely to be three or four pictures by Albert and his brothers on display in the gallery at any one time but should you wish to see more it is advisable to contact the Keeper of Fine Art and Applied Art prior to your visit. In the public catalogue listing fine art in Kent there is a work called *Saying Grace* by Arthur Hughes (1881) listed under Maidstone's collection.

The gallery and museum is open Monday - Saturday 11:00-17:15 and Sunday 11:00-16:00.

(The UNITED REFORM CHURCH in Week Street is an early nineteenth century building that houses a tapestry reproduction of a stained-glass window by Burne-Jones. ***The church is normally open for coffee mornings Mon, Tues, Wed 10:30-12:30.*** The design that this is based on is *The Good Shepherd* and the original glass panel dates from 1857 and was installed in the Congregational Church in King Street in 1861. At this early date Burne-Jones was in the employ of James Powell & Sons. He stayed with Arthur Hughes at Marsham Street in the town during 1858. The church was demolished in 1974 and the panel is normally to be seen in Maidstone Museum. The CHURCH OF ST. MICHAEL AND ALL ANGELS has over twenty windows by the company of Heaton Butler & Bayne installed between 1879-98.)

Leave the town via the A274 road to Headcorn. Look out for Gore Court Road on your left (still within the outskirts of Maidstone) and follow it until you can turn right along White Horse Lane. This soon turns into Otham Street and shortly a sign to Stoneacre will appear pointing right.

(2) STONEACRE is a wonderful yeoman's house of about 1480 made from local limestone and oak trees. It has a great hall with an oak screen at one end and a rare king-post high up in the ceiling. After the Ellys family sold the house in 1725 it was occupied by tenant farmers for almost 200 years and the fabric of the building deteriorated. Thus it was in 1920 when a writer and follower of William Morris came across it and decided to repair the house filling it later with, amongst other things, medieval furniture and Arts and Crafts furnishings. His name was Aymer Vallance and today he is best known perhaps as a biographer of Morris. Vallance was educated at Oxford and in 1885 was ordained into the Anglican Church later serving as curate at the Church of the Annunciation in Washington Street, Brighton. This church has Morris & Co. glass dating from twenty years before Vallance's appointment so it is possible that this glass had a profound influence on the interests that Vallance developed later. He joined the Catholic Church in 1889 probably as a result of his support for the Oxford Movement who emphasised the importance of ceremony in church services. He also championed Aubrey Beardsley early on in his short career who had interestingly attended the same Church of the Annunciation a few years earlier.

Vallance was in his late fifties when he started work on Stoneacre and was to marry the following year. As well as putting in appropriate fireplaces, panelling etc. he constructed a new wing or rather reconstructed one from a sixteenth century house that was due to be demolished at Chiddingstone. There is an excellent guide to the house published by the National Trust so I will only highlight details of the interior which may be of particular interest. The glass in the Great Hall with its clear quarries is beautiful and was designed by Vallance in conjunction with Geoffrey Webb, Horace Wilkinson and Maurice Drake. The six lustreware chargers from Spain on the mantelpiece in the hall may be later additions to the house but are very suitable, reminiscent as they are of the work of the potter William DeMorgan.

In the Parlour are some fine curtains with an Arts & Crafts design by Herbert Horne from about 1885 entitled *Praise of the Soul Cretonne* but sometimes called *Angel with*

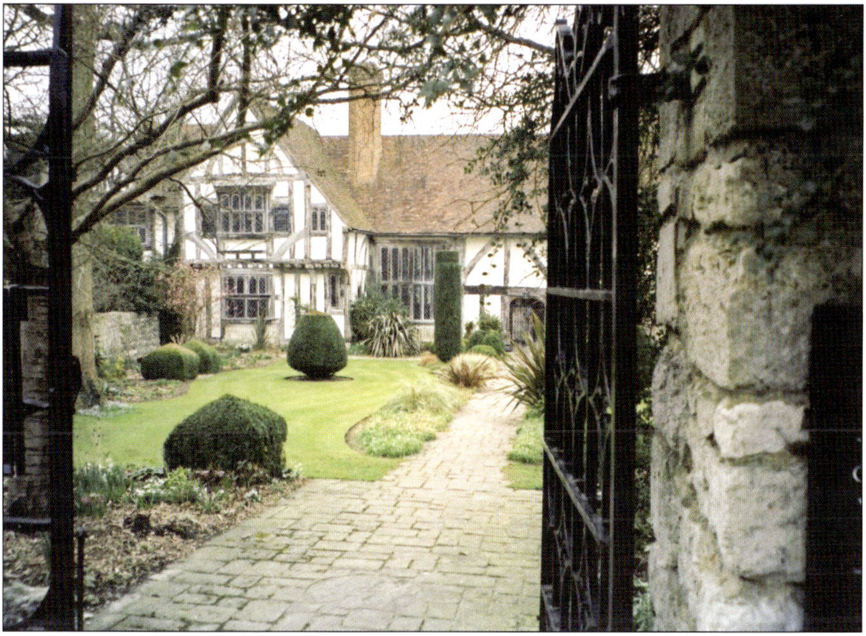

STONEACRE - BY KIND PERMISSION OF THE NATIONAL TRUST

the Trumpet.

Be sure to visit the garden before leaving, this offers elevated views of the building and is very peaceful especially considering its close proximity to Maidstone.

To get to Detling find the A249 Sittingbourne Road heading north out of Maidstone and follow it over the M20 until you see signs for Detling.

(3) DETLING church was painted by Rosa Brett, the talented artist and elder sister of the Pre-Raphaelite painter John Brett. In the interior is a particularly fine medieval lectern that is believed to come from Boxley Abbey after its contents were dispersed at the Dissolution. Rosa was born in Camberwell in 1829 and she spent periods of her life in Dublin and Manchester before coming to live in Kent. She lived with her parents at Lynchfield House in the village from the late 1850s probably as the daughter expected to look after them but perhaps also due to her own poor health. In 1859 she painted *The Artist's Garden* (Collection of David Dallas)which shows a horse chestnut tree which is likely to have been in the garden of the house. Unfortunately the house and garden were destroyed in order to build the road to Sittingbourne that the reader of this book may well have just travelled along. However, if one takes the Pilgrims' Way heading west out of the village another location for one of Rosa's pictures can be glimpsed. In *Thistles* (1860-Private Collection) she painted the view towards Boxley church with the woods on the North Downs at Boarley Warren shown in the distance. Both pictures show their subjects to a Pre-Raphaelite level of detail with particular attention to botanical accuracy and geographical truth. The paintings were both shown at the exhibition *Pre-Raphaelite Vision* in 2004.

To arrive at Bluebell Hill take a minor road through Boxley stopping at St Mary and All Saints church (painted by Rosa Brett)if you wish. Continue to head

westwards until you hit the A229 where you should turn right towards Chatham. The ancient megalithic burial chamber Kit's Coty is to the left of the road before coming into Bluebell Hill. This provided the subject for a drawing in a Rosa Brett sketchbook (1871) which she may have intended to use as a study for a later painting.

(4) BLUEBELL HILL is now close to a number of major road intersections but its position on a rise overlooking features such as the Pilgrims' Way made it a destination for John and Rosa Brett. Rosa painted the water-colour *From Bluebell Hill* (Private Collection)in 1851 whilst on one of a number of sketching sessions with her brother. Sometimes these were very tiring and the distances (despite being essentially local) were quite long.

(In 1862 Rosa lived about two miles south-west of Maidstone at East Farleigh close to the river Medway. Her place of residence was the Court Lodge which was the manor house in the village and belonged to Christ Church Priory in Canterbury. She painted it in wonderful detail as *The Old House at Farleigh* (Private Collection) and the picture may have been intended for exhibition at the Royal Academy. This did not happen and for a number of reasons her career never really seems to have taken off. She may have suffered the obvious disadvantages of being a female artist as well as having other commitments on her time and may also have experienced long term poor health. The house was demolished about 1874 with a half-timbered wing being reconstructed in the museum in Maidstone. The CHURCH OF ST. MARY has four windows by Powell dating from 1891-1917.)

Trail No. 5 By the Sea

Points of Interest

(1) RAMSGATE - THE CHURCH OF ST. AUGUSTINE *** & THE GRANGE - Pugin creations

(2) MINSTER-IN-THANET - Where Morris first began to appreciate Gothic architecture

(3) BIRCHINGTON - THE LOCATION OF ROSSETTI'S DEATH AND ALL SAINTS CHURCH*** - The tower bungalows by Seddon where Rossetti spent the last days of his life and the Celtic cross by Ford Madox Brown in memory of him as well as further stained glass

(4) WESTGATE-ON-SEA - THE CHURCH OF ST. SAVIOUR **- Kempe glass

(5) HERNE BAY and HUNTERS FORSTAL - Where an ill Rossetti fled in 1877 with Ford Madox Brown

(6) PEGWELL BAY - Location for William Dyce's seminal work of the same name

STARTING POINT: The Grange is found in St. Augustine's Road in Ramsgate.

HOW TO GET THERE: St Augustine's Road forms part of the B2054 and leaves the A255 on both sides of the town to run along Ramsgate's seafront.

FINISHING POINT: Pegwell Bay near Westcliff - a little to the west of Ramsgate.

REFRESHMENTS: Many opportunities in the town of Ramsgate and there are pubs near to the other locations.

TRANSPORT: Own car essential

DURATION: One day

Augustus Welby Northmore Pugin built (1a) THE GRANGE in 1843-4 as a family home. The idea was that his family would be close to a monastery and church which were both his intention to build next door. In the event his early death at the age of forty meant that his son Edward would complete these buildings which today still house a Benedictine community. The Grange is a wonderful Gothic house made of brick, tiles, slate and Caen stone which at the time it was built was very innovatory in design. Undoubtedly it provided a blueprint for later Gothic houses as well as Arts & Crafts buildings by Philip Webb, C.R. Ashbee, Charles Annesley Voysey and G.E. Street to name but a few.

Before designing The Grange Pugin had lived at Ellington Cottage in Ramsgate following his second marriage to Louisa Burton in 1833. Two years later they moved to a house he designed at Alderbury near Salisbury called St Marie's Grange. It was there

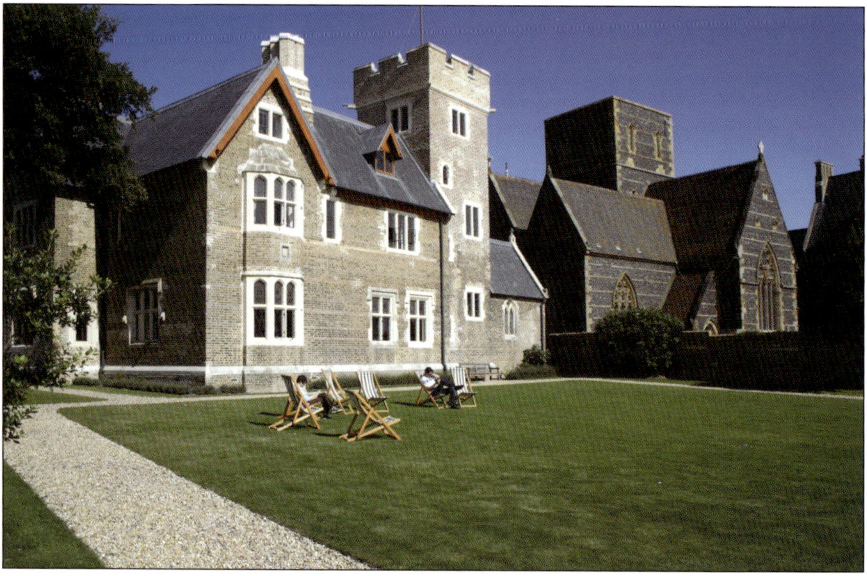

THE GRANGE - PHOTO BY BRIAN WISE

that he used red brick in a pioneering fashion some twenty-five years before Webb used similar materials at Red House. A little later he designed some interiors for King Edward VI Grammar School in Birmingham where Edward Burne-Jones would start attending as a pupil in 1844. Shortly afterwards Pugin converted to Catholicism which at that time was unusual and likely to adversely affect his professional career. Fortunately he secured work and was able to help Charles Barry in the designs for the new Houses of Parliament. Then in 1843 after a number of large successful commissions for Roman Catholic churches and cathedrals he started to build The Grange. It had a stunning location on the edge of a cliff and its exterior was simple and severe with few direct references to medieval work. A year later Louisa sadly died but Pugin, although distraught, continued work on The Grange and now began to build (1b) ST AUGUSTINE'S CHURCH adjacent as funds became available. He also continued to work on the extensive interior designs for the Houses of Parliament. St Augustine's was an ex-voto offering at his own expense- that is to say a man's gift to his own faith and was never used as a private chapel.

The church is to the Kent plan and houses amongst other fine artefacts a magnificent font which was shown at the Great Exhibition of 1851 as was the brass tabernacle on the high altar. There are also some delightful cloisters on the north side of the church with stained glass by Hardman on the north and west walls.

In 1847 the House of Lords was opened and a year later Pugin married for the third time to Jane Knill. He continued to devote much time to building St. Augustine's and the church was in use from 1850. The next couple of years saw a decline in Pugin's mental health brought on in particular by the Catholic churches predilection for Baroque-styled architecture to the detriment of his beloved Gothic. In 1852 the House of Commons was finally opened but Pugin was no better and Jane had to rescue him from London and his own demons and brought him back to The Grange. He died there on the fourteenth of September and was buried in a vault designed by his son and found in his chantry on the

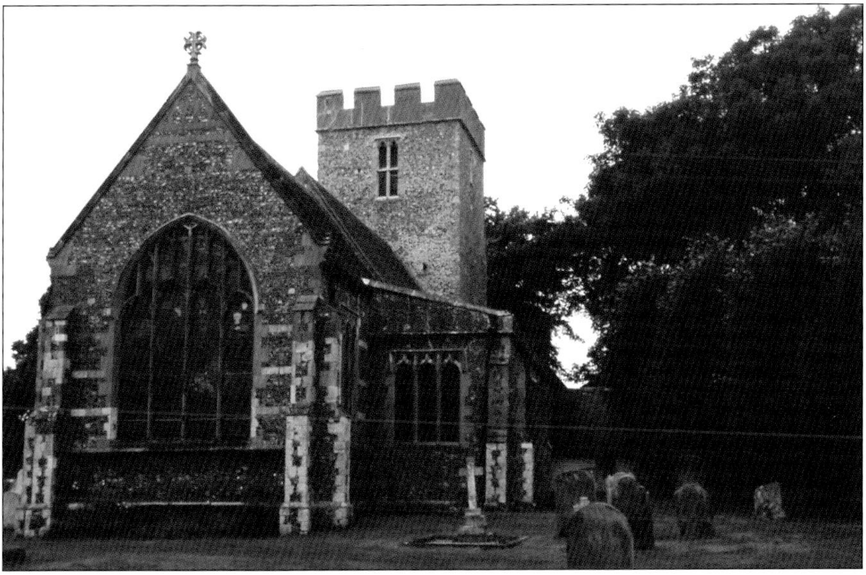

THE CHURCH OF ST. AUGUSTINE AT RAMSGATE - PHOTO BY AUTHOR

south side of the church. The same year the Bishop of Southwark (to whom the church was vested) handed it over to a group of Benedictine monks and further Abbey buildings and a school were later erected across the road

The Grange is as expected a functional house with its main rooms leading off a bright centrally-placed stairwell. There are glimpses of Pegwell Bay from the living room window which has a particularly impressive stone fire surround. A wider view of the goings-on in the Bay can be enjoyed from the lookout tower. The house is now owned by the Landmark Trust who with other benefactors have spent over two million pounds restoring it to Pugin's original designs.

The Grange is available for holidays through the Landmark Trust and the rooms on the ground floor are open by appointment every Wednesday afternoon.

Now make your way to Minster by going westwards along the B2054 London Road. Soon it joins the A299 Canterbury Road and follow this until you see signs for Minster at a roundabout. The abbey is found at the junction of the High Street and Church Street.

(2) MINSTER was once at the heart of Thanet and was also an early centre for Christianity in Kent. A nunnery was founded here in 669 but by the beginning of the eleventh century it had declined and was given to St. Augustine's Abbey, Canterbury. During the subsequent two centuries the church of St. Mary was rebuilt to a grand scale. Then in the thirties nuns returned to the Minster which is not the original building but a twelfth century grange.

When William Morris was aged about eight his father took him to see Canterbury Cathedral which had a profound impact on his emotional and aesthetic development. On the same trip he also visited the Minster and it too affected him deeply. In fact fifty years later he could still describe the building in very accurate terms as if he had only just visited the remains.

The church of St. Mary contains a giant Norman arch and a fine Early English chancel and there is good stained glass of 1861 by Thomas Willement in the east window.

Some parts of the abbey building can be seen including the Norman crypt. It is open Mon-Sat 11-12 with the additional times of 2-4:30 May to Oct.

To get to Birchington head north out of Minster down the High Street and Tothill Street and continue in the same direction along the B2190. At the next roundabout continue along Minster Road through Acol until you meet up with the B2050 heading into Birchington.

Dante Gabriel Rossetti died on the evening of Easter Sunday the tenth of April 1882. This occurred at Westcliff Bungalow which was in Beach Avenue a road that runs from near the railway station towards the promenade. The bungalow was provided by John Pollard Seddon. Unfortunately the building has been demolished although it is possible to see other bungalows in the town of a similar nature.

Thanet started to be developed as a resort in the late 1860s and the architect John Taylor built what were apparently the first bungalows in the British Isles in the area around Westgate-on-Sea a little to the east of Birchington. Taylor then began to build further bungalows on West Cliff at Birchington. John Pollard Seddon appears to have had a professional arrangement with Taylor but this may well have ended when Seddon himself began developing the area in about 1880.

Seddon's brother Thomas was an artist who was briefly very involved with the Pre-Raphaelite circle until his early death caused by dysentery at the age of only thirty-five. This occurred in Egypt in 1856 where he had previously travelled for more than a year from the winter of 1853 some of the time accompanied by Holman Hunt. His painting style was similar to Hunt's being very meticulous and he produced a number of pictures with a Pre-Raphaelite intensity to them. John Pollen Seddon met the prominent Pre-Raphaelites at his brother's studio and formed a great attachment to them before leaving London. He later returned and was able to commission works from some of the artists for Llandaff Cathedral. This included asking Thomas Woolner to produce models for

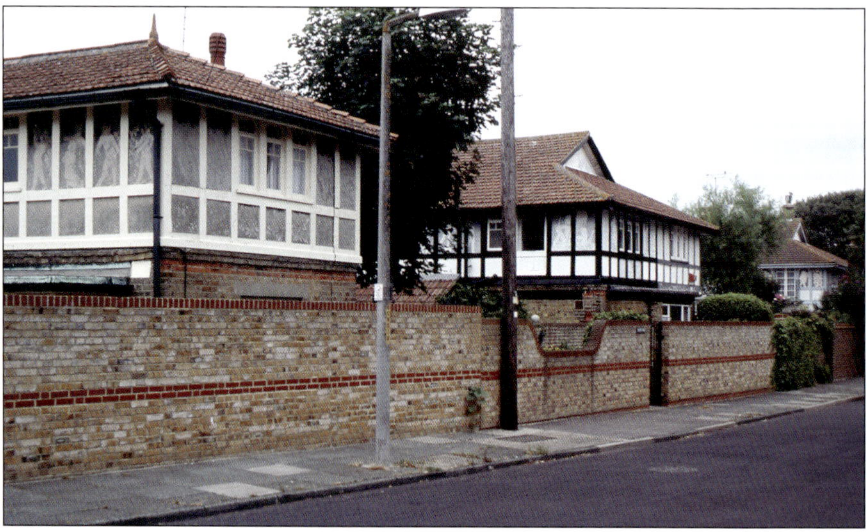

TOWER BUNGALOWS AT BIRCHINGTON - PHOTO BY AUTHOR

the pulpit and asking Rossetti to design the reredos. Seddon also commissioned paintings by both Rossetti and Madox Brown for the house he lived in at Llandaff. Following Rossetti's death Seddon collaborated with Madox Brown in the design of a monument to Rossetti that stands on Chelsea Embankment.

It is still possible to see examples of Seddon's bungalows in Birchington although despite extensive planning few were actually constructed. A vast hotel did not leave the planning stage and neither did terraces down to the sea and of the six blocks built only four now survive. These distinctive buildings - the 'Tower Bungalows' can be seen in Spencer Road which branches off Beach Avenue. They have some very attractive exterior decorations. Each of the buildings has a sturdy tower at the land-ward end. The artist Simeon Solomon was also at one time a resident of one of the bungalows.

(3) ALL SAINTS CHURCH was restored by C.N. Beazley almost twenty years before Rossetti's death and the nave roof dates from that time.

Gabriel's funeral took place on the fourteenth of April 1882 in the churchyard. A hearse and five mourning coaches left the bungalow for the short drive to the church in mid-afternoon and amongst the mourners were Gabriel's mother then aged 82 as well as William and Christina. His Aunt Charlotte attended as did the painter George Price Boyce and ex-Brotherhood member Frederic Stephens. Some of Gabriel's patrons were also there and after the short service most of the group went back to London. That was where a number of people had expected Gabriel to be buried but thoughts of Lizzie may have been the reason for his wish to be interred in Birchington. Christina wrote a poem simply called *Birchington Churchyard* and Madox Brown was called upon to design a gravestone. There was some argument over its design as Christina and her mother wished to have it in the form of a cross but William and Lucy thought this was inappropriate considering Rossetti's religious unbelief. In the autumn of 1884 Brown's 'runic' cross was erected on which pagan and Christian elements appear. These include a *Tree of Life* with a serpent representing Woman and the figure of *Divine Love* uniting Dante and Beatrice in Heaven. There is also the figure of the patron saint of painters *St Luke* at his easel and below that a maze or labyrinth the curves of which shape themselves at one point into the initials D.G.R. ***The headstone is found near the south door of the church.***

Inside the church are windows by Lavers & Westlake in the east and west windows but of more interest is the window in the south aisle to the memory of Rossetti. The right light was designed by Frederic Shields and installed in October 1884. It shows *Christ healing the blind* and was described by the vicar at the time as innocuous although he had been far less blase about the original subject for the left light. This was to have been an adaptation of Rossetti's *Magdalene at the door of Simon* but the vicar considered it unlikely to inspire deeply religious thoughts and instead *'fear(ed) that in some cases might rather do the reverse'*. The design that is seen today is based on Rossetti's *Passover in the Holy Family*.

The church is often locked and access may need to be sought via the church-wardens.

It is now possible to visit (4) THE CHURCH OF ST. SAVIOUR ***in Westgate-on-Sea by heading eastwards along the A28 Canterbury Road and once in the resort leaving it by Domneva Road and then turning right into Westgate Bay Avenue.***

This church was built in 1883-4 by C.N. Beazley the same architect responsible for the restoration work at Birchington. The building which is reminiscent of the work of Sir Arthur Blomfield contains stained glass by Kempe throughout. In the east window are five lights with the Crucifixion and Passion as subjects dating from 1887. In the west of

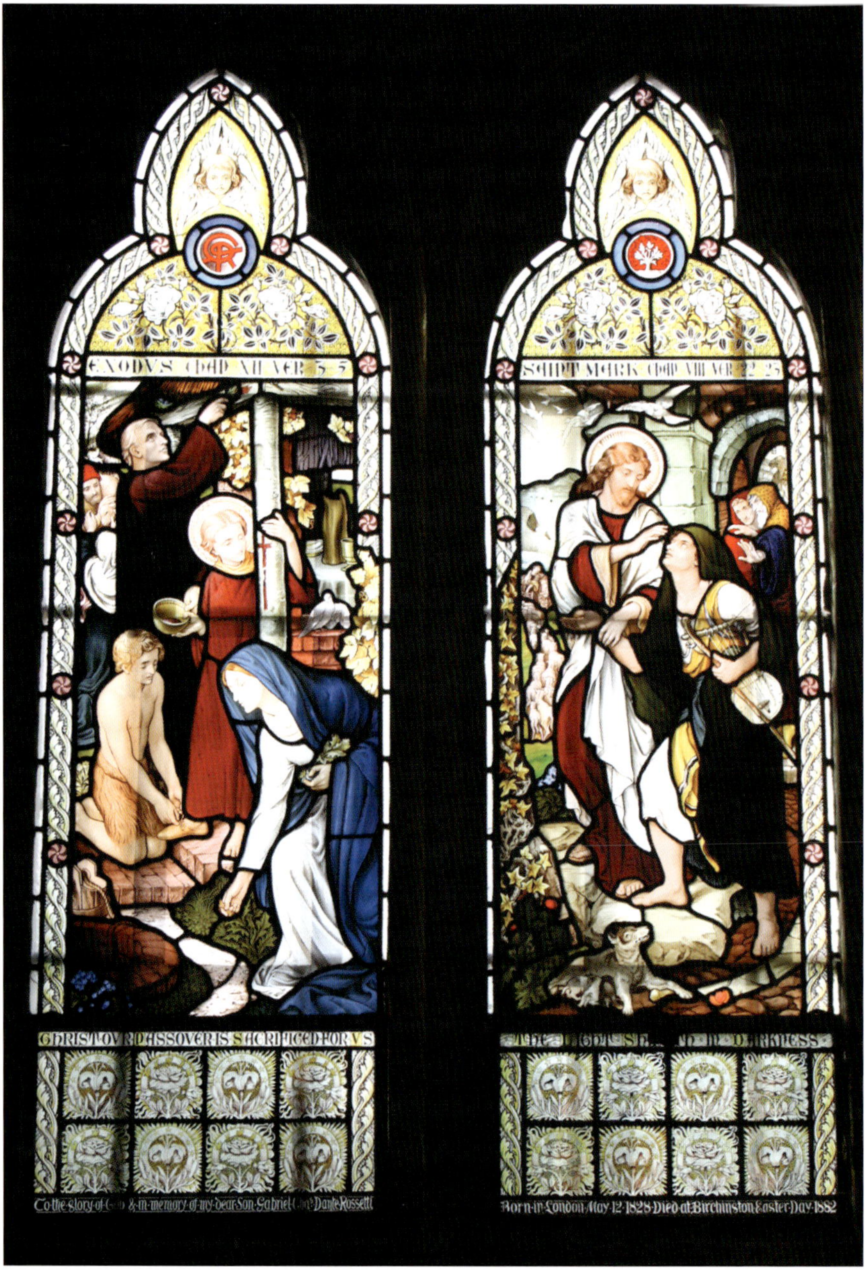

WINDOW BY FREDERIC SHIELDS COMMEMORATING ROSSETTI AT BIRCHINGTON CHURCH - PHOTO BY BRIAN WISE

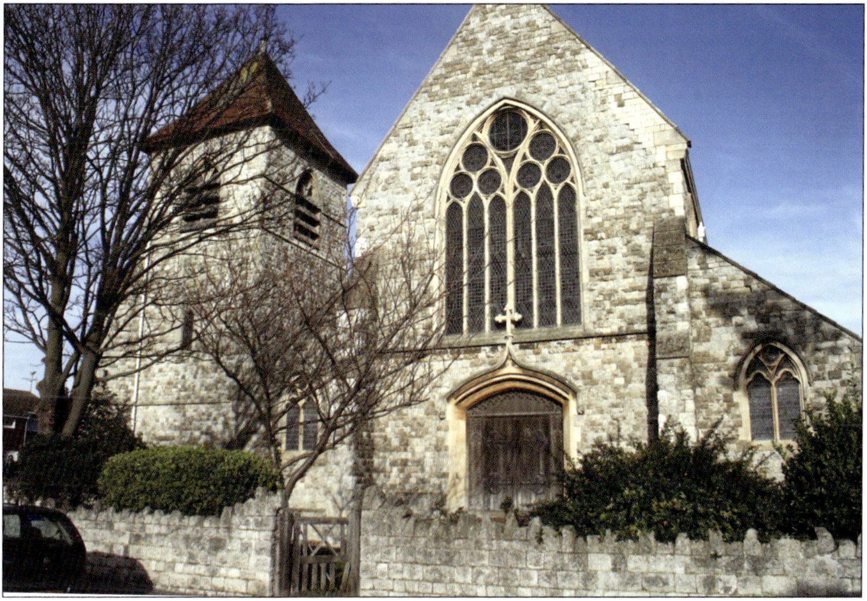

WESTGATE - ON - SEA CHURCH - PHOTO BY BRIAN WISE

the south aisle are the figures of *St Michael* and *St George* (1910)and opposite in the north aisle are the figures of *King David* and *Isaiah* (1919). Also in the north aisle at the westernmost end are the later figures of *St Luke, Elizabeth, John the Baptist* and *Zacharias* (1923). The remaining windows in the north aisle all date from 1919 and show *Christ blessing a child with angels* and going east *St Louis, Elijah* and *St Martin* and lastly at the easternmost end the saints *Alban, George* and *Oswald.* It's quite a collection and there was even more Kempe glass in the resort at the old St Michael's school but the current whereabouts of this glass is unknown.

The church may be locked but access is possible through the churchwardens.

To get to (5a) HERNE BAY ***head westwards along the Thanet Way(A299). This road now runs between Herne Bay(to the right) and*** (5b) HUNTERS FORSTAL.

Herne Bay is now a small quiet resort which had its heyday in the Victorian era. Planned in the 1830s its main landmark is the clock tower at the centre of the seafront. There used to be a pier that stretched out to sea for three-quarters of a mile but that was largely destroyed by fire and storm in the nineteen-seventies. St. George's Terrace, opposite the new pier, is probably the most impressive set of buildings in the town and there is also a good museum and art gallery. It was to this modest town that Madox Brown brought a poorly Rossetti in August 1877. Gabriel had been ordered by his physician to leave London or die seeing as he was both physically and mentally unwell. The main difficulty not for the first time was his addiction to the sleeping drug chloral. Their first attempt at accommodation proved to be less than ideal. Brown wrote '*Our first landlady proved a vixen, and we had to decamp, sacrificing a week's rent. But there was no help for it, for the house was small, and her tongue resounded all over it. She was indignant at our having baths; she was indignant at our late dinners; she was indignant at our wish to shut in the sound of her children's voices. She was most of all indignant at eggs being poached and macaroni eaten. We found this pretty house, and left. D.G. is really better since, and talks of painting again.'* The house of the 'vixen' was Mrs Joiner's in East Street which is described by William Rossetti in a letter to his wife Lucy of the eighteenth August 1877- *'a small house with a view to the sea up a side street - two sitting rooms and three bedrooms and four beds, at £4 for the first two weeks and less after. Gabriel was in favour of this house and your father seems not dissatisfied with it'.* Clearly opinions changed quickly. ***East Street runs between the High Street and the Promenade on the east side of the resort.***

The house that they moved to is found between the old villages of Hunters Forstal and Broomfield although the distinction between the two is blurred by modern development.

To get to what remains of this building called Ivy Cottage leave Herne Bay via the High Street (B2205) heading in the direction of Margate or Canterbury but leave this road at a roundabout with Mickleburgh Hill. This road later joins the Margate Road and then goes over the main A299.

Continue to follow Margate Road until you see the Grade II listed houses of Gothic House and Ivy Cottage. Only part of the cottage that Brown and Rossetti rented is still in existence, the building now consists of a bakehouse with a big chimney and an oven dating back to about 1800. As mentioned before the whole area is much changed following the demolition of Broomfield Hall in 1961 and its replacement by housing.

Rossetti spent about twelve weeks convalescing here and was later joined by his mother and sister Christina. Whilst there an exchange of letters occurred between him and Fanny Cornforth which led to her returning the keys to his Cheyne Walk address as she believed Rossetti had grown tired of her. This led to him becoming anxious of her whereabouts but despite this his health began to improve. The quantity of chloral that he was taking was much reduced and he was able to produce sensitive portraits of his sister and mother. Unfortunately towards the end of this stay Rossetti disagreed with Brown over issues to do with the chloral and there was a temporary break in their long-standing friendship.

(6) PEGWELL BAY is a large sea inlet lying to the south-west of Ramsgate. ***You can reach the area by going in the direction of Ramsgate along the A299 but turning off this onto the A255 at the roundabout just outside the town. At another roundabout shortly afterwards turn right down Chilton Lane to come to the old village of Pegwell. The road leads to West Cliff near to the start of this trail.*** From the Western Undercliff it is possible to gain access to the beach and to see the vast expanse of Pegwell Bay where William Dyce painted his masterpiece of the same name.

Dyce was born in Aberdeen in 1806 so he was about twenty years older than the members of the Brotherhood. He spent a short while studying at the Royal Academy but then came under the influence of the Nazarenes during two visits to Rome as Madox Brown would also later become. He was back in Scotland by 1829 mainly working as a portrait artist but also developing his interests in intellectual pursuits and science. Unlike Brown he was successful in the 1844 fresco competition to decorate the Houses of Parliament and these kept him busy right up to his death. Visiting the Royal Academy in 1850 he was impressed by the Pre-Raphaelite work there and suggested to John Ruskin that he should also take the time to see their paintings. He also began to paint under their influence and *Pegwell Bay, Kent - a Recollection of October 5th. 1858* (Tate Britain) is one of these pictures. It shows his family in the foreground collecting shells, a popular pursuit whilst on holiday. The figure on the far left of the oil painting is probably Dyce himself carrying artists' materials. There is also a water-colour of the subject entitled

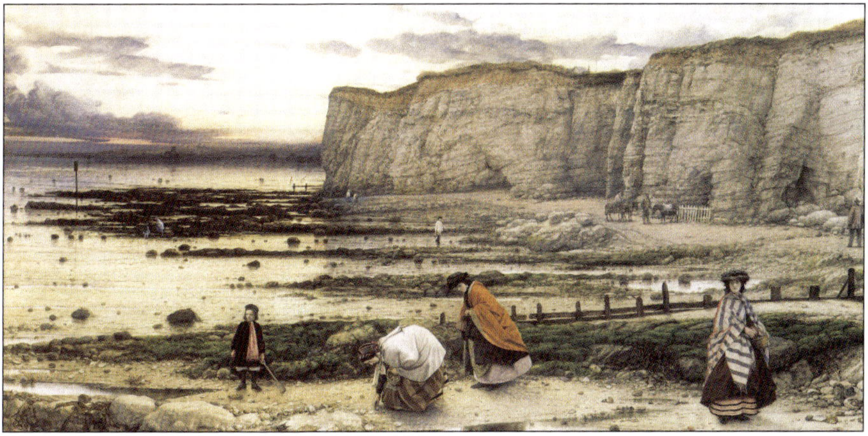

'PEGWELL BAY' BY WILLIAM DYCE - PERMISSION OF THE TATE

simply *Pegwell Bay* (Aberdeen Art Gallery and Museum) and dating from a year earlier which differs from the more well-known oil in not having any foreground figures and showing the bay at sunset. It is also painted in a broader style and was no doubt used as a study for the later oil that was completed in Dyce's studio. Some critics believe the oil picture was influenced also by photography. Certainly the painting's detail lends it a large amount of truth to nature some characteristics of which can also be seen in the water-colour. Both pictures also have an uncomfortable air to them - both being rather forlorn and not exactly having a holiday atmosphere. It is, for example, very different to Frith's *Life at the Seaside* (Royal Collection)painted nearby and concentrating instead on the figures depicted interacting with one another. The small figures in the Dyce oil seem distant from each other and interestingly do not notice the comet in the sky (except the artist). This might point to an underlying text to the work; commenting how science is all around but unnoticed and how advances in it will forever change the certainties of Victorian life, especially religious belief. Dyce was also interested in geology and because of this was perhaps drawn to Pegwell Bay with its fossil-rich chalk cliffs. These are certainly shown in amazing detail.

The area shown in the painting now has a sea wall at the bottom of the cliffs. In addition it does take some imagination to see the beach thronging with holiday-makers catching shrimps and going on donkey rides as would have been the scene in Victorian times. But the fact that the view is still identifiable today does show how accurate Dyce's picture was to the landscape at the time.

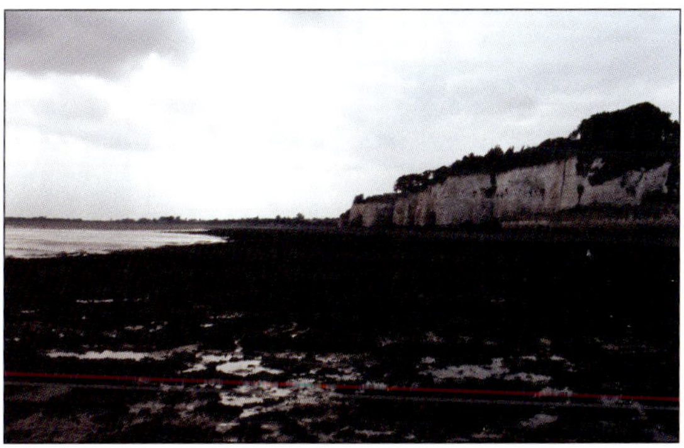

PEGWELL BAY TODAY - PHOTO BY AUTHOR

Trail No. 6 Around Cranbrook

Points of Interest

(1) CRANBROOK - MUSEUM AND CHURCH OF ST. DUNSTAN***- Paintings by the Cranbrook Colony of artists and locations associated with them plus stained glass by Paul Woodroffe amongst others.

(2) WOODCHURCH - ALL SAINTS CHURCH**- Kempe glass in a beautiful interior

(3) ORLESTONE - CHURCH OF ST. MARY THE VIRGIN***- Stained glass by Henry Holiday

(4) SMALLHYTHE PLACE - The home of Ellen Terry has a number of artefacts associated with members of the Pre-Raphaelite circle.

ALSO: ROLVENDEN - CHURCH OF ST. MARY THE VIRGIN**- Lutyens cross and GT. MAYTHAM HALL

STARTING POINT: Cranbrook Museum is in Carriers Road opposite the Church of St. Dunstan

HOW TO GET THERE: Cranbrook is positioned off the A229 Hurst Green to Maidstone road.

FINISHING POINT: Cranbrook (circular)

REFRESHMENTS: Pubs and cafes at Cranbrook and Tenterden. Pubs at Woodchurch and Rolvenden.

TRANSPORT: Own car essential

DURATION: A leisurely day.

The town of Cranbrook has a fine High Street gradually rising on a hill towards the south. Tucked away near the church is the local (1a) MUSEUM housed in an old timber-framed farmhouse dating from the sixteenth century. Room Nine of the museum is devoted to the group of artists known as the Cranbrook Colony. This is the title given to six painters who visited the town in the latter half of the nineteenth century, some choosing to stay and live. They were contemporaries of the Pre-Raphaelites but quite different stylistically although some of their genre interiors do have a high degree of detail. Nor did they have a shared need to rebel against established art practice, what they did share however was a mutual enthusiasm for painting somewhat idealised pictures of country life and of children. Their pictures generally reflect a time before the Industrial Revolution when most workers were involved in agricultural jobs. The artists included Frederick Daniel Hardy and his elder brother George who both attended the Royal Academy although the younger artist had little early formal tuition. F.D. Hardy was a more successful artist and lived in Cranbrook from the 1850s, later sharing The Studio in the High Street with Thomas Webster. Webster had been depicting subjects from town life in his work since the 1830s and lived in the town from the mid-1850s. He did have a Royal Academy training and managed to achieve a considerable level of success as a painter having a number of patrons in the north. He particularly enjoyed showing children in his sometimes humorous work which was not at the time always to everyone's taste. He later lived in the three-storey early Georgian house in the High Street later named after him. Another member of the group was John Calcott Horsley who preferred to paint historical scenes set in houses of the period. He has latterly achieved fame as the designer of the first Christmas card. The artist Augustus Mulready (the son of the more well-known William) was a visitor to Horsley's home at Willesley when he came to the town although his connections with the Colony are less pronounced. Finally, there was the artist George Bernard O'Neill who was related to the Hardys and who came to know Horsley choosing to live close-by him at Old Wilsley.

Although this group of painters belong to a very different strand of Victorian art, they are exact contemporaries of the Brotherhood with some offbeat connections. For example O'Neill's pictures of children such as *The Tete-a-Tete Tea* (Wolverhampton Art Gallery)have an uncanny resemblance to Millais' late sentimentalised style as typified by *Bubbles* (Uniliver) or *My First Sermon* (Guildhall Art Gallery).

More intriguingly a dark-haired child called Constance that O'Neill used in a work entitled *Gran's Treasures* (Guildhall Art Gallery) is thought to have later modelled for Burne-Jones' *The Golden Stairs.*

Whilst visiting Room Nine in the museum you should be sure to look at the engraving of F.D. Hardy's *The Chimney Sweep* (Wolverhampton Art Gallery) which was clearly painted in this actual room with its distinctive newel post on the landing beyond.

Before going into the church the aforementioned homes of the artists can be seen in the High Street with Old Wilsley and Willesley (Norman Shaw's first major commission) further afield along the A229.

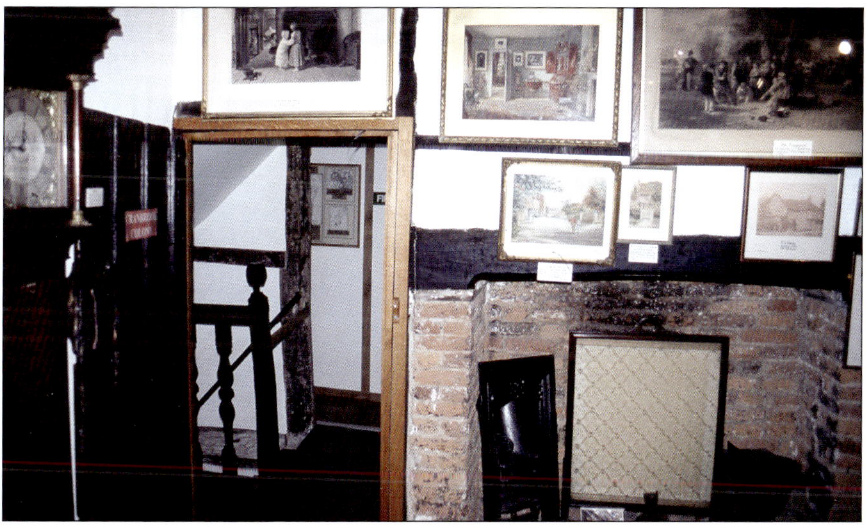

INSIDE CRANBROOK MUSEUM - PHOTO BY AUTHOR

The (1b) PARISH CHURCH OF ST DUNSTAN is sometimes referred to as the 'Cathedral of the Weald' because of its enormous scale, the building being funded by wealthy cloth-makers in the fifteenth and sixteenth centuries. It has some distinctive features such as the figure of Father Time above the tower clock and inside a total immersion font installed to lure Baptists back to the congregation and reportedly only used twice!

It is also a treasure trove of stained glass with examples from many Victorian companies and later work from the Arts & Crafts period. Before looking at the glass there are two monuments either side of the nave on the west wall. Nearest the entrance door is a marble relief in memory of Thomas Webster and showing him lying in a painter's smock and with the tools of his trade. It is by the well-known Victorian sculptor Hamo Thorneycroft and dates from 1889. As a pendant to it on the other side is a similar sized relief called the Alexander Memorial commemorating two brothers who died exploring Africa. The figure of Africa in the centre is wonderfully Art Nouveau. The monument is by W. Robert Colton and was completed in 1913.

Returning to near the Webster memorial there is a nice Victorian font in Gothic style and on the west wall above a large window by Paul Woodroffe, a pupil of Christopher Whall. It was donated by the same Alexander family as the memorial on the west wall.

Woodroffe (1875-1954) is a lesser known stained glass designer who also worked in book illustration. His first two books illustrated nursery rhymes and were praised by Walter Crane. After attending the Slade School of Art he joined the Art Workers' Guild and started to design stained glass. In the late 1890s he began to be much influenced by Whall with his emphasis on the need to understand all parts of the process for producing glass. He also lived for many years near Chipping Campden and was closely connected to C.R. Ashbee and his Guild of Handicraft although he ran a workshop on more formal lines. One of his more personal innovations was to abandon traditional

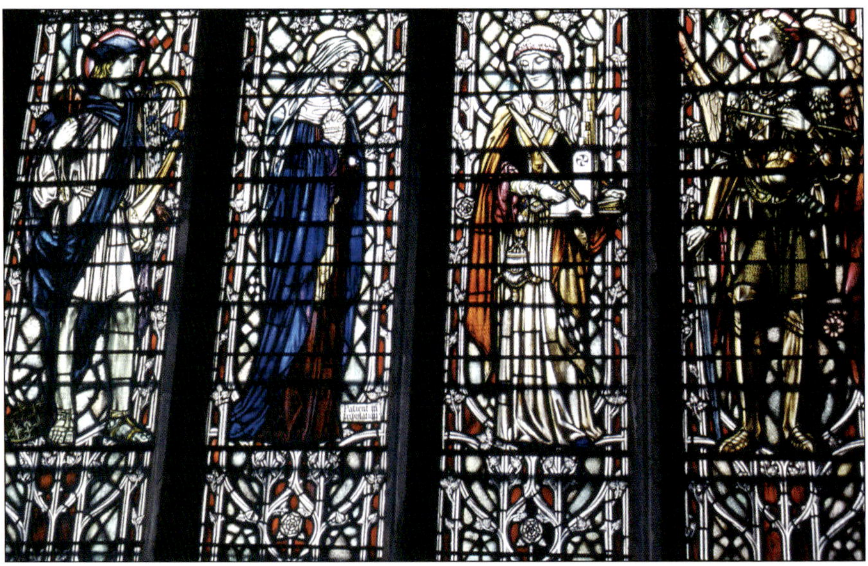

DETAIL OF THE WINDOW BY PAUL WOODROFFE IN CRANBROOK CHURCH - PHOTO BY AUTHOR

canopies above his figures in favour of foliage. Woodroffe spent some of the later years of his life at Mayfield in Sussex and died at Eastbourne.

Moving to the south wall of the nave we will see three large windows by Kempe with impressive main scenes across each of their three lights. His wheat-sheaf motif can be seen in each of the windows. They date from 1902, only four years before Woodroffe's work but are far less radical although a reasonable example of the output of the Kempe studio.

Further down the same wall is some Meyer glass which has as its subject the *Three Maries at the Sepulchre* and surprisingly has a rather Pre-Raphaelite angel as a dominant feature. Then there is lighter glass by Michael O'Connor to be seen(one window is in memory of Webster's wife) as one continues into the chancel with its considerably darker, busy but solemn east window by Powell and Co. This commemorates Queen Victoria and Robert Tooth and dates from 1904.

Stained glass by Heaton Butler & Bayne (in memory of Mr. Dennett a local printer) completes the main interior features of this impressive church although for those visitors who are particularly interested in the glass there are further windows to be explored.

To find your way to Woodchurch head north from Cranbrook (passing Old Wilsley and Willesley) and then take the A262 towards Tenterden. Go into the town via the A28 and turn left on the B2080 and then left again to go along the Woodchurch Road (B2067). Woodchurch is signposted to the left. The church is found by The Green on the left-hand side.

(2) ALL SAINTS CHURCH is both large and elegant and very much the focal point of the village. The spire is a landmark for miles around. The building was sympathetically 'restored' by the Victorians in 1858 and has a beautiful interior. In addition to some medieval stained glass there is also a good east window by Kempe. The three long lights date from 1896 and show the *Crucifixion*, the Saints *Mary* and *John* with *Resurrection* scenes. Kempe's wheat-sheaf can be seen which is the logo that he used from about 1895 until 1907.

The church is open most days.

Our next stop is Orlestone which is found by retracing your steps back to the B2067 and continuing along in the same direction as previously until you arrive at Hamstreet. Go through the village leaving it to go north along Ashford Road and shortly the church is to be found along a lane to the right leading to Court Lodge Farm.

The (3) CHURCH OF ST. MARY THE VIRGIN was largely restored in 1883-4 and its simple interior is dominated by the three windows in the chancel. The two facing each other on the north and south walls were designed by Henry Holiday in 1893. Holiday also designed the main east window of similar date which is arguably an even better window and appears stylistically to be in a late Morris & Co vein. The art historian Nikolaus Pevsner found there to be an *'unpleasant emphasis on the bodies of the saints'* and this is perhaps not surprising as he also found the late designs of Burne-Jones to be offensive on occasion. The windows seem to benefit from their austere setting. Before leaving be sure to look at the font with its *Signs of the Evangelists* and a panel referring to Thomas Paine being the churchwarden here.

The church can be locked but access is possible through the churchwardens.

It is possible to get to Smallhythe via the outskirts of the Romney Marsh and the Isle of Oxney. This beautiful drive is found by retracing your steps along the B2067 but leave on the road signposted Kenardington where its isolated church has fine views over the marshes. Continue on through Appledore Heath over the B2080 and

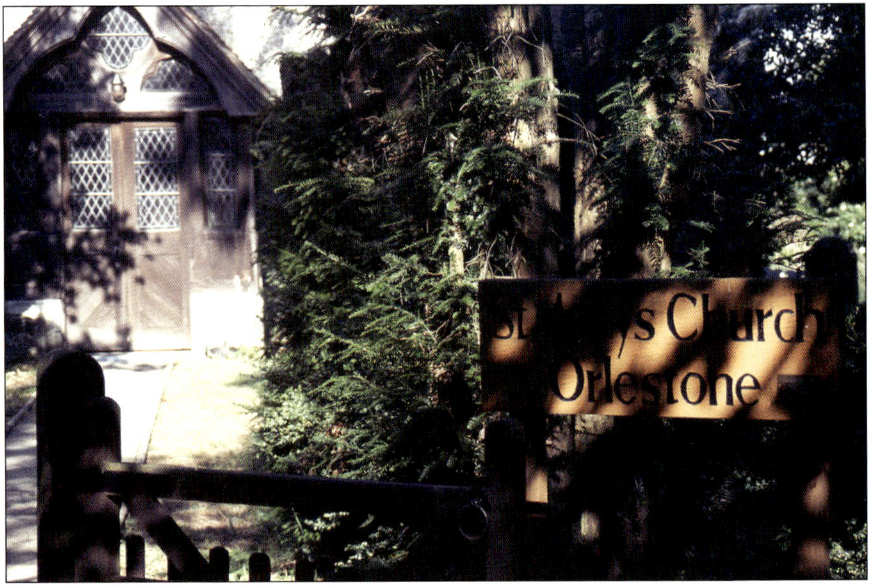

ORLESTONE CHURCH - PHOTO BY AUTHOR

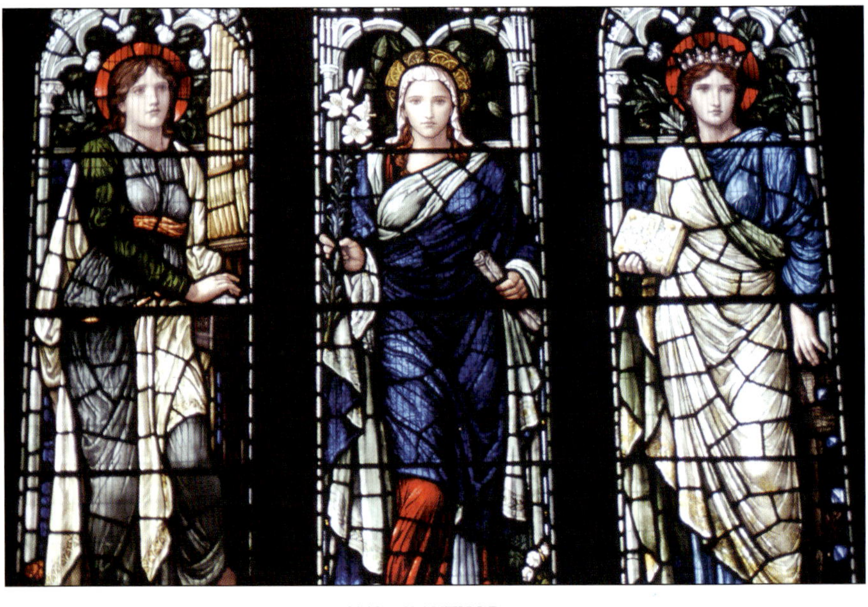

EAST WINDOW AT ORLESTONE - PHOTO BY AUTHOR

through Stone in Oxney until the road joins the B2082 near Wittersham. Heading in the direction of Tenterden the road will soon bring you to the next destination on this trail.

(4) SMALLHYTHE PLACE is a timber-framed yeoman's house dating back to 1480. It was called Port House before the ancient harbour hereabouts ceased to function when the river silted up. It served the nearby town of Tenterden and in its day was very busy, Henry VIII visiting in 1538 to inspect a warship.

The house is well known today as the home of the actress Ellen Terry from 1899-1928. She fell in love with it whilst driving around the area with Henry Irving in the late 1890s and when an opportunity presented itself she promptly bought it. Ellen had at the time enjoyed a long and largely happy professional partnership with Irving at the Lyceum Theatre although this was nearing its end.

She had up to this point led a rich and successful life although an unconventional one. At the age of only sixteen she was married to the painter G.F. Watts who was over thirty years older than her. She had become acquainted with him through attending his studio in Little Holland House in London where he lived permanently with Mr and Mrs Thoby Prinsep. The latter was one of the Pattle sisters who included Julia Margaret Cameron the pioneering photographer (the house has copies of her photographs of Ellen). It was in this social milieu that Ellen Terry would have come across the likes of Hunt, Millais and Rossetti in addition to such luminaries as Tennyson, the Brownings and Thackeray.

The marriage was only to last a short while but Watts produced several fine portraits of his young wife including *Choosing* which is in a style reminiscent of Rossetti. It shows her in the wedding dress that was designed by Holman Hunt (there is a copy of this painting in the Hall). Watts, an older artist, was probably closest to Hunt of all the Pre-Raphaelites.

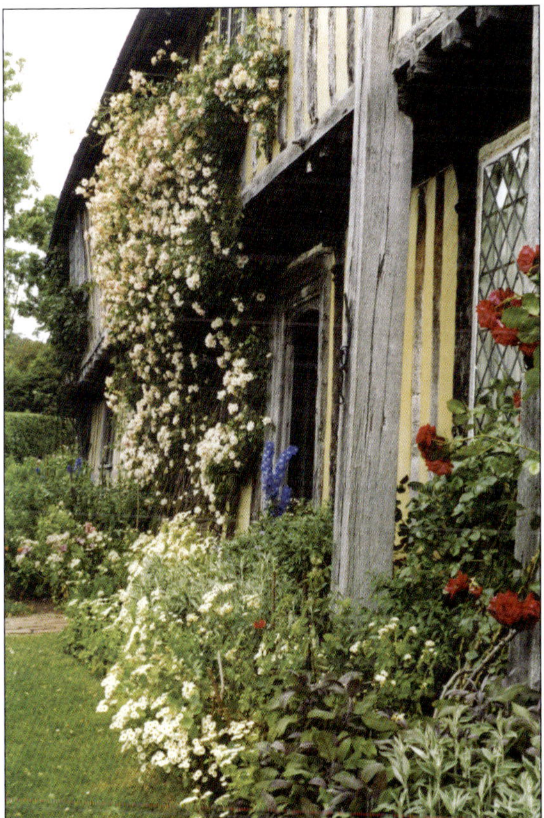

SPRING AT SMALLHYTHE - BY KIND PERMISSION OF THE NATIONAL TRUST

EDWARD GODWIN

Although only separated from Watts, Ellen then eloped with the architect/designer Edward Godwin whom she had met before in her stage career. She subsequently had two children by him, Edith Craig and Edward Gordon Craig(their surnames were changed by deed poll) in a relationship that lasted about six years. Godwin was a highly original talent who was close friends with Whistler and William Burges but was also argumentative on occasion and very poor in his financial dealings. This last characteristic was instrumental to the end of their relationship as Ellen found herself alone with the children in their home at Fallows Green, Harpenden with the bailiffs at the door. Ellen would later remarry twice and Godwin met and married Beatrice Philip (the daughter of the sculptor John Birnie Philip), with whom he frequently visited **Sheerness** and **Broadstairs** regularly in the summer. He also kept up an increasingly amicable relationship with Ellen advising her on costumes and theatre sets as well as home decoration although this did not include any work at Smallhythe as he died in 1886.

The interior of the house today contains a number of pieces of furniture designed by Godwin who shared some of the ideas associated with the Arts & Crafts Movement. These include a concern for cleanliness in the home and simplicity of design. His designs fall into many styles such as Gothic, Georgian, and Anglo-Greek although he is most known for his Anglo-Japanese pieces. It is true to say however that his work is always interpreted distinctively and is not just a reproduction of an historical style. A number of his pieces were made by the firm of Collinson and Lock who were associated with a number of top designers at the time. One of these was the *Lucretia* cabinet with panels executed by Charles Fairfax Murray for the Paris Exposition Universelle of 1878. This design and many others show how Godwin had a penchant for furniture with thin spindly forms with little ornamentation.

In the Terry Room at Smallhythe is an interesting canterbury (or music bookcase) which shows the influence of Chinese cane furniture in its splayed legs and cut-in ring decoration. Quite different is his Shakespeare armchair in the Lyceum Room of about 1881 which shows Godwin's interest in the Jacobean period. Yet another style can be seen in Ellen's bedroom where a dressing table displays Egyptian-inspired origins. I gather that the National Trust who own the property have also recently found other pieces of Godwin furniture and intend to restore these and perhaps show them in the house. Not to be seen at Smallhythe but in a style coming much nearer to the Morris & Co. range of *Sussex* chairs is Godwin's *Old English* armchairs of around 1867, an example of which can be seen relatively close-by, at Standen in West Sussex.

Although Godwin did not share William Morris' complete dislike of the machine he did share his admiration for medieval craftsmen and also his concerns that his furniture should be affordable.

To return to the present house there are some particular items of interest - in the Terry Room are two costume designs by Burne-Jones above the fireplace. There are also copies of paintings by Watts that show Ellen and an original oil that shows her in the guise of *Joan of Arc*. Nearby is a study of *Lady Macbeth* by Sargent and a signed lithograph of his more famous treatment of the same subject.

Other items of interest in a house packed with memorabilia are some blue and white plates given to Ellen by Whistler and shown on the dresser in the Dining Room.

Smallhythe Place is under the care of the National Trust. It is open from early to mid-March on Sat and Sun 11-5 and from late Mar-Oct on Mon-Wed, Sat, Sun 11-5.

(In the CHURCH OF ST. JOHN THE BAPTIST **nearby there are a number of windows by A. O. Hemming).

To return to Cranbrook head into Tenterden and then take the A28 in the direction of Hastings. At Rolvenden turn right along the B2086 towards Cranbrook.

In Rolvenden it is possible to see work by Sir Edwin Lutyens in the church and a house called Great Maytham that he designed in 1909-10 is also in the village. Lutyens was the architect responsible for some excellent country houses in the Art and Crafts style although Great Maytham is a very large Neo-Georgian pile. In the church there is also glass in the chancel by Powell showing the *Three Maries at the Sepulchre* and dating from 1907.

Trail No. 7 Coast and Marshes

Points of Interest

(1) FOLKESTONE - No.6 (now 8) EARL'S AVENUE - Site of private commission for Morris windows /HOLY TRINITY CHURCH***- Henry Dearle window /CHURCH OF ST. MARY AND ST. EANSWYTHE***- Murals by Hemming and glass by Kempe

(2) SANDGATE - Where Ruskin convalesced in 1887-8

(3) HYTHE - CHURCH OF ST.LEONARD***- Sculpture by Henry Hugh Armstead / SALTWOOD CASTLE - Restoration work by Arts and Crafts architect Philip Tilden

(4) ST. MARY IN THE MARSH - CHURCH OF ST. MARY THE VIRGIN***- Holman Hunt's *Light of the World* in glass

(5) NEW ROMNEY - CHURCH OF ST. NICHOLAS***- The location for an early SPAB victory

(6) LYMPNE CASTLE - Site of work by Robert Lorimer and Phoebe Traquair

(7) ELHAM - CHURCH OF ST. MARY***- A neo-medieval interior by Frederick Charles Eden

STARTING POINT: West side of Folkestone

HOW TO GET THERE: A259 coming into town from Rye

FINISHING POINT: Elham about 4 miles to the north of Folkestone

REFRESHMENTS: Plenty of opportunities in Folkestone and Hythe. Pubs at New Romney and Elham.

TRANSPORT: Own car essential

DURATION: One day.

This trail offers less to see in terms of actual artefacts but is rich in other associations to the Pre-Raphaelites and has the bonus of being set in wonderful landscapes.

Just off the main A259 on the west side of FOLKESTONE look out for (1a) EARL'S AVENUE ***and turn into the seaward end of this road.*** On the left number eight soon appears (previously number six), a large and probably Edwardian semi-detached house. It was here that Morris windows were installed in 1913 for a J.A. Roberts Esq. who had most likely recently retired to this popular part of the town. It is possible he may have already have commissioned glass from Morris and Co. The windows supplied here were nine in total and the subjects were the *Sun, Moon, Thor, Odin, Frey, Karlsefne, Gudridr, Leif the Lucky* and a *Viking Ship*. These largely Teutonic subjects were all to original Burne-Jones designs. They have since been removed and were sold (with the exception of *Gudridr*) at Christie's in 1975.

A short walk away further along the road you came in by (Sandgate Road) is (1b) HOLY TRINITY CHURCH. ***An alternative walk to it can be made via The Leas,*** a development built along the promenade from the early 1840s. The church was built piecemeal from 1866 and nave and chancel were completed by 1868. The south aisle and transept were added in 1882 and within the following six years its complementary north aisle and transept were built together with the tower and spire. The architect was Ewan Christian, who had previously been in the offices of G.E. Street and it is Christian who is responsible for the incredible width of the nave. The building suffered damage particularly during World War II when a bomb fell to the north of the building and took out a number of the windows. These were quickly and temporarily repaired when the church was opened again for worship after the nearby Christ Church was destroyed except for its tower in 1942.

In today's church there are a number of fittings that bid for attention - the marble font on granite base with its carved wooden cover is close to the entrance. Then there is the pulpit with the use of black labrador granite. The apse-shaped chancel has a fine reredos and mural decoration which due to damage is no longer complete in the roof. The reredos dates from 1889 and although it is now incomplete is a fine example of High Victorian work. The church guide suggests that the angels shown on the right-hand side are more Pre-Raphaelite in style than the rest of the work and perhaps it has a point.

The Morris glass is on the south wall of the side chapel and dates from 1922. Known as *The River of Life* it shows *St. Gabriel* on the left-hand side with the figure of *St Raphael* on the opposite side. In the centre *Christ with Angels* is shown. Much of the remainder of the glass appears on stylistic grounds to be by Clayton & Bell. ***The church is open Mon, Wed, Fri 9-5, Thurs 9-1, Sat 9-12, closed Tues.***

Just off the main shopping street in the centre of town is the ancient (1c) CHURCH OF ST. MARY AND ST. EANSWYTHE, the latter being the first English abbess and the founder of the first religious community for women in about 630 AD. Her remains are believed to be in a lead casket found in the church in 1885. The exterior of the church (as so often) does not prepare one for the sumptuous detail of the inside. One of the main reasons for the lavish interior

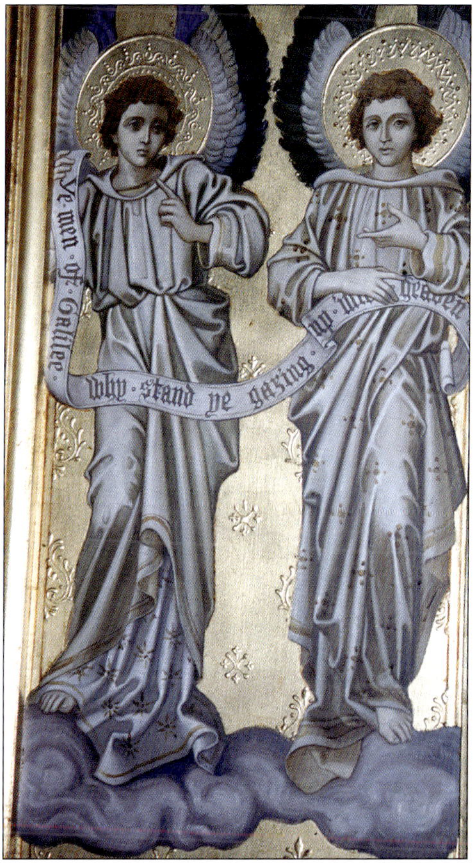

PART OF THE MURALS IN HOLY TRINITY CHURCH, FOLKESTONE - PHOTO BY AUTHOR

lies with the mural decorations (largely devoted to the Stations of the Cross) by A.O. Hemming and completed between 1889 and about 1901. Hemming trained with Clayton & Bell and also designed stained glass and by this time he had set up his own business. There were even more murals but some were removed including a huge *Tree of Jesse* on the wall leading into the Lady Chapel. The murals and much of the stained glass formed part of the extensive restoration and decoration completed under the guidance of Matthew Woodward who became Vicar in 1851. A wealthy church commissioned the beautiful sanctuary arcading by Hems and other work such as the mural by Alfred Oake on the south side of the chancel. There was more stained glass but that on the north wall was lost during World War II. We are left with glass by Clayton & Bell and O'Connor but the glass by Kempe is of greater interest to the subject of this book. Most notable is the west window or Harvey memorial window of 1874 with its subjects of the *Tree of Life* and the *Four Miracles.* The two small lower lancets are particularly satisfying on the same wall. Kempe was also used for the three lights that form the east window with the right window showing *St Eanswythe* (1885). More of his work is found in the south and north aisles as well as the Lady Chapel. As mentioned before, some of his windows were lost in the war whilst some of those that survive have needed varying amounts of restoration.

It all adds up to a stunning High Victorian space despite its later losses and one typical of the Oxford Movement whose advocates provided many commissions for the Pre-Raphaelite artists. The church guide also mentions vestments and altar frontals by Bodley and a Gothic Revival chalice that belonged to Cardinal Manning being amongst other church treasures.

The church is often open weekday mornings.

Head out of town along the A259 in a westerly direction and The Leas soon merges into (2) SANDGATE.

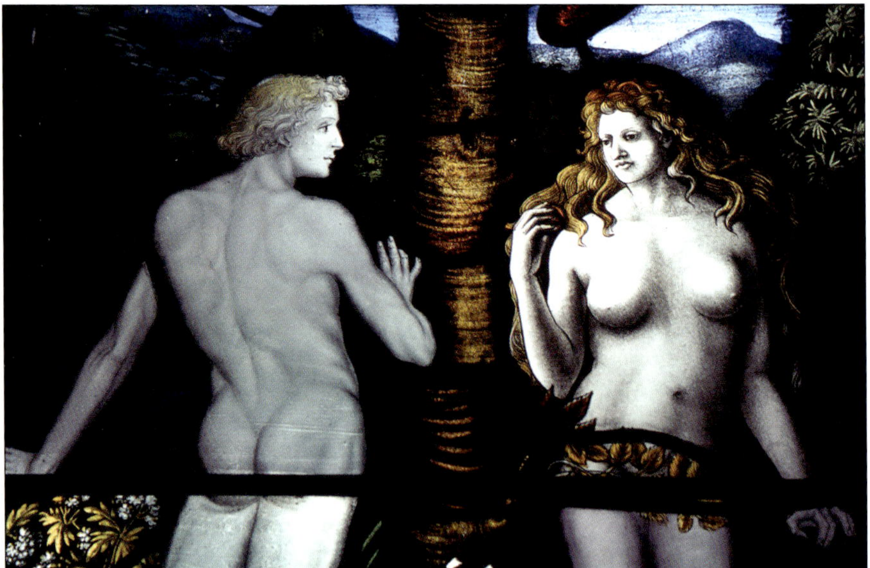

DETAIL OF KEMPE GLASS IN THE CHURCH OF ST. MARY AND ST. EANSWYTHE, FOLKESTONE - PHOTO BY AUTHOR

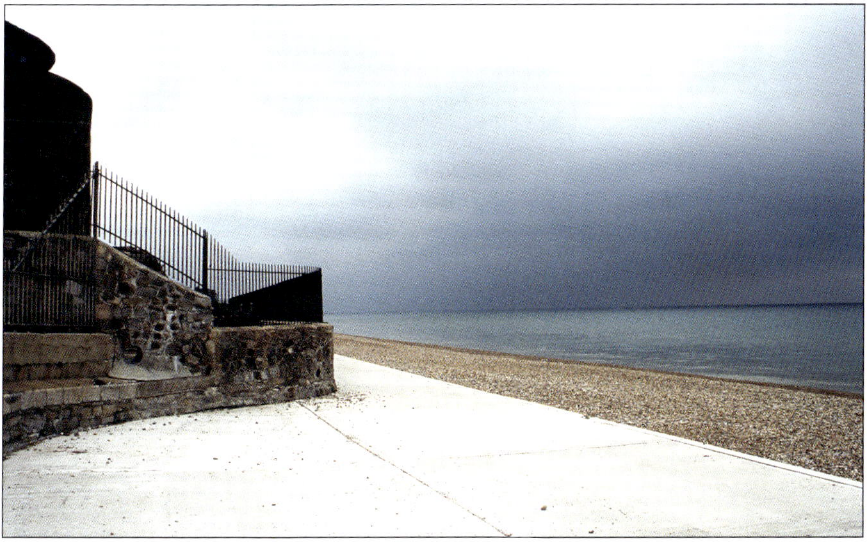

THE COAST AT SANDGATE - PHOTO BY AUTHOR

In the summer of 1887 and following a mental breakdown, the art critic John Ruskin came to stay at the Paris Hotel in Folkestone. There had been recent friction with his appointed guardians Joan and Arthur Severn as well as a manservant called Peter Baxter. Subsequently Ruskin was left to his own devices but unfortunately injured himself when walking along the beach. A local man Edwin Trice came to his rescue and arranged for Ruskin to stay at a boarding house in nearby Sandgate. This was at 2 Devonshire Terrace which was then newly built. Just before Xmas he was visited there by the Severns but they did not take him back to Brantwood, Ruskin's home on the side of Coniston Water in the Lake District. Instead he spent the festive period on his own looking out to sea. It was a despairing time for the ageing professor particularly as the third of January was the anniversary of the death of Rose La Touche. She was the young woman whom Ruskin had become obsessed by and to whom he proposed marriage. Ruskin was still devastated by her death aged twenty-seven in May 1875 following long-term mental health problems and physical illness.

It was also at Sandgate that Ruskin wrote a chapter of *Praeterita*, his autobiography, which tellingly speeds through the years 1850-60 when he was married, and then divorced, from Effie Gray who then eloped with John Everett Millais to whom she was later married.

Ruskin later referred to his time in Sandgate as '*ten months* (of) *misery*' and he was certainly far from well whilst in the town although by April of 1888 he was revived enough to visit museums and exhibitions in London. He finally left with Baxter and Arthur Severn in June to travel with them on the continent.

The house where Ruskin stayed has been demolished but the town retains some of its latter-day charm with its weatherboarded cottages, quiet seafront and adjacent castle.

Continue westwards along the A259 until HYTHE is reached and where the church is located high on the hill just to the north of the town centre.

The (3) CHURCH OF ST. LEONARD is sometimes referred to as 'the church with the bones' because of its amazing collection of human remains in the crypt. William

Morris visited the church in the spring of 1881 and although he considered it to be *'terribly restored by Street and Pearson'* (in 1875) he admired a number of its Early English/Norman style features. He described its location distinctively as *'high up on the steep hillside over the queer little market-town in a lovely place amidst gardens and old stone walls'*. As you enter its cool interior you will see a window dedicated to St Leonard who is the patron saint of prisoners, and a little further on you will have your first glimpse of its beautiful chancel. This was built in the thirteenth century at a time of great prosperity for the town when it was one of the prestigious Cinque Ports. On the right-hand side of the chancel is a great treasure - the marble reredos that used to be positioned behind the main altar. It was given by a former curate in memory of his wife and has a naturalistic Pre-Raphaelite style and is full of movement. It depicts *The Entombment* and the angels on both sides have a definite Rossettian intensity. It is reputed to have been carved from a single piece of Carrera marble to the design of G.E.Street who in earlier times had both William Morris and Philip Webb as apprentices in his architect's office.

This wonderful piece of sculpture dates from 1881 and was carved by Henry Hugh Armstead who also contributed extensively to both the Albert Memorial and the Arts & Crafts interior of the Holy Trinity church in Sloane Street, London. The reredos is one of the fittings introduced to the church at the time of its restorations in the latter half of the nineteenth century.

Before departing the Victorian pulpit can be viewed as should the window commemorating Robert Hildyard who died in the Great War which has a dreamy almost Art Nouveau style. This was designed by A. L. Moore in 1916.

The church is open most days.

At this point you can visit (3b) SALTWOOD CASTLE ***by going a mile north along***

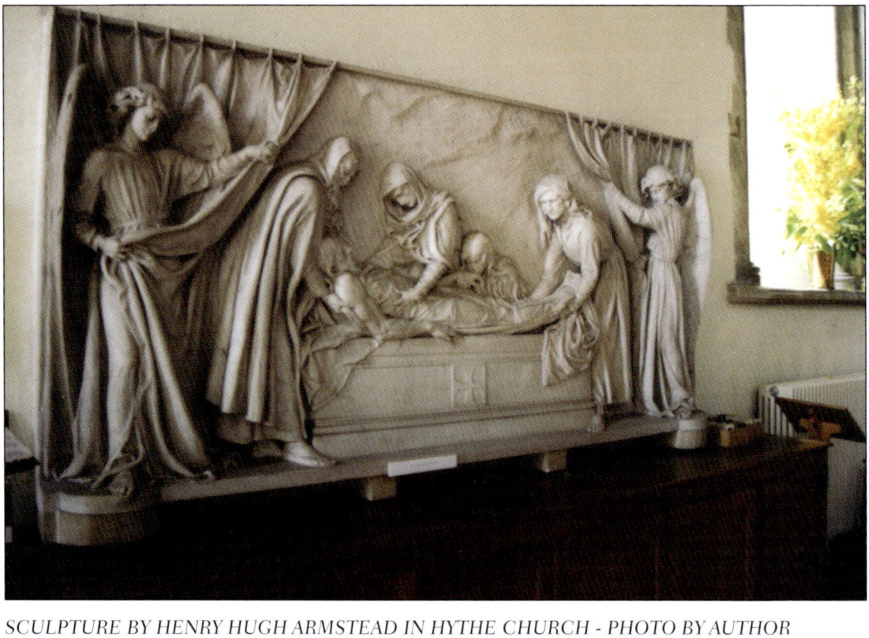

SCULPTURE BY HENRY HUGH ARMSTEAD IN HYTHE CHURCH - PHOTO BY AUTHOR

Tanner's Hill from the roundabout between Prospect Road and East Street. This joins Castle Road and the castle itself is soon found on the right. A footpath offers views of the castle.

The building is largely Norman but with many later additions and together with Lympne Castle it defended the then important town of Hythe. It is said that the plan to assassinate Thomas Becket was plotted here on the twenty-eighth of December 1170 by four knights who performed the grisly deed the next day at Canterbury. In 1580 the castle became uninhabitable due to an earthquake but the building was restored in the nineteenth century as a residence of the Archbishop of Canterbury. Morris came to the castle in 1891 and thought it to be *'restored out of all knowledge'* and *'a swell house'*. However, he found its circle of walls to be *'left untouched'* and consequently *'interesting'*. In the nineteen-thirties Philip Tilden restored one of the great halls of the castle spending many months here. It was a quiet time for the architect who had in the past been busy as an exponent of the Arts & Crafts style. Growing up he had known Basil Gimson and by 1906 he had taken himself off to Chipping Campden to learn more of his trade from C.R.Ashbee. He later built the celebrated Porth-en-alls house in Cornwall before working in Kent at both Chartwell and Allington Castle. Saltwood was purchased by the art historian Kenneth Clark in 1955 who was interestingly a great collector of Pre-Raphaelite pictures. His son Alan was the Conservative MP and writer of the well-known political diaries. He is buried in the grounds of the castle.

The castle is not open to the public.

Once again resume going westwards along the main coast road until arriving in Dymchurch. Then look for signs to ST. MARY IN THE MARSH where the (4) CHURCH OF ST. MARY THE VIRGIN ***is to be found.***

This simple and rather remote building has parts that date from the twelfth century.

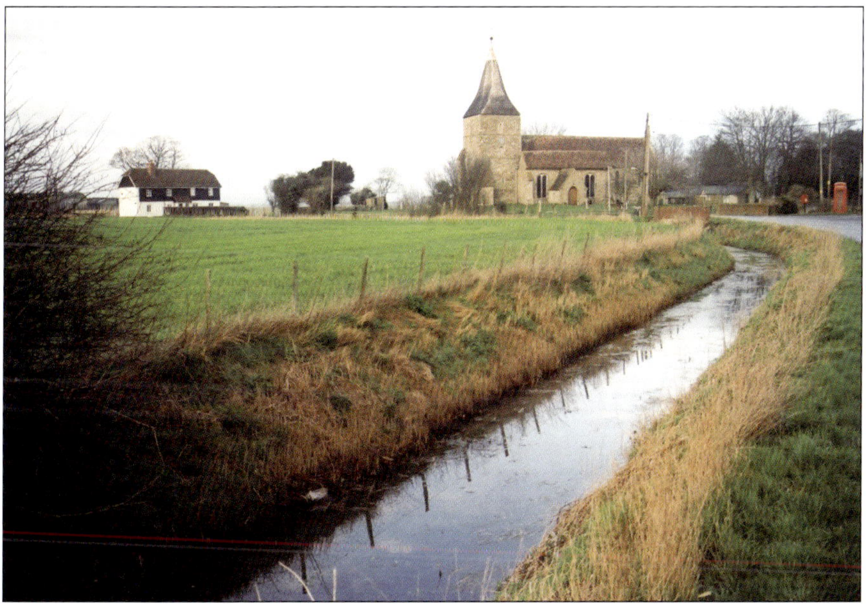

ST. MARY - IN - THE - MARSH CHURCH - PHOTO BY BRIAN WISE

One of the windows has stained glass depicting the *Light of the World* and its date of erection (1906) shows the long popularity of Holman Hunt's original work. The first version of the painting was shown at the Royal Academy in 1854 where it was poorly received. However, Ruskin jumped to its defence describing it as *'one of the very noblest works of sacred art ever produced in this or any other age'*. Its popularity was increased by its successful translation into engravings and photographs. Hunt also produced two copies of the work and a large version toured the colonies at the same time that this window was produced. This version has the inscription *'Behold I stand at the Door and Knock'* a part of the quote from Revelations that accompanied the original picture when first exhibited.

Upon leaving the visitor may like to see the grave of E. Nesbit, author of *'The Railway Children'* who lived in this parish.

The church is open most days.

Now follow St. Mary's Road south to New Romney where the (5) CHURCH OF ST. NICHOLAS ***is just south of the main High Street.***

This church is undoubtedly one of the delights of the area dating as much of it does from about 1100. Its massive tower has an amazing variety of stonework and the Norman zigzag decoration at the west door is almost awe inspiring. Noticeably the floor of the church is completely unrestored with its original brick, tile and ledger stones. This is most unusual and is the result of the direct intervention of William Morris in his role as the secretary of the Society for the Protection of Ancient Buildings (SPAB).

In 1878 John Oldrid Scott had began to over-restore the building as was a regular custom in Victorian times. This was also the year in which SPAB was formed and it had one of its first major triumphs when it protested at the scale of the work that Scott was doing to the church. Initially the vicar was not happy at SPAB's interference and Scott remained quiet about it but later SPAB published all the documents about the case in the local newspapers and no more of the 'restoration' occurred after 1880. The

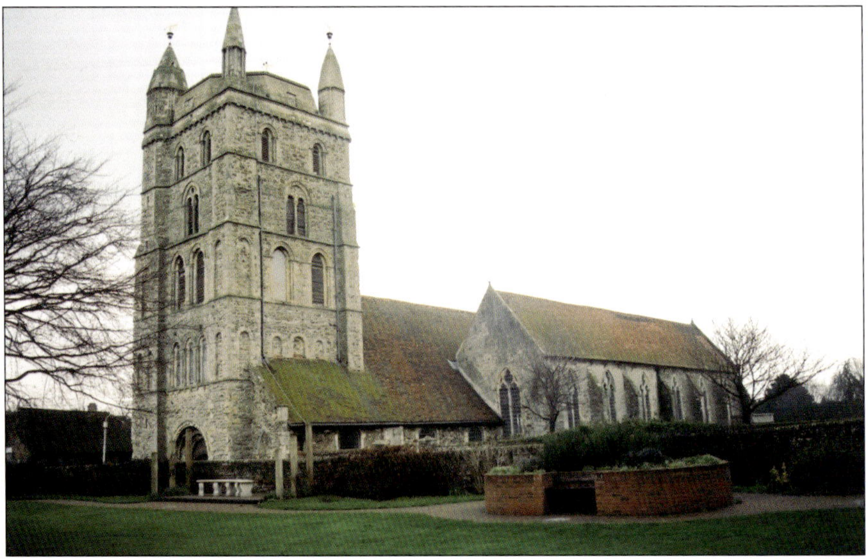

NEW ROMNEY CHURCH - PHOTO BY BRIAN WISE

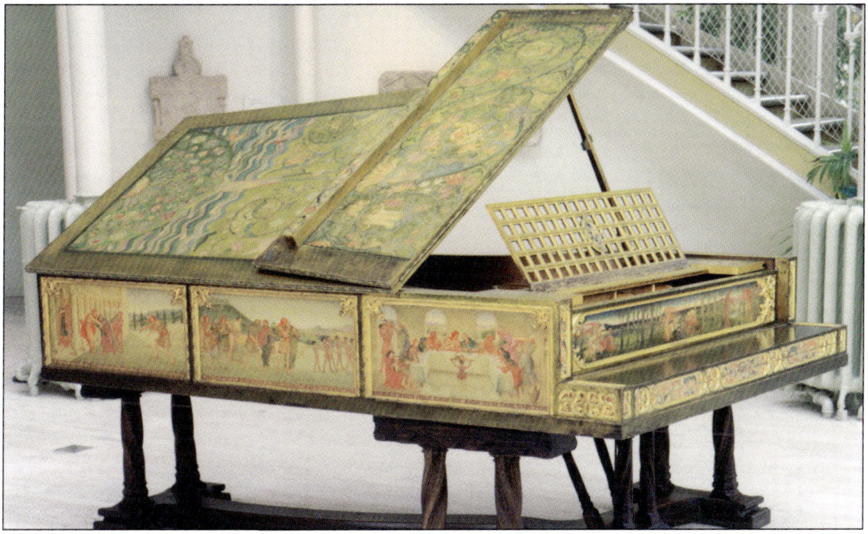

'THE WILLOWWOOD PIANO' PAINTED BY PHOEBE TRAQUAIR © NATIONAL MUSEUMS OF SCOTLAND

grand proportions of the building reflect New Romney's status as a Cinque Port prior to the River Rother altering its course. It is now hard to imagine ships moored up close to the church.

The church is open most days.

To reach (6) LYMPNE CASTLE ***head towards Rye on the A259 and then take the A2070 in the direction of Ashford. Turn off at Hamstreet and go along the B2067 until you arrive at Lympne.***

The ragstone castle dates from the thirteenth century and although fortified was also always a comfortable residence. William Morris paid a visit to the castle in July 1896 in the company of the artist Frederick Walker. Morris later wrote to Philip Webb describing the building as *'a most exceedingly beautiful house'*. He also looked at the Church of St. Stephen (just to the east) and in the same letter pronounced it to be *'once a noble EE* (Early English) *and Norman* (church) *ruined by fakement various'*. It had been restored by James Piers St. Aubyn in 1878-80. He liked its location though *'the whole churchyard lies all along the brow of a steep hill. It is a strange and beautiful place'*. The castle was mainly ruins in 1906 when Robert Lorimer was commissioned to do restorative work and to add buildings to the north-west in addition to the cottages that line the road. Early on in his career Lorimer discovered the ideas of William Morris and began to design to an Arts and Crafts style and in 1896 he was elected to the Art Workers Guild. Many of his finest buildings are to be found in his native Scotland. By the time he came to work at Lympne the direction of his work had inevitably begun to change with the decline in the popularity of the Arts and Crafts. However, as part of the restoration work Lorimer commissioned Phoebe Traquair to decorate a Steinway piano, one of only three pieces of furniture she ever worked on. Traquair was a key figure in the Arts & Crafts Movement producing enormous murals for churches and other buildings mainly in the Edinburgh area. She also made fine embroideries, did enamel work and produced illuminated manuscripts. The piano had a stand designed by Lorimer and was painted by Traquair with scenes from *The Song of Solomon* as well as an illustration of *Willowwood,* a sonnet by Rossetti. There was also a *Tree of Life* on the outer lid of the piano and a scene with *Pan* and *Psyche* on the inner side. The work on the piano was very much in the mode of Burne-Jones' piano decoration for William Graham completed in 1879-80. The piano is now in the collection of the National Museum of Scotland.

The castle is available for functions but is not generally open to the public.

(Nearby a mile to the west at Port Lympne is a large house that was adapted by Philip Tilden to include a Moorish patio and neo-Roman gardens. It has beautiful views over the Romney Marshes.)

The house is open to the public as part of Port Lympne Zoo.

The final stop on this trail is at Elham to the north-east. To get there go through the village of Lympne along Stone Street and continue straight ahead when this becomes Ashford Road. Just before the road joins the M20 take the A20 turning on the right. After crossing over the motorway take the next road on your left towards Lyminge. This road will eventually lead you to the village of Elham where the church is behind the square.

The (7) CHURCH OF ST. MARY is predominantly thirteenth century but its interior was refitted between 1908-1917 by F. C. Eden. He was an architect as well as a stained glass designer who was employed by William Butterfield for a short period of time before spending ten years in the office of G. F. Bodley. After 1910 he began making his own windows having previously only designed them for others to execute. In this church he was careful not to over-restore and he added furnishings of high quality. He is responsible for features such as the black and white pavement in the sanctuary, the panelling and fine carvings (by the same workers who restored Grinling Gibbons' carvings in St. Paul's Cathedral in London) and the altar rails. He also introduced the organ loft, font cover and Tabernacle. As well as contemporary pieces he also found older artefacts that could be integrated into the whole scheme. In the west window of the south aisle is a window by him and dating from 1915. Another unusual window in the chancel shows the Victorian celebrities Madame Patti and Thomas Carlyle (as *David* and *Saul* respectively) with the figures of Gladstone and Disraeli behind and three of Queen Victoria's daughters attending. It was designed by Frank Wodehouse who was the then vicar's brother. The large reredos was painted by J.R. Wilmer. Lastly, after seeing Saltwood Castle earlier in the trail, it is interesting to see a depiction of the murder of Becket on one of the alabaster panels behind the altar. ***The church is open most days.***

Trail No. 8 Canterbury and Environs

Points of Interest

(1) CANTERBURY - CATHEDRAL**** - Has stained glass by Christopher Whall and the building was much admired by William Morris

(2) WICKHAMBREAUX - CHURCH OF ST. ANDREW***- Art Nouveau-styled window by Arild Rosenkrantz

(3) PATRIXBOURNE - CHURCH OF ST. MARY***- Location for a Pre-Raphaelite photograph

(4) BISHOPSBOURNE - CHURCH OF ST. MARY***- Morris glass

(5) CHILHAM - CHURCH OF ST. MARY***- Sculpture by Alexander Munro

ALSO: BLEAN CHURCH** and ADISHAM CHURCH** can be visited as an option.

STARTING POINT: Canterbury Cathedral

HOW TO GET THERE: Parking for the Cathedral is available at several points in the city centre

FINISHING POINT: Chilham, a little to the west of Canterbury and a short drive along the A28

REFRESHMENTS: Many outlets in Canterbury and pubs at Chilham

TRANSPORT: Own car essential

DURATION: Whole day

When William Morris was eight years of age his father took him to see (1) CANTERBURY CATHEDRAL. Prior to this Chingford church in Essex had been his only real contact with Gothic architecture. Morris was overawed as he stood in the magnificence of the lofty building and later revealed that he felt the Gates of Heaven had been opened up for him. He told this to Wilfrid Scawen Blunt(lover of Janey Morris but also worshipper of William) sometime after he met him in 1884 and Blunt subsequently visited the Cathedral as a result of the accolade. But when Blunt went in 1896 he was not so impressed and this was probably due to the heavy restoration work that was going on at the time. It is possible that this may also mar your own visit but the Cathedral certainly still has the power to impress.

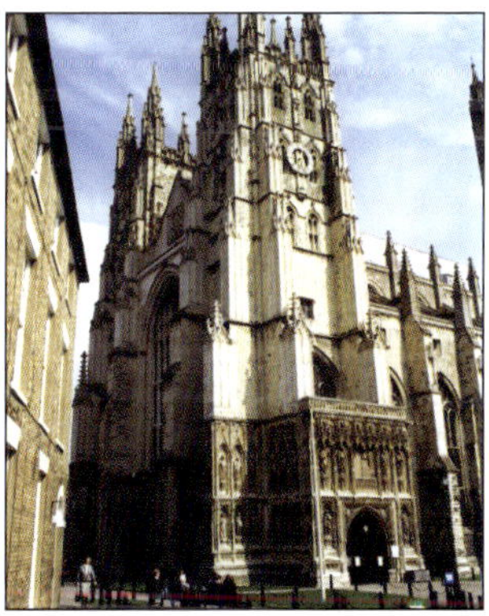

CANTERBURY - PHOTO BY BRIAN WISE

There are many good guides to the building and these will direct you to some of the sights that so aroused Morris' admiration. These no doubt included the wall paintings in St. Gabriel's Chapel and the stained glass that dates from the twelfth century. Since Morris' time the Cathedral has gone through many more changes primarily as a result of damage in 1942 and the subsequent additions and restorations since the war.

The subject of this book suggests that the windows by Christopher Whall are of important interest although these were of course installed after Morris' death. They are to be found in the south-west transept and date from 1902. Whall was an advocate of the Arts & Crafts movement and was deeply committed to making stained glass participating in all stages of the process. At Canterbury he has used the thickly moulded slab glass that was devised by Edward Prior a leading Arts & Crafts architect. His use of this type of glass shows how the material has determined the style of the window with its tendency to be lighter and thinner at the edge.

The highest row of lights with figures show *The Resurrection* in the middle with *St Uriel* and *St Michael* on either side. The figure of *St Michael* has been wisely compared to Burne-Jones' Prince entering the wood in his *Briar Rose* series. On the row below are the figures of the Saints *John the Baptist* and *John the Evangelist* with an emotional *Agony in the Garden* in the central two lights. At the bottom of the window is *The Nativity* with *St Bartholomew* and *St. James the Major.* It is perhaps in the *Agony* that the unique luminescence possible through the use of slab glass is most apparent.

There was further glass by Whall in the St. Andrew's Chapel that was installed in 1900 but this was a casualty of the war destruction in 1942. Some glass by Clayton & Bell can be found in the north aisle of the nave.

Amongst the many diverse delights of Canterbury is the Royal Museum and Art Gallery (High Street) housed in a Victorian red brick building that was previously named the Beaney Institute. James Beaney was a doctor who spent some of his life in Australia as well as participating in the Crimean War. His career as a surgeon was blotted by his being tried for murder and manslaughter on more than one occasion following operations that went wrong. However, when he died in 1891 he left monies in order to set up the Institute. Inside the art gallery's collection includes a copy of Millais' *Vale of Rest* by Captain Stephen Swinney as well as other Victorian pictures.

Leave Canterbury by the A257 road to Sandwich and having reached Littlebourne turn left along Nargate Street. This later leads you into Wickhambreaux where the church is on the left by the village green.

The (2) CHURCH OF ST. ANDREW is pleasantly located to the north-west of the village green along an avenue of lime trees. It is essentially of fourteenth century origin but its chancel was extensively restored in 1878. The tiling used has its own charm but does rather resemble a dairy at times. There are also murals which show angels in the chancel and a *Christ in Majesty* figure (also with angels) appears high in the nave with more foliage.

However, the obvious highlight is the main east window which is a rare and stunning piece of Art Nouveau. Although this style is not the central subject of this book the stained glass here is contemporary to the late work of Burne-Jones and does share a number of features. There is, for example, no architectural setting for the figures and instead they are surrounded by the swirling lines of flags, wings and drapery that so much relate to the style of Art Nouveau. A number of Morris & Co windows achieve a similar effect by the use of abstract backgrounds such as at Allerton near Liverpool. Where this window is different is in its extensive use of semi-opaque glass which means that some areas let in much less light than others. The artist responsible was a Dane by

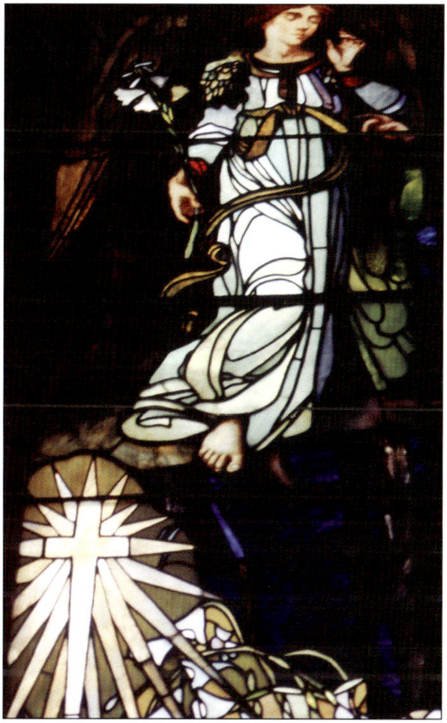

DETAIL OF EAST WINDOW AT WICKHAMBREAUX - PHOTO BY AUTHOR

the name of Arild Rosenkrantz and he has signed the glass, having exhibited the work in New York before bringing it here. It was commissioned by Count James Gallatin (a somewhat mysterious figure whose mother lies in the churchyard) and may have been the first commission in Europe given to American glass-workers. The man credited with making this window and pioneering the use of mottled glass is John la Farge but perhaps Louis Comfort Tiffany is more commonly associated with this type of material. The window's use of dark greens and orange still divides public opinion but in more recent years the general view of those visiting is a positive one. ***The church is usually open during daylight hours.***

The next stop is Patrixbourne which is found by returning along Nargate Street until you are back at its junction with the A257. Go straight across down Bekesbourne Lane until you come to Patrixbourne. Turn left at a small roundabout and shortly the church is on your right.

The (3) CHURCH OF ST. MARY was the subject of a photograph by Benjamin Brecknell Turner in the 1850s that in its high detail has been compared to the approach of the Pre-Raphaelite artists. Turner is perhaps better known for his image of the church at Hawkhurst where the pioneer of early photography Sir John Herschel lived at the time. His presence may have been the reason for Turner coming to the area and he could have come to Patrixbourne on the same visit. The south door of the church was the subject of the photograph with its magnificent tympanum having a figure of *Christ* in a mandorla being held by angels. There are further exquisite carvings on the lintel and around the arch. The original photograph was cropped to also include the adjacent ivy-covered walls but little else thus appearing to show its subject in great detail. This is particularly noticeable in the contrast between the doorway and the ivy. The photograph formed part of the exhibition *Pre-Raphaelite Vision* at the Tate in 2004. The rest of the church built about 1170 is worthy of exploration with another smaller doorway with Norman carvings on the south side of the chancel. There is also sixteenth and seventeenth century stained glass. ***The church may be locked but access is possible through the churchwardens.***

Leave the village via Keeper's Hill and follow this until it joins Bramling Road and then turn right to go along Coldharbour Lane. You go under the A2 and arrive in Bishopsbourne where the church is on the right-hand side.

The thirteenth century (4) CHURCH OF ST. MARY is located in this peaceful village once the home to the novelist Joseph Conrad. Surprisingly since the old Roman road Watling Street (but now the busy A2) runs comparatively close-by, the village still seems

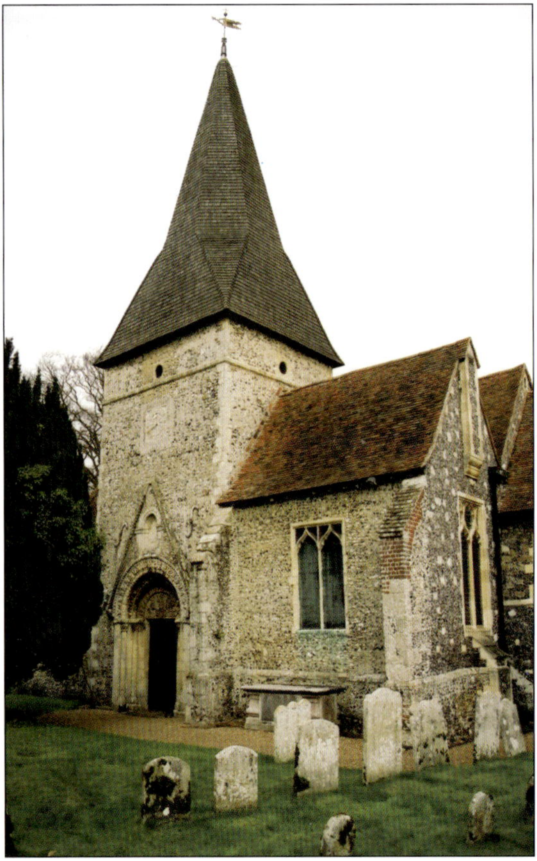

PATRIXBOURNE CHURCH - PHOTO BY BRIAN WISE

to nestle quietly in the Elham Valley. In the church is a bust in memory of another writer Richard Hooker who came here in 1594 so that he could have the opportunity to write. He was a contemporary of that Pre-Raphaelite 'immortal' William Shakespeare and was well known in his own time.

The church chancel has wall tiles, mosaics and a lovely reredos that appears Morris inspired in places. The west window in the tower is the real thing being mid-period Morris & Co. glass dating from 1875. The three lights show two symbolic figures in each division with backgrounds of foliage up to the shoulders of the main figures. There are pale quarries above with the title scrolls and angels to be seen in the tracery. On the left the figure of *Hope* is twinned with that of *Despair.* In the centre is *Charity* above *Envy* and on the right *Faith* is seen over the figure representing *Folly.* The Latin inscription beneath is in memory of Doctor Sandford who was the rector here in 1870 and later the Bishop of Gibraltar. Burne-Jones designed all the figures and the main ones were first used about five years before at Christ Church, Oxford. The combination with the lower figures was only used on one other occasion at St Chad's church in Rochdale in 1873 although the tracery was very different and there were other more minor differences to the backgrounds used. C.W. Sandford also asked John Pollard Seddon to prepare drawings for a proposed fireplace and other decorations to the dining room of the nearby parsonage in 1871. ***The church is usually open during daylight hours.***

ALSO: At this point there is an option of visiting ADISHAM CHURCH nearby which has glass by Lavers, Barraud & Westlake.

The quickest route to proceed to Chilham is via the A2 towards Canterbury and the A28 in the direction of Ashford. The village is signposted from the A28.

This picturesque village is built around a square with the gates of the castle at one end and the (5) CHURCH OF ST. MARY at the other. Our third church of this dedication has a fine Perpendicular tower and inside are several impressive tombs usually to members of the Digges family. Amongst works by Chantrey and Westmacott is a sculpture in the north chapel by Alexander Munro which shows Arthur and Edmund Hardy, from the same family who own the castle. They are shown with their arms affectionately around one another reading from *The Babes in the Wood*. The piece might be described as sentimental but it does also have a truthfulness to nature and a tendency to attempt to portray character. It dates from 1858 so is later than Munro's more famous *Paolo and Francesca* at Wallington Hall (1851) but a similar time to Munro's tympanum at the Oxford Union completed during that building's decoration by Rossetti, Burne-Jones and Morris amongst others.

Munro had been born at Inverness in 1825 and was accepted into the Royal Academy twenty-two years later. A short while after this he became close friends with Rossetti and shared a studio with Arthur Hughes in the 1850s. It was at this point that he began to specialise in portrait groups of children such as this work. Unlike Thomas Woolner, another sculptor, he was never a fully-fledged member of the Brotherhood but for a good time his work showed the influence of the ideas of the Pre-Raphaelites. He was married in 1861 but went to the south of France in 1865 for health reasons where he died on the first of January 1871 aged only forty-five.

Also in this lovely building are several windows by C. E. Kempe and C.E Kempe & Co. Ltd dating from 1906 (north transept),1914 (north windows in the chancel with the Arms of the Hardy family in the tracery) and 1916 (south windows in the chancel).

The church is open most days.

ALSO: Another option before returning to Canterbury is to visit the CHURCH OF ST. COSMAS AND ST. DAMIAN at Blean which contains stained glass designed by Henry Holiday and made by Powell. It dates from 1866 and is Morrisian in style.

Trail No. 9 Faversham and Sheppey

Points of Interest

(1) FAVERSHAM - CHURCH OF ST. MARY OF CHARITY***- Medieval relics in a fascinating building

(2) EASTLING - CHURCH OF ST. MARY**- Powell stained glass in a charming rural setting

(3) LEAVELAND - CHURCH OF ST. LAURENCE**- Kempe glass

(4) EGERTON - CHURCH OF ST. JAMES*** - Very late Morris & Co. glass

(5) BOUGHTON MALHERBE - CHURCH OF ST. NICHOLAS***- An ecclesiological delight.

(6) MURSTON - ALL SAINTS CHURCH****- Designed by William Burges.

(7) EASTCHURCH - ALL SAINTS CHURCH***- Glass by George Edward Cook and Karl Parsons.

ALSO: It is possible to visit the CHURCH OF ST. JAMES** at BICKNOR which was the subject of work by Bodley in 1859-61.

STARTING POINT: The centre of Faversham near the Tesco Supermarket
HOW TO GET THERE: The town is sign-posted from the M2 junction 6
FINISHING POINT: Eastchurch on the Isle of Sheppey
REFRESHMENTS: Multiple outlets in Faversham plus good pubs in Egerton and Eastchurch
TRANSPORT: Own car essential
DURATION: One day

This trail is through largely rural areas providing an opportunity to see unspoilt parts of the county that was probably Morris' favourite at least until he lived at Kelmscott. There are few direct associations to the artists themselves but a wealth of contemporary artefacts.

The (1) CHURCH OF ST. MARY OF CHARITY ***is found in the centre of Faversham close to the Tesco supermarket and signposted Parish Church.***

This enormous building was unfortunately the subject of an attack by people of the town in 1301 following which large parts of it needed to be rebuilt. Also in 1753 its massive central tower largely collapsed leading to the erection of a new Georgian nave in classical style. The present crown spire was erected between 1794-7. There were also Victorian 'restorations' which changed the fabric of the building but despite all of this or perhaps because of it the present building fascinates.

One of its main attractions (which no doubt would have been of interest to Rossetti et al should they have come this way)is the painted column in the north transept. This is medieval dating from about 1306 and surprisingly not obliterated during the Reformation. The skilled paintings show ten scenes from the *Life of Christ*. There is all around a multitude of nineteenth century stained glass mainly by the firm of Lavers, Barraud & Westlake although the main east window is credited to A L. Moore and dates from 1911. The former were established in London in 1855 and only ceased production a few years after the death of N. H. J. Westlake in 1921. The windows at Faversham largely date from 1870-90. ***The church is open most days.***

There is also reputed to be glass by Wilhelmina Geddes depicting *Joseph of Arimathaea* in a church in the town but the author has been unable to verify this.

To find Eastling leave the town via the B2045 Western Link road and turn right at the roundabout with the A2. Take the first left along Faversham Road and follow this under the M2 until there is a left turn down North Eastling Road. The next right is Eastling Road which leads into the village, the church is found by going left along Kettle Hill Road for a few yards.

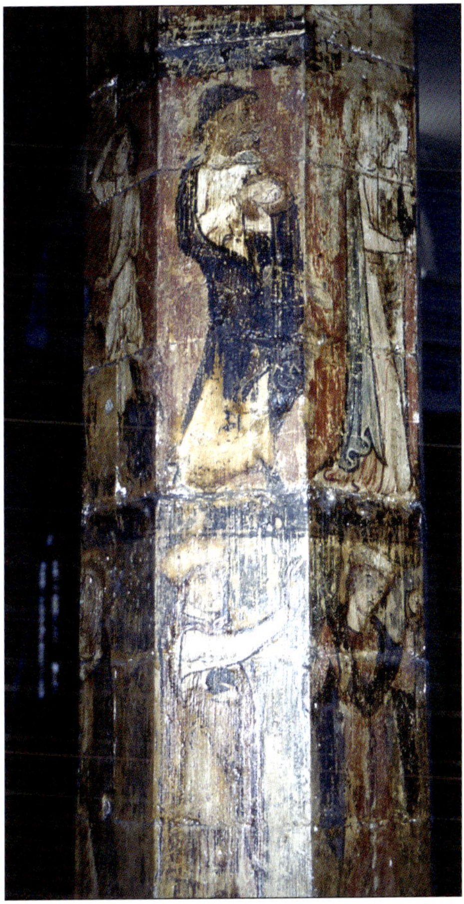

MEDIEVAL DECORATION IN THE CHURCH OF ST. MARY OF CHARITY, FAVERSHAM - PHOTO BY AUTHOR

The (2) CHURCH OF ST. MARY at Eastling was *'grossly over restored by R.C. Hussey (as usual)'* according to the architectural historian Nikolaus Pevsner. This occurred in 1855-6 and involved the rebuilding of much of the church and may have followed a small fire. Its exterior today is a good one although once inside there are worries that whatever medieval features it may have once had are mostly gone.

The chief item of interest is a lancet window on the north wall of the chancel. This shows *The Presentation* and is by James Powell and Sons despite its atypical appearance. It is early dating from 1863 the year coincidentally when Henry Holiday joined the firm. Outside is an enormous and extremely old yew tree. ***The church may be locked but access is possible through the churchwardens.***

There is a longer drive to Egerton; however, a short stop can be made at the small (3) CHURCH OF ST. LAURENCE ***at Leaveland. To do this turn left along Kettle Hill Road and follow it until you arrive at the hamlet of Hockley where you should***

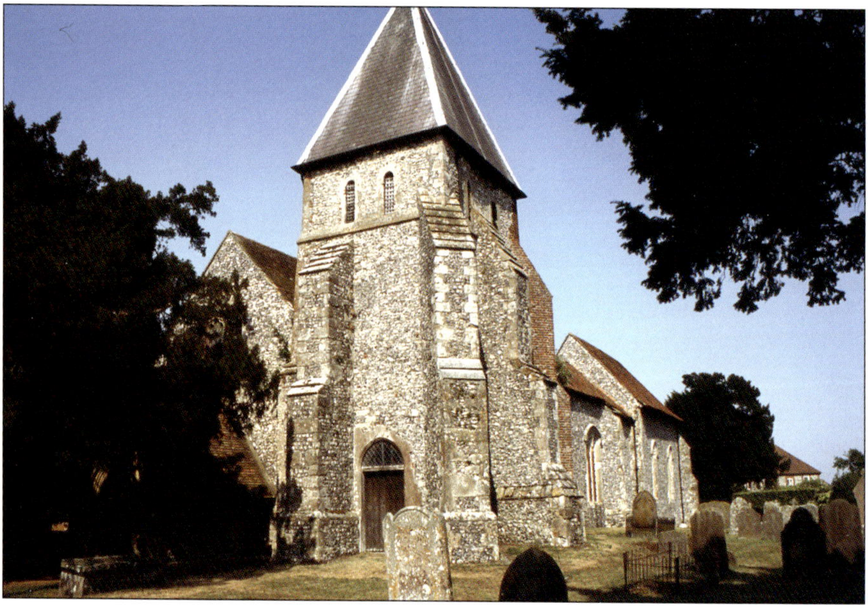

EASTLING CHURCH - PHOTO BY AUTHOR

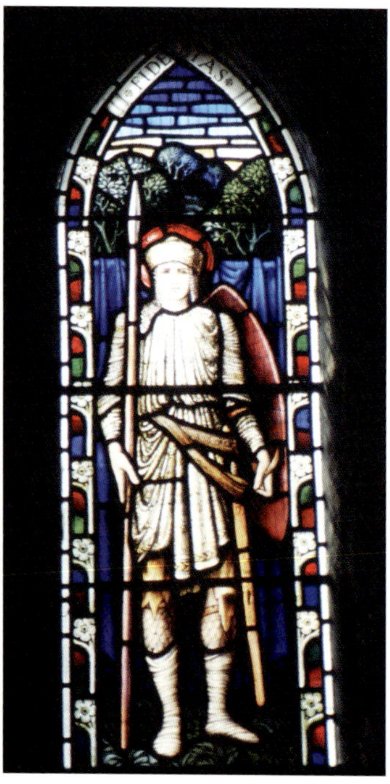

turn left. Take the first right along Haywards Hill turning first right to go through Throwley. Take Workhouse Road on your left and this will lead you to Leaveland church which soon appears on your left.

Inside there are two nice lancets by Kempe of 1888 one with the *Crucifixion* and the other showing *Mary* and *St John*. The silver and gold townscape behind both scenes is an attractive feature and typical of Kempe's work at this time. ***The church is open most days.***

Now follow the A251 southwards to its roundabout with the A252 where you should turn right. At a further roundabout with the A20 go right and then take the first road on the left by the name of Hook Lane. Although the road changes name follow it ignoring all turns off over the M20 until a right-hand turn into Pivington Lane. This soon has a T-junction with Egerton Road where you should turn right to arrive at Egerton. The church is opposite the Post Office.

Once in the (4) CHURCH OF ST. JAMES it may take some minutes to locate the late Morris &

MORRIS WINDOW IN EGERTON CHURCH - PHOTO BY AUTHOR

Co. window high up as it is on the south wall. This single light of a figure representing *Fidelity* has an emotive inscription to a John Hodge who died in 1934 in Nigeria - *'fear no more the heat o' the sun'*. The window is very late and was installed in 1935 only five years before the company ceased trading. The design was originally from Burne-Jones and is derived from his *Abraham* figure first used in 1895 at Ashton-under-Lyne. The same design was used in 1912 for the figure of *Fortitude* at St. Stephen's church in Tonbridge (see Trail No.3). ***The church is open most days.***

To find Boughton Malherbe leave the village along Stonebridge Green Road and follow it past Bramley Farm until its T-junction with Coach Road where you turn left. Keep right and Coach Road will eventually take you to a crossroads with Boughton Road where you should go left. The church soon appears on the left-hand side.

The (5) CHURCH OF ST. NICHOLAS had its chancel rebuilt by a local man, Alexander Apsley, in 1848-50 who surprisingly was buried in the churchyard only two years after completing the work. Inside there are three large marble lions in the chancel that used to support a black marble pyramid of a monument dating from 1663. Also, there is a pulpit with linen-fold panelling from Elizabethan times but the main feature of the church is its ensemble of fittings by Apsley and forming what Pevsner describes as an *'ecclesiological interior'*. This relates to the influence of the Cambridge Camden Society that was formed around 1839 with their premise of supporting Gothic architecture. In fact the Society shared a number of ideals with Ruskin and the Pre-Raphaelites with their advocacy for a return to the use of medieval style in churches. They were particularly influential at the time of the alterations to this building.

On the half screen that divides the nave from the chancel are some appealing carvings of acorns, ivy etc. and more can be seen on the choir stalls. It seems that a recent incumbent wished to remove some of the stalls to be closer to his congregation

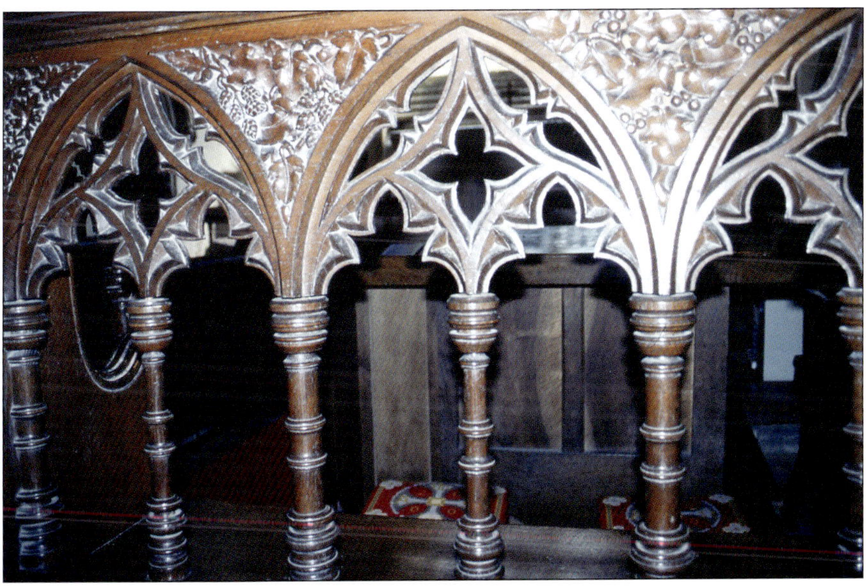

PART OF THE ECCLESIOLOGICAL INTERIOR AT BOUGHTON MALHERBE - PHOTO BY AUTHOR

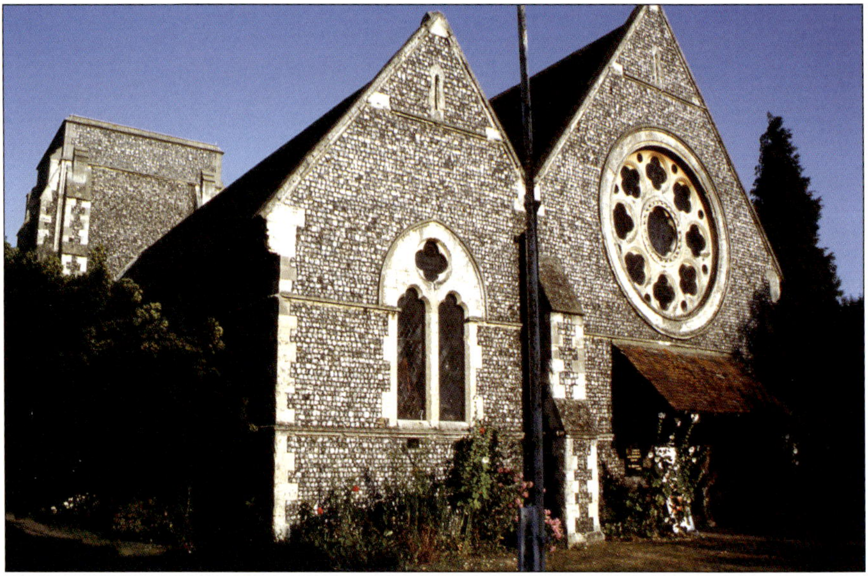

MURSTON CHURCH DESIGNED BY WILLIAM BURGES - PHOTO BY AUTHOR

and this is understandable as the chancel is further hidden by being several feet up from the body of the church. However, the Victorian Society visited the building after hearing of such plans and advised that this would effectively be despoiling the interior. Also dating from the 'restoration' is the altar with its pelican carving and some fading decoration below the main east window. The two other screens are later but the lectern dates from the time of Apsley's work with its bright use of colours.

There is a Kempe window in the tower area from 1894 showing the patron saint of the church with *St Augustine.*

In the area that was a south chapel but is now used for the Sunday school is a reminder of the Pre-Raphaelites who were so active at the time of the 'restoration' - a large print of Holman Hunt's *The Light of the World.*

The church is sometimes locked but access is possible through the churchwardens.

(On the way to the next location at Murston it is possible to visit BICKNOR CHURCH. This is by using a long cross-country route on minor roads via Lenham, Frinsted and Wormshill. The church there had a 'restoration' by G.F. Bodley in 1859-61 and contains early Clayton & Bell glass.)

The quickest way to arrive at Murston is probably by using the M20 via junction 7 changing onto the A249 heading towards Sittingbourne and then changing onto the A2 towards Faversham. Murston is signposted on the left.

As soon as one sets sight on the large and impressive rose window of (6) ALL SAINTS CHURCH there is a feeling of being in the presence of a very distinctive architect. Those readers who are aware of the church at Lowfield Heath in Sussex may also have some sense of deja-vu because there is a similar window and porch there. The architect is one and the same - the most individual William Burges. This church was built in 1874 at a cost of £3000 and replaced an older building that was half a mile or

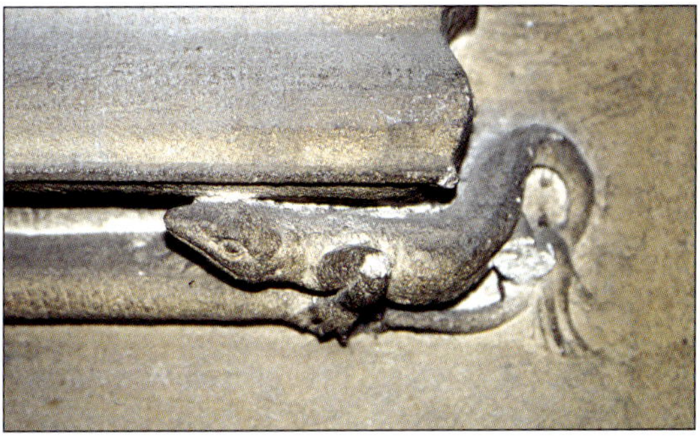

SIGNATURE LIZARD BY BURGES AT MURSTON - PHOTO BY AUTHOR

so to the north. Part of that church was used to construct a mortuary chapel and this is still standing although it has a variety of newer uses. Other parts of the fabric were also incorporated into All Saints where the arches between the nave and north aisle use stone from the previous building. In addition the restored fifteenth century screen was reused to form a vestry at the east end of the north aisle. The chancel is apsidal with lancet windows four of which are filled with glass possibly by Ninian Comper and dating from the 1920s. There are also some fine Burges features in the interior as one would hope. Firstly there is the roof with its turned tie-beams at two levels. There are in addition two corbels either side of the chancel arch representing the Old and New Testaments and at the other end of the nave is a fine font by the architect. Looking up at the rose window one can see it has only recently been installed with coloured glass previously having had just plain glass. This has been very successful, the work being designed by Ronald Page of Shepherdswell and installed in 1991. Before making your exit look on the north wall of the chancel where one of Burges' signature motifs is to be found - a lizard carved in stone.

The only real disappointment is that the tower of All Saints was never completed with the wooden tower roof being dismantled in 1959.

The church may be locked but access is possible through the churchwardens.

To reach Eastchurch retrace your way back along the A2 until you reach the major roundabout with the A249 and then head in the direction of the Isle of Sheppey. Once on Sheppey take the B2231 which leads you to the outskirts of Eastchurch and then follow the High Street to the church which will be seen on the left.

The (7) ALL SAINTS CHURCH is little changed since it was built soon after the site for it was acquired in 1431. Its interior boasts an effigied monument of 1622 to Gabriel Livesey. The Victorian tabernacle in the Lady Chapel is also of interest. But it is once again the stained glass that showcases the work of craftsmen inspired by Pre-Raphaelite style. The east window of 1872 is by George Edward Cook who is rather an unknown figure. What is clear is that as well as designing windows he was also a painter who exhibited landscapes at the Royal Academy between 1872-94. Prior to this he had a number of contacts with Henry Holiday who supplied him with cartoons. Between 1873-4 he shared a Gower Street studio with Bruce J. Talbert, a prominent designer of art furniture. Later he shared another studio with the architect J.M. Brydon and Cook produced a window for a private house designed by Brydon at Crockham Hill. The window at Eastchurch certainly has a Morrisian inspiration.

Another window of great interest in the church is to be found in the south aisle. This commemorates two pioneers in aviation - Charles Stewart Rolls (of Rolls Royce) and Cecil Stanley Grace both of whom died in the earliest fatal flying accident. This occurred in 1910 and the window was located here as the two men had completed much of their flying practice on Sheppey. The window shows the figures of *Fortitude* and *Hope* and it

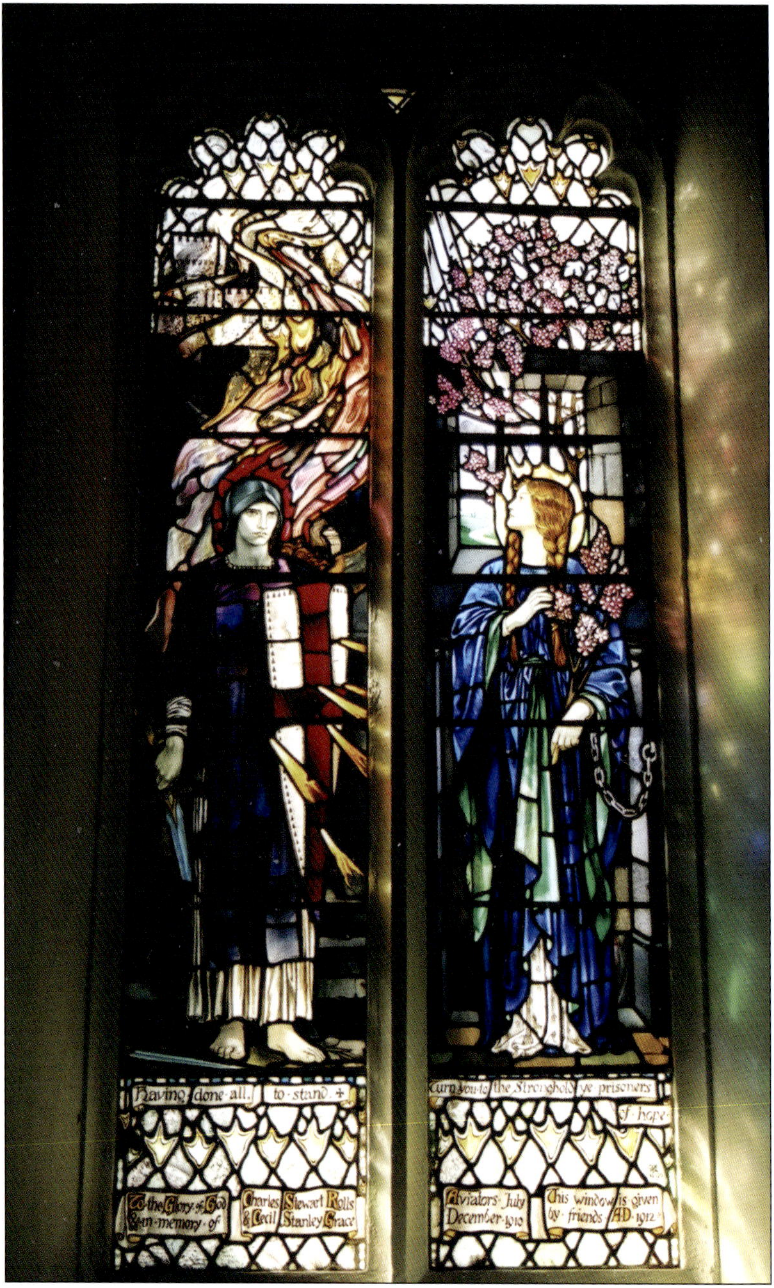

WINDOW DESIGNED BY KARL PARSONS AT EASTCHURCH - PHOTO BY BRIAN WISE

was dedicated at the church by the then Archbishop of Canterbury in 1912.

The designer was Karl Parsons who was a pupil of Christopher Whall from the age of fifteen. As he became more confident in his craft Parsons collaborated with Whall on commissions and in 1908 they jointly designed windows for the Cape Town Cathedral in South Africa. Four years later he was asked to make the windows for Eastchurch and he exhibited his designs for the window at the Arts and Crafts Exhibition the same year. One of the key tenets of his apprenticeship with Whall was that inspiration should be sought from nature and to this end Parsons and other pupils were encouraged to bicycle to rural areas and make detailed drawings of the flora and fauna that they came across. At Eastchurch the almond blossom seen in the right light was adapted from preliminary drawings that Parsons had executed in a garden at Northwood in Middlesex. He also recorded in his diary that the flames seen in the other light caused him some anxiety but that he was pleased with the end result. The window was restored in 1990 by Rolls Royce.

Parsons later worked with Robert Lorimer the Scottish architect (see Trail no.7) and he produced a number of windows for buildings north of the border. In addition he knew the Irish stained glass designer Harry Clarke well and they worked together. Unfortunately Parsons' health was never particularly strong and he died in 1934 at the early age of fifty.

The church is open most days during daylight hours.

Trail No. 10 Rochester to Meopham

Points of Interest

(1) ROCHESTER - CATHEDRAL****- Cope chest by George Jack - CASTLE - Where Holman Hunt once painted - CHURCH OF ST. MARGARET***- Has more work by Jack

(2) GAD'S HILL PLACE - Home of Charles Dickens

(3) HIGHAM - CHURCH OF ST. MARY***- Glass by Robert Bayne

(4) SHORNE AND SHORNE RIDGEWAY - CHURCH OF ST. PETER AND ST. PAUL***- Stained glass by Reginald Hallward who also had his workshop in the area. Madox Brown painted here.

(5) COBHAM - CHURCH OF ST. MARY MAGDALENE****- More glass by Hallward in a rich and fascinating interior.

(6) LUDDESDOWN - CHURCH OF ST. PETER AND ST. PAUL****- Surviving Victorian murals.

(7) MEOPHAM - CHURCH OF ST. JOHN THE BAPTIST**- Where Ford Madox Brown married his first wife.

ALSO: CHURCH OF ST. JOHN THE BAPTIST** at HALLING - Kempe glass. Plus churches in Gravesend, Chatham and Gillingham(listed at the end of the trail).

STARTING POINT: Rochester Cathedral

HOW TO GET THERE: The Cathedral is found at the junction of the High Street and College Yard in the old town.

FINISHING POINT: Meopham

REFRESHMENTS: Restaurants and many other opportunities in Rochester, good pubs in Cobham and Luddesdown.

TRANSPORT: Own car essential.

DURATION: One Day.

(1a) ROCHESTER CATHEDRAL has a spectacular West Front with a giant Norman door that has seen modifications throughout the centuries but did not get its present appearance until 1888 when J.L. Pearson completed some restoration work. The enormous Perpendicular window was also restored in the nineteenth century being originally installed in 1470. Inside the choir walls were worked on by another heavyweight Victorian architect Sir Gilbert Scott in the 1870s and are easily seen with their gold lions and fleur-de-lys on a red and blue ground. There is a precursor to Burne-Jones on one of the choir pillars where a *Wheel of Fortune* seen as a treadmill can be found.

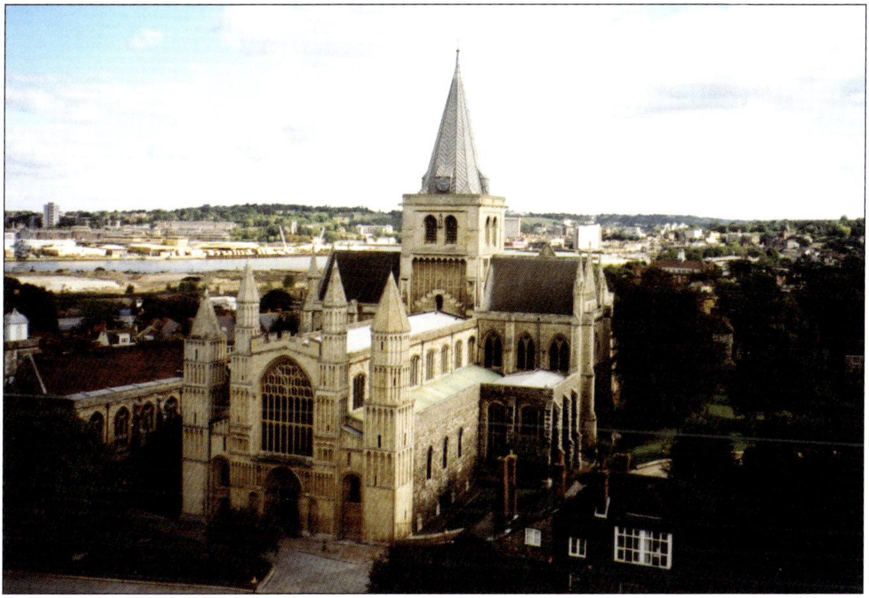

ROCHESTER CATHEDRAL - PHOTO BY AUTHOR

W.R. Lethaby was at one point the surveyor of the cathedral and in 1894 had become the first principal of the London Central School of Arts and Crafts set up on Morris' ideals. Lethaby's position at the Cathedral is no doubt the reason for a cope chest designed by George Jack being present in the building. It dates from 1924 and has five carved panels depicting the *Lamb of God* and the signs of the Evangelists. Also on view in this historic interior are a number of Kempe windows - three windows of two lights dating from 1899 are to be seen on the east side of the south transept. In addition there is a further window at the westernmost end of the north aisle showing the Saints *George* and *Elizabeth* and dating from two years later. Glass by Powell and Clayton & Bell as well as a number of other nineteenth century stained glass companies can be found throughout the expansive interior. ***The Cathedral is open most days.***

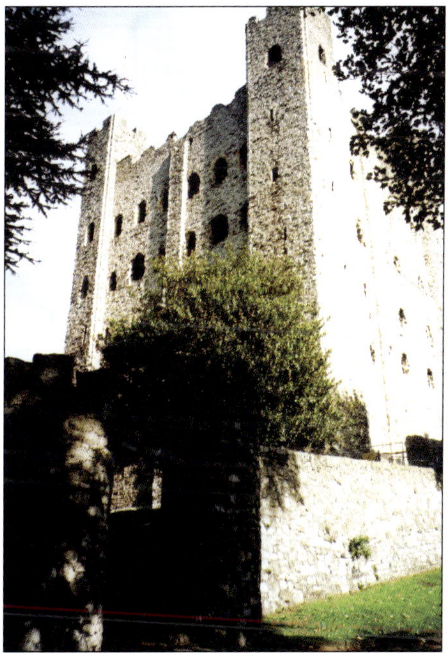

ROCHESTER CASTLE - PHOTO BY AUTHOR

Opposite the Cathedral is (1b)

ROCHESTER CASTLE rising sharply above its surrounding lawns. The keep is over a hundred feet tall and was built at the beginning of the twelfth century. It was to Rochester that Holman Hunt and Rossetti came in August 1848. They were at the time both members of the Cyclographic Society and firm friends who would later share a studio at Fitzroy Square in Bloomsbury. It was during this visit that Hunt probably painted his *Sketch of a Staircase at Rochester Castle, Kent* (Private Collection). It is likely that this work illustrates the winding staircase in the east angle of the great tower. ***The castle is in the care of English Heritage. It is open daily April-September 10-6 and October-March 10-4. Closed 24-26th. December and 1st. January.***

High on the hill above the cathedral is (1c) THE CHURCH OF ST. MARGARET which also has work by George Jack at Lethaby's instigation. He was engaged to design a mahogany font cover for the church in 1919. Also on view inside is Jack's medallion on the reredos dating from 1921-2. This is brightly painted and depicts the *Lamb of God* with a verdure background and a blue, white and gold border The main east window was designed by Lavers & Barraud in about 1869. ***The church may be locked but access is possible through the churchwardens.***

The Foord Almshouses in Priestfields off the Maidstone Road have stained glass designed by Robert Anning Bell and date from the 1920s.

There are a number of buildings in Rochester with connections to Charles Dickens. These include Restoration House in Maidstone Road which was the inspiration for Miss Havisham's house in *Great Expectations*. There is also Eastgate House near the High Street which contains the Charles Dickens Centre and in the garden is the chalet where he wrote some of his late novels originally located at Gad's Hill. He was writing *'The Mystery of Edwin Drood'* in the chalet the day before he died.

The next stop on this trail appropriately is (2) GAD'S HILL PLACE. This is found halfway between Rochester and Gravesend on the Old Dover Road. ***Go across the Rochester Bridge and stay on the A2 until you can turn right on the A226 Gravesend Road. After two roundabouts Gad's Hill Place can be seen on the left.***

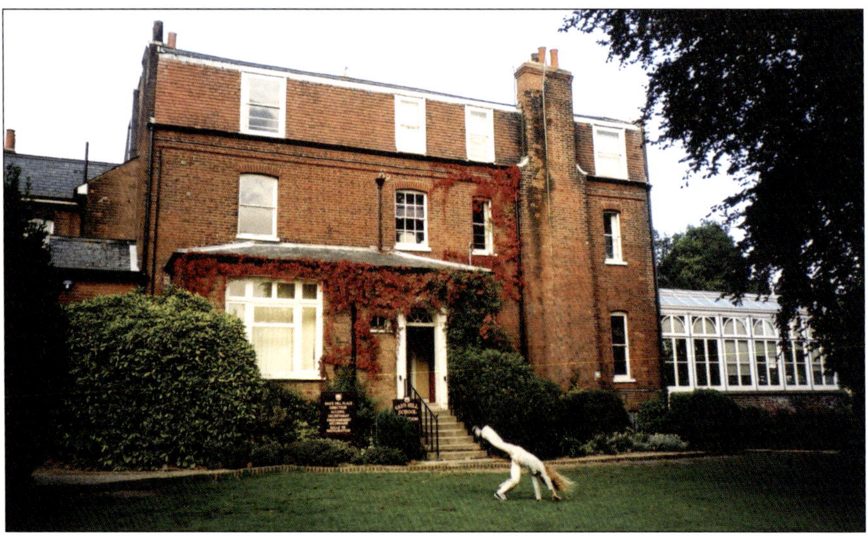

THE REAR OF GAD'S HILL PLACE - PHOTO BY AUTHOR

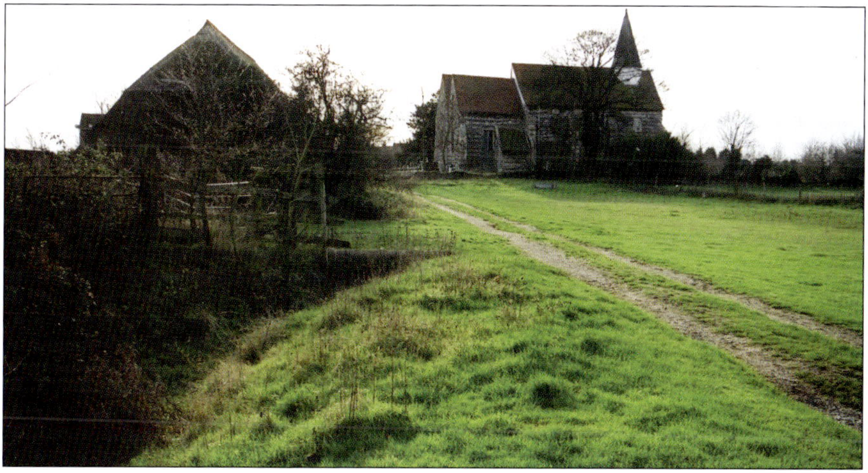

HIGHAM CHURCH - PHOTO BY BRIAN WISE

The house is described in the chapter William Holman Hunt and Gad's Hill Place. ***Next on this trail is Higham Church which is located by leaving Gad's Hill and turning left along the A226. After a short distance turn right down Villa Road into Higham village. At a crossroads turn left to go down School Lane towards Lower Higham. Then go right over the railway and follow Church Street where the church is soon found on the left-hand side.***

(3) ST. MARY'S CHURCH is now in the care of The Churches Conservation Trust and is sited admirably on the edge of the Thames marshes. The old building has a number of medieval fittings including the font from the thirteenth century and a wonderful pulpit from a little later. The interior was the subject of a 'restoration' in 1863 by Robert Speechly when the windows were renewed. The main east window and its glass dates from this time and shows *Jesus* as the *Good Shepherd* with the *Virgin Mary* and *St John* on either side. The glass is the work of Robert Bayne of the firm Heaton Butler & Bayne. He may well have trained with J.R Clayton of the rival company Clayton & Bell but then went on to become one of the more original stained glass artists working within the Gothic Revival style. Clayton was also of course a close friend of Rossetti's in his formative years. However, the arrival of Morris' firm in 1861 would lead to Bayne making stylistic changes some of which may be in evidence here. When leaving the church more Victorian changes to the building by Robert Speechly can be seen passing through his porch also of 1863. ***The church may be locked but access is possible through the keyholder.***

Retrace your way back to the A226 this time using Forge Lane and turn right. Take the second turning on the left (another Forge Lane) to arrive at Shorne.

The (4) CHURCH OF ST. PETER AND ST. PAUL is something of a puzzle historically as it has parts dating from the eleventh to the sixteenth centuries plus a 'restoration' of 1874-5. The architectural historian Nikolaus Pevsner found this nineteenth century work to be *'aggressive'* especially as the man responsible, T.H. Wyatt, had only a year before written knowingly about the original windows in the church before he promptly replaced them. The west window in the north aisle is in memory of Adelaide Hallward who died in 1925 and was designed and erected by her husband who for some

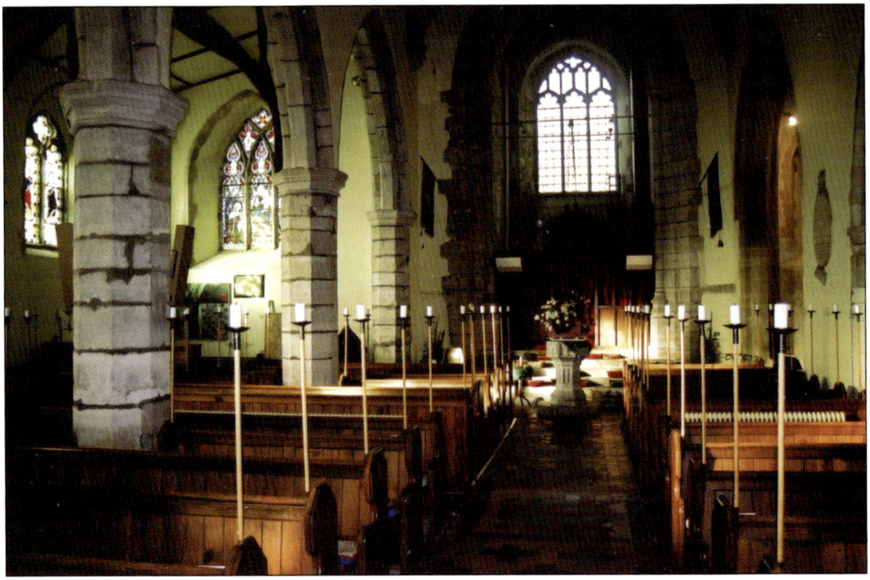

INTERIOR OF SHORNE CHURCH - PHOTO BY BRIAN WISE

years had his studio at his house Woodlands in Woodlands Lane at nearby Shorne Ridgeway. Even now apparently lumps of stained glass from the kilns can be found. Reginald Hallward was a pupil of Christopher Whall, joining him at his small cottage near Dorking from about 1885 to work on stained glass design with only characteristically primitive facilities. This is typical of the approach to developing craftsmanship skills advocated by the Arts & Crafts Movement. The window at Shorne is in a Pre-Raphaelite style and quite different from others in the church. The angel in it is said to be a likeness of a village child who served as a model (information from the church guide). Hallward also designed children's books and had his own press at his home which not surprisingly went by the name of the Woodland's Press. The church also has glass by Herbert Bryans and A.O. Hemming. ***The church may be locked but access is possible through the churchwardens.***

It is in this same area that Ford Madox Brown started painting *View from Shorne Ridgeway, Kent* (National Museums and Galleries of Wales)in July of 1849 which looks towards the Shorne Marshes with the River Thames in the distance.

The next stop is the village of Cobham which is found by going south up Tanyard Hill and then turning right into the fore-mentioned Woodlands Lane. Continue right along Brewers Road over the A2 to a roundabout on the other side. Here take the first exit Halfpence Lane (with Cobham Hall on your left) and then the first right which takes you into the village where the church is on the left.

The (5) CHURCH OF ST. MARY MAGDALENE forms the centrepiece of this unspoilt village which also has Dickensian connections. The pub opposite called the Leather Bottle was used by the novelist both as a boy and later when resident at Gad's Hill. It was not far from here that the artist Richard Dadd stabbed his father to death whilst mentally unstable in 1843. This spot is now called Dadd's Hole and it lies in Cobham Park to the east of the church.

The church itself is well known for its memorial brasses and fifteen of them form a pavement in the chancel. They were last restored and repositioned in the 1860s. The second window from the east in the south aisle is by Reginald Hallward (see Shorne) and its original design means it stands out from the other glass in the church. It was illustrated in Christopher Whall's seminal book *Stained Glass Work* of 1905 after its design was first exhibited at the Arts and Crafts Exhibition Society two years before. The main east window is by the firm of Lavers & Barraud (designed by F.P. Barraud and J.M. Allen, the latter known for his robust figures) and dates from about 1861. There is further work by the same company in the church and the west window is probably by Heaton Butler & Bayne. Stained glass by Powell and Herbert Bryans is found in the chancel. Before leaving the building be sure to look at the organ of about 1860 which was constructed by Richardson, the organ builder to Queen Victoria.

The countryside around Cobham provided the inspiration for three paintings by John Samuel Raven about whom little is known except that he was taught to paint principally by his father. In 1857 he produced a sketch now entitled *Study for 'Saint-foin in Bloom'* (Tate Britain)the title referring to a much larger oil painted two years later from the sketch. Both works show the church at Cobham in the background and are painted from a location near the Cobhambury Road and Woods (to the south-east of the village). Sain-foin (or saintfoin) was a crop in Victorian times that was used to provide winter fodder. Raven also produced another picture from a very similar viewpoint called *Rooks Parliament* (1858-Private Collection) which shows birds of the crow family in the foreground of a landscape of a similar nature to *Saint-foin in Bloom*. The subject may have been a play on other members of Raven's family (his father and two brothers were all clergymen) who after all had an appropriate surname. The artist was befriended by Henry Holiday and the three paintings undoubtedly have a Pre-Raphaelite attention to detail and colour. They were all exhibited at the exhibition *Pre-Raphaelite Vision* in 2004.

In addition there is a house in the vicinity designed by the leading Arts and Crafts architect Robert Weir Schultz. Scalers Hill is found about a mile to the north of the

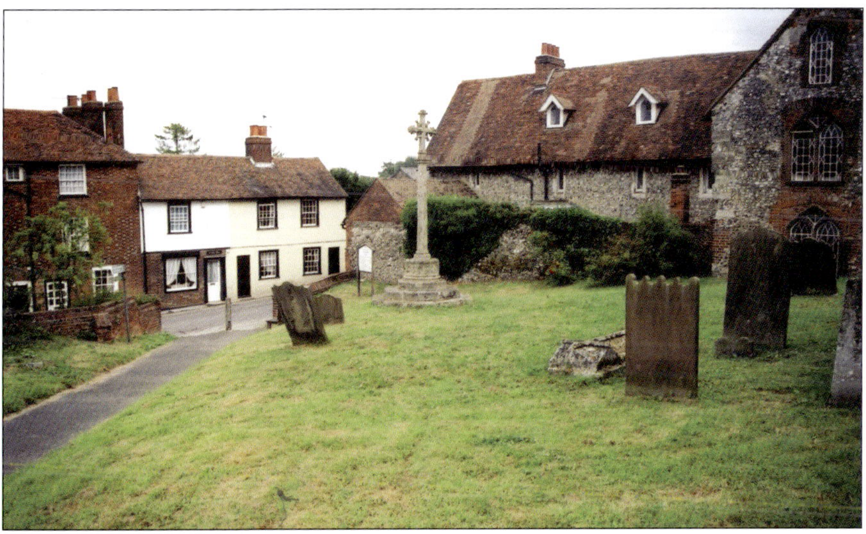

VIEW FROM THE CHURCHYARD, COBHAM - PHOTO BY BRIAN WISE

village close to the A2. It was designed for A.W. Booth who was a friend of Herbert Baker another architect who designed a number of buildings in South Africa particularly between 1892-1912. ***The house is privately owned.***

To arrive at Luddesdown leave Cobham by heading east past the Primary School on your left. Take the first right and then go right again along Batt's Road. Follow this to a T-junction and go left - this road brings you to another T-junction and you should again turn left to come out at the Golden Lion pub. Turn slight right to drive into Luddesdown where the church is seen to the left.

Set in hills in a comparatively remote location the (6) CHURCH OF ST. PETER AND ST. PAUL from the outside is truly charming. However, the interior is even more beautiful as it is unexpected. The building had a major 'restoration' in 1866 when the chancel was slightly lengthened and the tower heightened. However, the work was not as drastic as it might have been following the collapse of the nave roof through decay. The architect Robert Philip Pope produced plans for a new church but then the Rev. Alfred Wigan sought the advice of Joseph Clarke who was a representative of an organisation devoted to the sensitive repair of ecclesiastical buildings. A compromise was reached whereby much of the material of the old church was re-used in the new building. It was about four years later that the marvellous murals were started although records of their completion are vague. Certainly the west wall was worked on in 1877 with the grisaille (depicting *Children being presented to Christ*) in the baptistery and decoration over the south door being added a year later. The major murals on the north wall are in memory of the Rev. Wigan and his son who succeeded him as rector and were completed in 1894. These show the *Donation of the Keys to St Peter* and the *Pentecost*. The chancel ceiling has delightful golden stars on a blue background with half angels holding biblical texts and panels of *Wheat* and *Vine* to the sides of the reredos. All the murals are the work of Heaton, Butler & Bayne as is the east window showing the *Life of Christ* that replaced a single lancet window. This was installed in 1870 and all the other stained-glass windows in the church are likely to have come from the same company during that next decade. Since 1860 their work had been in the ascendancy due to the high levels of competition with other glass firms. This coincides with the arrival of Robert Turnill Bayne joining the partnership of Heaton & Butler. His considerable design skills may well have been responsible for the particularly beautiful murals in the baptistery area. As has been noted before Bayne probably received training from J.R. Clayton (of Clayton & Bell) and was a friend of Henry

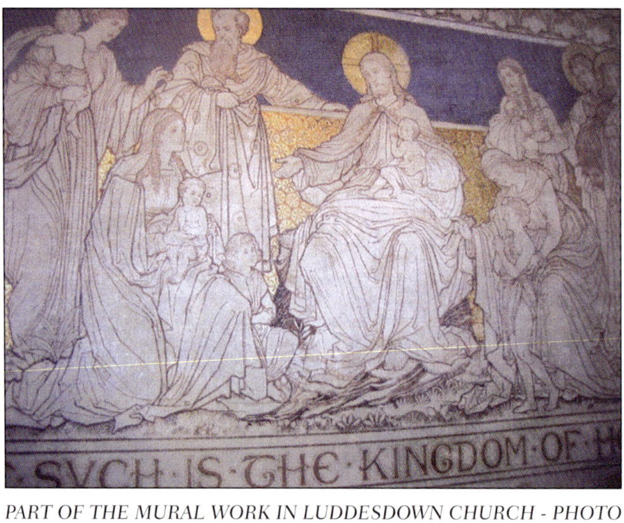

PART OF THE MURAL WORK IN LUDDESDOWN CHURCH - PHOTO BY AUTHOR

Holiday - both these men had contact with the Pre-Raphaelites and their influence is evident in the extensive murals at Luddesdown.

The church may be locked but access is possible through the churchwardens.

(At this point there is an option to visit the CHURCH OF ST. JOHN THE BAPTIST at Halling which has fairly extensive glass by Kempe completed in 1892 and 1900.)

The final stop on this trail is Meopham found by continuing westwards out of the village along Oakenden Road which becomes Foxendown Lane before coming to a junction with the A227. Turn to your right and the church is visible on the right-hand side.

Meopham is strung out along the A227 with the church being over a mile north of the village green. The area is rich in farms and it was nearby that Lucy Madox Brown lived with her Aunt Helen following the death of her mother in 1846. She was visited at Melliker Farm by her father occasionally who knew the house from his courting days with Elisabeth.

Melliker Farm is to the north - drive along the A227 to Hook Green where Melliker Lane is a turning on the left just past the pub. Follow this to its junction with the B260 where the farm is just opposite.

The (7) CHURCH OF ST. JOHN THE BAPTIST is a large mainly fourteenth century building which contains a wooden pulpit made for St. Margaret's Church in Westminster

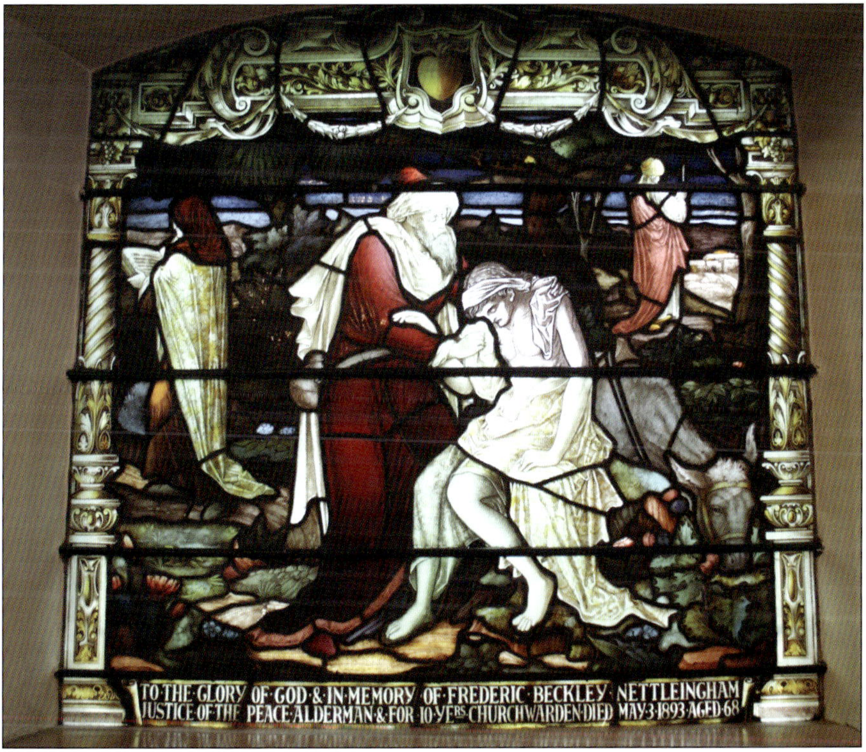

STAINED GLASS BY HEATON BUTLER & BAYNE IN THE CHURCH OF ST. GEORGE, GRAVESEND - PHOTO BY BRIAN WISE

in 1682. It was transferred here in 1800 by a vicar who was a teacher at Westminster School and it has wonderful carvings. The main reason for the church's inclusion on this trail is that Ford Madox Brown married his first wife Elisabeth here on the third of April 1841, the bride being given away by her brother Augustus. Apparently Brown looked so young that the clergyman officiating the ceremony asked where the bridegroom had got to! Much of the stained glass in the church would have been completed after Brown's happy day and includes designs by Lavers Barraud & Westlake and Hardman.

The church may be locked but access is possible via the churchwardens.

The easiest way to return to Rochester is to drive towards Gravesend on the A227 changing onto the A2 to the north of the town.

OTHER CHURCHES OF INTEREST IN THE VICINITY.

GRAVESEND - CHURCH OF ST. GEORGE**- Has glass by Heaton Butler & Bayne from the 1890s and by James Powell and Sons from the same period and later.

The church is open occasionally but access can also be arranged via the Tourist Information Centre nearby.

CHURCH OF ST. ANDREW**- Built by G.E. Street in 1870-1 with stained glass by Clayton & Bell.

The building is now an art centre with daytime opening hours.

CHATHAM - CHURCH OF ST. MARY - Built by A.W. Blomfield, it has an east window by Kempe. ***Closed and boarded at time of writing.***

CHRIST CHURCH contained Kempe glass and a reredos but was demolished many years ago. Present whereabouts of the glass and reredos unknown.

GILLINGHAM - CHURCH OF ST. MARY **- Restored by A.W. Blomfield in 1868-9 it has some glass made by Heaton Butler & Bayne in 1869 which may have been designed by Henry Holiday in the east window. In addition there is a window in the north aisle that may well be by Reginald Hallward and dating from 1908. ***The church is normally locked but keys may be available through the vicarage adjacent.***

Appendix 1

OTHER CHURCHES WITH MORRIS GLASS

FARNBOROUGH (ORPINGTON) - CHURCH OF ST. GILES THE ABBOTT - On the north wall are two lights showing *St. Peter and St. Paul* which appear to be early windows by Morris & Co (1860s). They do not however appear in Sewter's catalogue of the same. There is also glass by Powell dating from 1885-95.

The church may be locked but access is possible through the churchwardens.

FARNINGHAM - CHURCH OF ST. PETER AND ST. PAUL - Morris & Co. glass in the chancel on the south side. The single lancet window dates from 1903 and the *Virgin and Child* shown are from a Burne-Jones design. There is also glass inspired by Charles Winston in the church (but designed by Charles Clutterbuck) who was largely responsible for the revival of medieval-styled stained glass practiced in the nineteenth century. He was the son of the vicar at the time(1832).

The church is usually open.

KESTON CHURCH (UNKNOWN DEDICATION) - Has Morris & Co. glass dating from 1909 depicting the figure of *Love*. This is from a Burne-Jones design and is found in a north-west window of the nave. Other glass by Morris & Co. was destroyed in World War II -these were the windows of *Faith, Hope* and *Prayer* of the same date and designer.

The church may be locked but access is possible through the churchwardens.

PENGE - CHURCH OF ST. JOHN THE EVANGELIST - Stained glass by Morris & Co. at the westernmost end of the north aisle. The figures of *Hope* and *Temperance* are from Burne-Jones designs and date from 1911.

The church may be locked but access is possible through the church-wardens.

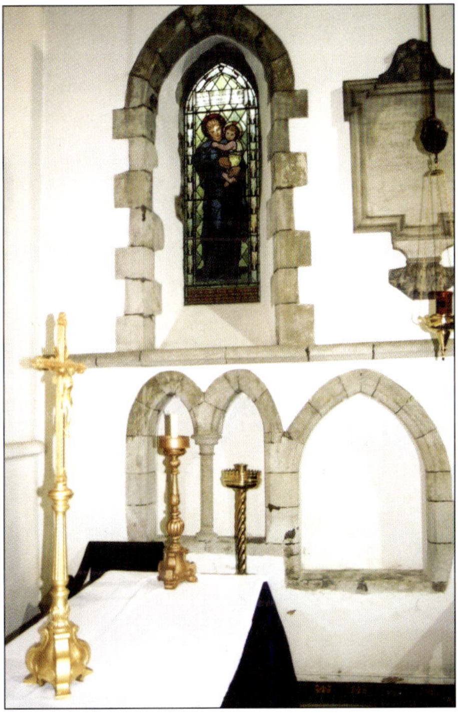

VIRGIN AND CHILD WINDOW BY BURNE - JONES IN FARNINGHAM CHURCH - PHOTO BY BRIAN WISE

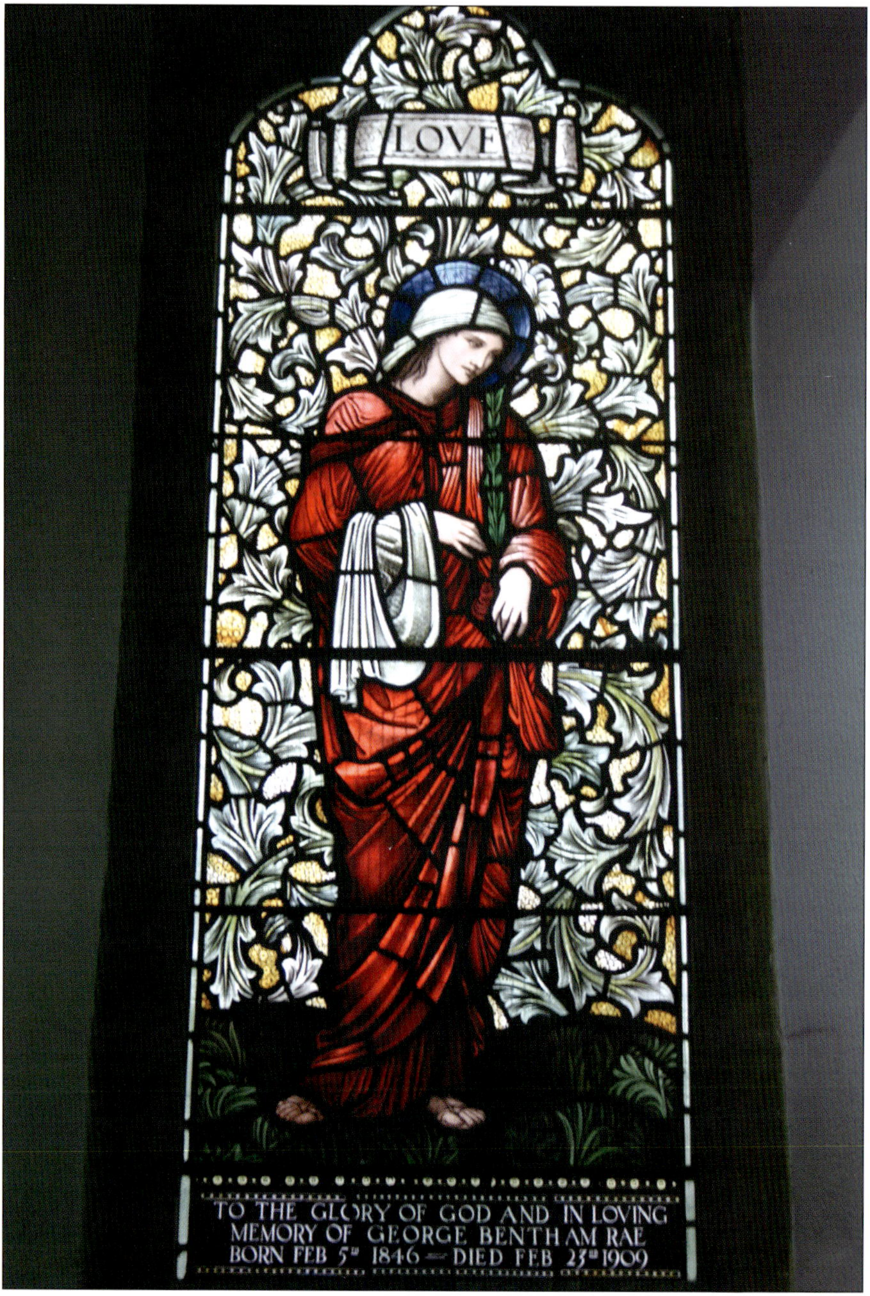

FIGURE OF 'LOVE' WINDOW IN KESTON CHURCH - PHOTO BY BRIAN WISE

Appendix 2

OTHER CHURCHES OF INTEREST

Access arrangements need to be checked except where otherwise noted.

ASHFORD - CHURCH OF ST. MARY - Extensive glass by Lavers Barraud & Westlake dating from 1857-82 plus glass by Powell and Kempe.

BEARSTED - HOLY CROSS CHURCH - Four windows by Heaton Butler & Bayne 1875-94.

BECKENHAM - CHURCH OF ST. BARNABAS - Two windows by Karl Parsons dated 1913 and 1918.

BROMLEY - CHURCH OF ST. LUKE - Ensemble of sixteen small windows by Powell (1891-1914).

CHELSFIELD - CHURCH OF ST. MARTIN OF TOURS - In the chancel are windows by Veronica Whall (1925) and Christopher Whall. There is also a west window by Powell and a work by Gerald Moira (1920) on the north wall.

CHISLEHURST - CHURCH OF ST. NICHOLAS - The building was adapted by Bodley and Garner in 1896 who also supplied the reredos. There is much Victorian glass by the likes of Kempe, Burlison & Grylls and Herbert Bryans.

The church is normally open.

CLIFFE - CHURCH OF ST. HELEN - Three windows by Heaton Butler & Bayne dating from 1912 and one window by Powell from 1889

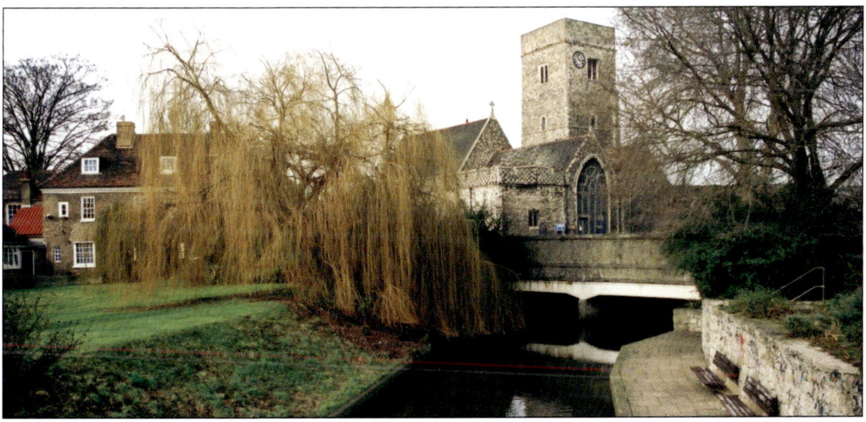

HOLY TRINITY CHURCH, DARTFORD - PHOTO BY BRIAN WISE

DARTFORD - HOLY TRINITY CHURCH - The town is one of the oldest in Kent and was a staging post on Watling Street in Roman times. More recently it played an important role in the development of steam power and the church has a memorial to Richard Trevithick. He built a steam-powered road vehicle in 1801 and three years later a steam locomotive to run on rails. Despite these developments and other innovations he died penniless and was buried in a pauper's grave in the upper burial ground on East Hill.

The church was also visited by Queen Victoria and restored by the architect A.W.Blomfield in 1862-3. Of interest to readers of this book are the 1859 west window by Powells and the east window by Heaton Butler & Bayne dating from the final year of the restoration. The church was also home to some Kempe glass showing the figures of *Saint Michael* and *Saint Gabriel* but the former was destroyed in World War II with *Gabriel* removed and re-sited elsewhere in the town at West Hill Hospital Chapel.

ERITH - CHRIST CHURCH - Was built in 1874 by J.P. St. Aubyn to serve the enlarging population brought into the area by increasing industry. It is brick built in an Early English gothic style with an apse at the east end, the tower being added in 1915. It is its interior however that particularly warrants a visit with the walls of the nave and chancel having extensive murals and painted decoration. The east end has a Renaissance-styled triptych of the *Adoration of the Magi* by A.O. Hemming dating from 1904 and there is glass by him in the south aisle. Hemming was employed by the firm of Clayton & Bell before working independently of them from about 1883 (more of his decorative work can be seen at the church of St Mary and St Eanswythe in Folkestone also included in this book).

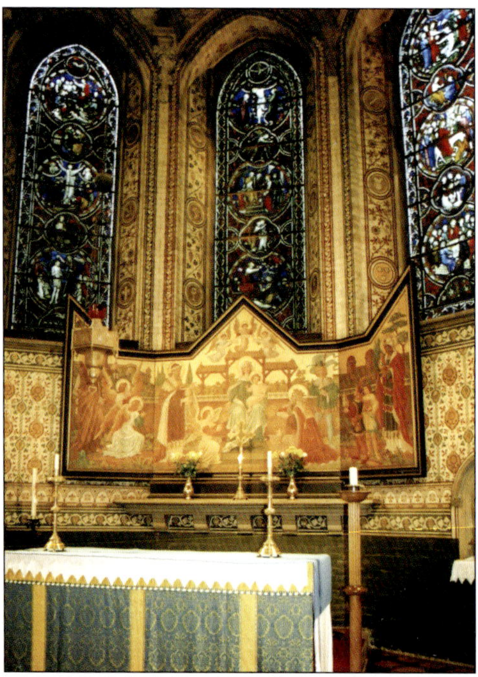

TRIPTYCH BY A.O.HEMMING IN ERITH CHURCH - PHOTO BY BRIAN WISE

The majority of the mural work is by another company, Ward & Hughes, that was completed between 1906-9. The north wall of the chancel has a *Resurrection* with the *Angels of the Ascension* on the south wall opposite. Around the same time (1906) they also painted the west wall of the nave with its three scenes of *Suffer the Little Children, Noah and the Ark* and *Moses Parting the Red Sea.*

A couple of years later the same firm were used for the twelve scenes in the north and south aisles of the nave showing the history of the English church. The overall effect of such a comprehensive scheme is enhanced by the colours of the Hardman & Sons glass in the lancets of the east window in what is a wonderfully rich interior.

The church may be locked but access is possible through the churchwardens.

FRINSBURY - ALL SAINTS CHURCH - Three windows by Heaton Butler & Bayne (1869-79) and extensive glass by Clayton & Bell (1888).

GROOMBRIDGE - CHURCH OF ST. JOHN THE EVANGELIST - Extensive glass by Kempe dating from 1894-99).

GOUDHURST - CHURCH OF ST. MARY - Contains a window in the south aisle by Paul Woodroffe depicting *Christ in Majesty.*

LEEDS - CHURCH OF ST. NICHOLAS - Includes glass by Powell (1908-11), Heaton Butler & Bayne (1914-25) and Kempe & Co, Ltd. (1930).

MEREWORTH - CHURCH OF ST. LAWRENCE - A *Raising of Lazarus* window by Frederic Shields (1888) is found in the south aisle of this unusual church. The east window is by Lavers Barraud & Westlake (1875) and there is also glass by Powell (1912).

NORTHFLEET - CHURCH OF ST. BOTOLPH - The building was restored by E.W. Godwin in 1862 and has tile-work designed by him. There is in addition glass by Lavers & Barraud (1863) in the east window and a number of other windows by Lavers Barraud & Westlake dating from 1870-74.

NURSTEAD - CHURCH OF ST. MILDRED - The east window was designed by Christopher Whall (1916).

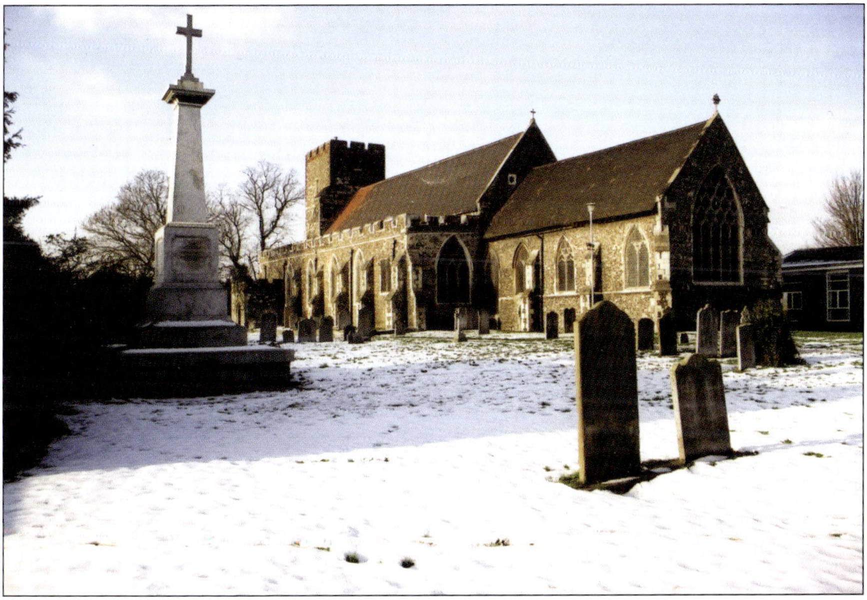

NORTHFLEET CHURCH - PHOTO BY BRIAN WISE

SANDHURST - CHURCH OF ST. NICHOLAS - A window by Henry Holiday whilst he was with Powell & Sons (1875).

TILMANSTONE - CHURCH OF ST. ANDREW - There is a small but jewel-like window under the tower. It shows the figure of *Faith* unusually unaccompanied by either *Hope* or *Charity*. Even in the rather unpromising location the window begs to be noticed with the red 'velour' of the allegorical figure's dress being an electrifying red. The halo above her head is a suitably vibrant blue. The glass was designed by the ubiquitous Henry Holiday and dates from 1897 and is in memory of Fanny Master. The Kempe windows nearby are rather jaded but a number of them do have the wheat-sheaf monogram. They date from 1897-1906. The mosaic reredos was funded by the Rice family of nearby Dane Court.

The church may be locked but access is possible through the churchwardens.

UPNOR - CHURCH OF ST. PHILIP AND ST. JAMES - Contains five windows by Heaton Butler & Bayne dating from 1887-1906.

WEST WICKHAM - CHURCH OF ST. JOHN THE BAPTIST - an unusually high number of windows (five) by Herbert Bryans installed between 1896-1907 plus glass by Kempe(1896) and Powell(1903).

WITTERSHAM - CHURCH OF ST. JOHN THE BAPTIST - In the north aisle is a window of two lights produced by Mary Lowndes in 1897. She was a close follower of the Arts & Crafts Movement for some of her career.

Appendix 3

OTHER BUILDINGS OF INTEREST

BICKLEY, NEAR CHISLEHURST - BULLERS WOOD - A house remodelled by Ernest Newton in about 1889 for the Sanderson family which had inside decoration by Morris & Co. Nearly all this has gone except in the drawing room which has pattern-work on the ceiling and cornices. The room was decorated under Morris' personal direction and contained a hand-knotted carpet designed by him and John Henry Dearle (V & A). The house is now a school.

NONINGTON - ST. ALBAN'S COURT - Built by George Devey in the 1870s in an Elizabethan style. It is deliberately constructed to look older than it is using local ragstone so that it fits into the landscape. It thus adheres to the idea of faithfulness to its surroundings - a central tenet of Arts & Crafts architecture.

ORPINGTON - 15 STATION ROAD (THE SHOEHORN) - C. R. Ashbee designed this compact building and it was built in 1900. It was most likely called The Shoehorn because of the quantity of accommodation that was fitted into such a small house. At the time there was considerable interest in designing smaller houses as the middle classes found themselves increasingly able to buy holiday cottages and the like. Six years later Ashbee himself published a book on the same subject.

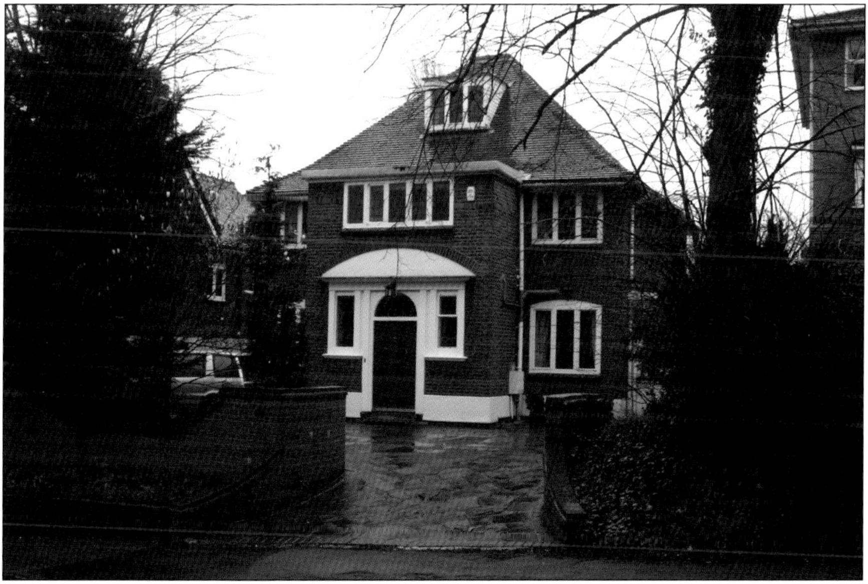

THE SHOEHORN BY C.R.ASHBEE IN ORPINGTON - PHOTO BY BRIAN WISE

Further Reading

Amor, Anne Clark, *William Holman Hunt: The True Pre-Raphaelite,* (Constable, London, 1989)

Davey, Peter, *Arts and Crafts Architecture,* (Phaidon, London, 1980)

Fitzgerald, Penelope, *Edward Burne-Jones,* (Sutton Publishing, Stroud revised 1997)

Fleming, G. H., *John Everett Millais: A Biography,* (Constable, London, 1998)

Harrison, Martin, *Victorian Stained Glass,* (Barrie & Jenkins, London, 1980)

MacCarthy, Fiona, *William Morris,* (Faber & Faber, London, 1994)

Marsh, Jan, *Dante Gabriel Rossetti: Painter and Poet,* (Weidenfeld & Nicolson, London, 1999)

Newman, Teresa and Watkinson, Ray, *Ford Madox Brown,* (Chatto & Windus, London, 1991)

Prettejohn, Elizabeth, *The Art of the Pre-Raphaelites,* (Tate, London, 2000)

Stavridi, Margaret, *Master of Glass:* Charles Eamer Kempe 1837-1907(John Taylor, Hatfield, 1988)

Thirlwell, Angela, *William and Lucy: The Other Rossettis* (Yale, New Haven and London, 2003)

Wood, Christopher, *The Pre-Raphaelites,* (Weidenfeld & Nicolson, London, 1981)